PERFORMANCE AND POPULAR MUSIC

Annette, Eleanor, Christopher and Susannah
All My Loving

Performance and Popular Music

History, Place and Time

Edited by

IAN INGLIS
University of Northumbria, UK

LONDON AND NEW YORK

First published 2006 by Ashgate Publishing

Published 2016 by Routledge
2 Park Square, Milton Park, Abingdon, Oxon OX14 4RN
711 Third Avenue, New York, NY 10017, USA

Routledge is an imprint of the Taylor & Francis Group, an informa business

British Library Cataloguing in Publication Data
Performance and popular music : history, place and time. –
   (Ashgate popular and folk music series)
   1. Popular music – Performances
   I. Inglis, Ian, 1948–
   782.4'2164'078

Library of Congress Cataloging-in-Publication Data
Performance and popular music : history, place and time / edited by Ian Inglis.
         p. cm—(Ashgate popular and folk music series)
   Includes bibliographical references.
   1. Popular music—Performances. I. Inglis, Ian, 1948– II. Series.

   ML3470.P45 2005
   781.64'078—dc22

                                                                2005005231

ISBN 9780754640561 (hbk)
ISBN 9780754640578 (pbk)

Typeset in Times Roman by N²productions.

Contents

Notes on contributors

Sean Albiez is Senior Lecturer in Popular Music Studies at Southampton Institute. He has contributed chapters to *Madonna's Drowned Worlds: New Approaches to Her Cultural Transformations*, edited by Santiago Fouz-Hernandez and Freya Jarman-Ivens (Ashgate, 2004) and *Pop Sounds: Klangtexturen in der Pop und Rockmusik*, edited by Thomas Phleps and Ralf Von Appen (Bielefelder, 2003). His current research interests include German and British electronic music in the 1970s, Detroit and Techno, and issues of gender in alternative rock and punk in the 1980s.

Philip Auslander is Professor in the School of Literature, Communication and Culture at Georgia Institute of Technology. His books include *Presence and Resistance: Postmodernism and Cultural Politics in Contemporary American Performance* (University of Michigan Press, 1992), *From Acting to Performance: Essays in Modernism and Postmodernism* (Routledge, 1997) and *Liveness: Performance in a Mediatized Culture* (Routledge, 1999), which won the Callaway Prize for the Best Book in Theatre or Drama. He is the editor of the four-volume reference collection *Performance: Critical Concepts* (Routledge, 2003) and (with Carrie Sandahl) co-editor of *Bodies in Commotion: Performance and Disability* (University of Michigan Press, 2005). He is currently preparing *All the Young Dudes: Performing Glam Rock* (University of Michigan Press).

Gary Burns is Professor and Assistant Chair in the Department of Communication at Northern Illinois University. He is the editor of *Popular Music and Society*, and his articles have been published in a wide variety of journals, including *Popular Music*, *South Atlantic Quarterly*, *Goldmine*, *Wide Angle* and *Journal of Popular Film and Television*. He co-edited *Television Studies: Textual Analysis* (Praeger, 1989) and *Making Television: Authorship and the Production Process* (Praeger, 1990).

Jeffrey Callen is currently writing his doctoral dissertation on contemporary Moroccan music. After graduating from the University of California, Berkeley, he received his MA in music from the University of California, Santa Barbara. In 2002, he was awarded a Fulbright-Hayes fellowship and in 2003–2004, he was a teaching fellow at the University of California, Los Angeles. His research and publications have examined the significance of popular music in a variety of contexts, including the blues in California, North African popular music and the use of music by the Hindu nationalist movement in India.

Norma Coates is Assistant Professor of Communication at the University of Wisconsin-Whitewater. Her articles about rock and gender and rock on television have appeared in several anthologies and journals. She is currently writing a book about rock music on television before MTV for Duke University Press.

Mike Daley is a producer at CBC Radio in Toronto and has taught courses at Guelph University and York University. He is currently completing a doctoral dissertation on the role of Jimi Hendrix in rock history narratives; his Master's thesis, which examined Bob Dylan's early vocal style, won a York University Thesis Prize in 1998. His articles have been published in numerous journals, including *Popular Music and Society, Journal of Popular Music Studies* and *Popular Music*. His research interests range across the music of Patti Smith, Elvis Presley, disco and ska.

Susan Fast is Associate Professor of Music and Director of the Graduate Programme in Music Criticism at McMaster University. She is the author of *Houses of the Holy: Led Zeppelin and the Power of Rock Music* (Oxford University Press, 2001). Her articles have been published in journals including *American Music* and *Canadian University Music Review*, and she has contributed essays to a wide variety of books, including *Expression in Pop-Rock Music*, edited by Walter Everett (Garland, 2000), *The Garland Encyclopedia of World Music* and *The New Grove Dictionary of Music and Musicians*. She has also written about late medieval music and music theory, and is a member of the editorial board of the *Journal of the Royal Music Association*.

Sarah Hill is Lecturer in Popular Music at the University of Southampton. Her doctoral research investigated Welsh-language popular music and cultural identity, and she is currently working on a cultural history of popular music in the San Francisco Bay area.

Tim Hughes recently completed his Ph.D., which analysed the music of Stevie Wonder, at the University of Washington. He was the multimedia editor for *The Jimi Hendrix Gallery, The Next Rock Record* and *The History of Recorded Sound* at the Experience Music Project in Seattle, and is a former chair of the Society for Music Theory's Popular Music interest group. His research interests include the analysis of soul and funk, repetition and the music of Ligeti and Stravinsky.

Ian Inglis is Senior Lecturer in Sociology at the University of Northumbria, Newcastle upon Tyne. He edited *The Beatles, Popular Music and Society: A Thousand Voices* (Macmillan, 2000) and *Popular Music and Film* (Wallflower, 2003). His doctoral research considered the significance of sociological, social psychological and cultural theory in explanations of the career of the Beatles. He is a member of the editorial board of *Popular Music and Society* and his articles have been published in numerous journals, including *Popular Music*, *Journal of Popular Culture*, *International Review of the Aesthetics and Sociology Of Music*, *Visual Culture in Britain*, *American Music*, *Popular Music and Society* and *Journal of Popular Music Studies*.

Jaap Kooijman is Assistant Professor of Media and Culture Studies at the University of Amsterdam. He gained his Ph.D. in American Studies, and his writings on American politics and popular culture have been published in a number of books and journals, including *Presidential Studies Quarterly*, *The Velvet Light Trap*, *Post Script* and *European Journal of Cultural Studies*. He has taught courses on 'Motown and the Civil Rights Movement' and 'The Politics of Soul and Disco', and is currently completing a study of Diana Ross and the Supremes.

Lee Marshall is Lecturer in Sociology at the University of Bristol. He is the author of *Bootlegging: Romanticism and Copyright in the Music Industry* (Sage, 2005) and the co-editor (with Simon Frith) of *Music and Copyright* (University of Edinburgh Press, 2004). He has written extensively on the music and career of Bob Dylan, and is currently preparing a book about him.

Emma Mayhew currently works for the Federal Department of Communications, IT and the Arts in Canberra. She taught at the University of Wollongong from 1992 to 2002, and completed a Ph.D. entitled 'The Representation of Women in Popular Music: The Feminine, Feminist and Musical Subject'.

Laurel Sercombe is the Archivist for the Ethnomusicology Program at the University of Washington in Seattle. She received a BA in Music from Humboldt State University, an MLS from the University of Washington and her Ph.D. in Ethnomusicology from the University of Washington in 2001; in 1998, she received a pre-doctoral Smithsonian Research Fellowship for her studies into Salish myth narratives. She is the co-editor (with William R. Seaburg) of *Our Stories: Skagit Myths and Tales* (Lushootseed Press, 2002) and a contributor to *Spirit of the First People: Native American Music Traditions of Washington State*, edited by Willie Smyth and Esme Ryan (University of Washington Press, 1999). Her particular interests include Coast Salish literature and songs, the history of ethnographic research in the Pacific North-West and the Beatles.

Sheila Whiteley is Professor of Popular Music at the University of Salford. She was General Secretary (1999–2001) of the International Association for the Study of Popular Music and is now Publications Officer. Her publications include *The Space Between the Notes: Rock and the Counter Culture* (Routledge, 1992), *Women and Popular Music: Sexuality, Identity and Subjectivity* (Routledge, 1998) and *Too Much Too Young: Popular Music, Age and Gender* (Routledge, 2004). She was editor of *Sexing the Groove: Popular Music and Gender* (Routledge, 1998) and co-editor (with Andy Bennett and Stan Hawkins) of *Music, Space and Place: Popular Music and Cultural Identity* (Ashgate, 2004).

General Editor's preface

The upheaval that occurred in musicology during the last two decades of the twentieth century has created a new urgency for the study of popular music alongside the development of new critical and theoretical models. A relativistic outlook has replaced the universal perspective of modernism (the international ambitions of the 12-note style); the grand narrative of the evolution and dissolution of tonality has been challenged, and emphasis has shifted to cultural context, reception and subject position. Together, these have conspired to eat away at the status of canonical composers and categories of high and low in music. A need has arisen, also, to recognize and address the emergence of crossovers, mixed and new genres, to engage in debates concerning the vexed problem of what constitutes authenticity in music and to offer a critique of musical practice as the product of free, individual expression.

Popular musicology is now a vital and exciting area of scholarship, and the *Ashgate Popular and Folk Music Series* aims to present the best research in the field. Authors will be concerned with locating musical practices, values and meanings in cultural context, and may draw upon methodologies and theories developed in cultural studies, semiotics, poststructuralism, psychology and sociology. The series will focus on popular musics of the twentieth and twenty-first centuries. It is designed to embrace the world's popular musics from Acid Jazz to Zydeco, whether high tech or low tech, commercial or non-commercial, contemporary or traditional.

Professor Derek B. Scott
Chair of Music
University of Salford

Acknowledgements

The preparation of this book has been an overwhelmingly positive experience, due in no small part to the enthusiasm of my fellow contributors. As a result of their encouragements and insights, it has been – like successful research should always be – informative and enjoyable, and I am enormously indebted to all those who have participated, and from whom I have learned much. I am, as ever, immeasurably grateful to Annette Hames for her patience, understanding and support. If I can conflate the words written and sung by my two favourite performers of the twentieth century, without her love I'd be nowhere at all, and it really would be a long, cold, lonely winter.

Introduction

History, place and time: the possibility of the unexpected

Ian Inglis

> Although the musical product yields its greatest source of income in recorded and written form, its authenticity, or validity, is very much dependent upon the music's being on view in the live performance. In this context the musical product is being produced and consumed in the same moment; there is an inextricable association between the musician and his music (White 1987: 187).

> History is never tidy, but rock and roll history is particularly resistant to neatness and order (Palmer 1995: 11).

> Q: Was your family in show business?
> John Lennon: Well, my Dad used to say my Mother was a great performer (Norman 1981: 214).

One of the distinguished contributors to this volume has pointed out that although music is always 'performative', in the sense that it only truly exists when performed, the performance of much contemporary popular music is routinely 'mediatized', reaching its audiences through an array of increasingly sophisticated audio-visual technologies, rather than live. Although (as, for example, several of the televised broadcasts of live concerts discussed in this book demonstrate) live and mediatized performance are parallel forms that are mutually dependent, it is undoubtedly true that 'mediatized forms enjoy far more cultural presence and prestige – and profitability – than live forms' (Auslander 1999: 162). In fact, live music performance has become the exception of musical perception and experience, to the extent that our retelling of popular music history often tends to be reduced to familiar and verifiable dates of 'important' recordings – either singles (Elvis Presley's 'Heartbreak Hotel'; the Sex Pistols' 'Anarchy in the UK'; the Sugar Hill Gang's 'Rapper's Delight') or albums (the Beatles' *Sgt Pepper's Lonely Hearts Club Band*; the soundtrack of *Saturday Night Fever*; Michael Jackson's *Thriller*) – many of which, of course, were created several months before audiences eventually got to hear them. While not denying the centrality of these records (and their associated movie and video releases) within rock culture(s), the end result has been to withdraw attention from music-making as an immediate theatrical act and to refocus it on music-making as a phased industrial process.

A similar neglect of live musical performance has been evident in many academic contributions to popular music studies. With some honourable exceptions (several of whom are represented in this collection), many writers have fashioned an intellectual terrain on which music is frequently approached as an economic system, as an industrial practice, as a political vehicle, as a developing technology, as a subcultural agent (all of which are, of course, wholly proper perspectives). But only rarely has it been considered as an opportunity for reciprocal exchange between those on the stage and those in front of it, in which 'the pulse of life, the imaginative charge generated when actors and audience come together' (Harwood 1984: 13) can have long-lasting and far-reaching consequences for both the production and the consumption of music, and for its shifting form and content.

In both cases, these oversights are not only regrettable, but puzzling, since the live performance of (any) music has traditionally been one of the most valued ways in which audiences and musicians can effectively interact. From the position of the performer, there are substantial benefits to be derived from such interactions:

> Jeff Beck: Most people have never heard me get the best out of a guitar. Recording puts a barrier between the artist and the audience. I only get the feeling I'm putting my true self across when performing live. Records never have, never will, show my real potential. If it's a good night on the road ... and if the audience is dynamite, there's a real chance of my 'going off' into a state of altered consciousness (Martin 1983: 143).

While articulated in different terms, the rewards gained by members of the audience, such as these Canadian teenagers who attended concerts by the Beatles in 1964, often refer to similarly altered states of mind:

> Eric Twimane: Never in all the years since have I been as emotionally high as I was during that concert. The music and the charisma ... simply can't be matched. You couldn't take your eyes off them. I still compare every concert to that one. None have measured up.

> Edith Manea: It's difficult to even describe my feelings. I was exactly where I had dreamed of being for months. I went to see them. And, my god, there they were (Kendall 1997: 128–9).

And, of course, the impulse is frequently mutual:

> Patti Perry: It was like a different Elvis. It was like a light coming on that stage – the electricity from the audience and the electricity from him, it was unbelievable (Guralnick 1999: 351).

Each of these testimonies (and many others reported in the accounts that follow) would seem to indicate the possibility of a kind of profound, even spiritual, response to the experience of personal participation in live musical performance. It has been frequently observed that 'transcendence, performance, and authenticity bear subtle relations to each other' (Kemal and Gaskell 1999: 1).

In addition to acknowledging the importance of specific or individualized accounts of the emotional cathexis forged between audiences and performers, there is a further, equally pertinent, historical reason for investigating the live performance of popular music. In its ability to simultaneously reflect and influence patterns of socio-cultural activity, it is one of the principal avenues along which musical change and innovation can be introduced and recognized. Indeed, since the emergence of rock'n'roll in the early 1950s, there have been a number of live performances which have had great significance for the subsequent trajectory of popular music. They can be characterized as moments of transition, in which old traditions are challenged and new ones established. Each has, in its own way, introduced new styles, confronted existing practices, disrupted accepted definitions and provided templates for others to follow. They have not only punctuated, but redirected the narrative of popular music. In short, they have been key moments in the evolution of rock'n'roll, and it is these historical moments that this book seeks to explore and understand.

It is essential to point out that the events discussed in the following chapters are not, in any way at all, intended to replicate the 'best concert/most exciting show/favourite gig' exercises that occasionally appear in the music press. Not only are the criteria by which such verdicts are reached necessarily subjective, but they are inconsistent and weakly defined. Metamusical components, such as facial expressions, body movements, microphone/instrument handling, spatial interrelationships and performer/audience topography may impact on the way in which a performance is evaluated (Middleton 1990: 242). So too might stage mobility and costume, particularly in terms of the sexual or 'rebellious' interpretations they encourage (Friedlander 1996: 289). A distinction must also be drawn between performers and performances. The two are not synonymous: what is spontaneous and what is rehearsed will almost certainly overlap. In addition, an inexperienced musician may deliver a memorable live performance; celebrated bands can (and do) give disappointing performances (Frith 1996: 207–15). Fears surrounding performance anxiety have been shown to be the major source of stress for musicians; often internally imposed, they range across a variety of potential problems, including maintenance of musical standards, faulty equipment, and degree of difficulty (Wills and Cooper 1988: 74–103).

The existence of such contradictions has prompted the observation that 'there seems to be something about the performance relationship which is fundamentally volatile, given to interruption and undecideability' (Toynbee 2000: 60). Ironically, it may be that it is the very unpredictability generated by these tensions – the possibility of the unexpected – that lends the live performance the energy and excitement lacking in 'mediatized' performance. Indeed, 'the unexpected' is a major facet of almost all of the events considered in this book.

I prefer to forego the normal editorial convention of summarizing each of the contributions that follow. They speak for themselves, and far more eloquently than I could ever hope to do. Taken together, however, they illustrate the enormous variety (size, location, expenditure, duration) of musical performance. Some (Madonna's performance at the MTV Video Music Awards) were over in a few minutes; others (the Woodstock festival) were spread over several days. Some performers (like those at Live Aid) were watched by hundreds of millions of television viewers around the world; while others (the Sex Pistols at Manchester's Lesser Free Trade Hall) were seen by no more than a few dozen people. Some (Patti Smith's television performance of 'Horses') took place with little or no advance publicity; others (the introduction of the Beatles to US TV audiences) received unprecedented attention before and after the event. And some are significant because of the ways in which they challenge the very definition of what a 'performance' is: the central facet of Sinéad O'Connor's performance at the Bob Dylan 30th Anniversary Concert was that it did not take place.

In all the accounts contained within this book, analysis of the performance is placed within a broader discussion of its contexts and consequences; it is, after all, not merely the music, but the opportunities for association, identification and resistance that the music permits – and all that is subsequently inferred – between performers and audience, between the musical and the non-musical, between the old and the new, which gives rock'n'roll its peculiar distinction. The vocabularies through which music is encoded, assessed and decoded rarely remain static for long, but are subject to an ongoing process of adjustment, refinement and change, in which we all, as consumers or producers of popular music, participate on a regular basis. Popular music, like popular culture generally, is always in motion, yet the impacts and influences that a particular event has are not always apparent immediately. The time and place in which cultural forms emerge are as relevant as the forms themselves: 'codes are immensely plastic and are constantly being reworked ... [and] to a large extent consequent upon combinations of existing meanings and the historical moment in which they come into being' (Nava 1992: 164). In concentrating on such historical moments, the chapters that follow may therefore be seen as dramatic enactments of those more subtle negotiations and transactions that routinely help us to define the structures and cultures of popular music, and our relationship to them. At the same time, they may provide a series of signposts to the turbulent, unpredictable and constantly surprising history of rock'n'roll.

Chapter 1

'Ladies and gentlemen …' The Beatles: *The Ed Sullivan Show*, CBS TV, February 9, 1964

Laurel Sercombe

The Beatles were most of all a moment (Bangs 1987: 299).

The Beatles' appearance on *The Ed Sullivan Show* on the evening of Sunday, February 9, 1964 marked the beginning of a new era in American popular music and culture as well as a new standard for its promotion and marketing. During 1963, the Beatles had gained extraordinary popularity throughout Britain; by the time they arrived in the United States, they had also performed in Sweden and France, sold millions of records, and had a huge, often frenzied, following whose behaviour had already been labelled 'Beatlemania' by the British press. With an intensively orchestrated publicity campaign in motion in the US, the Beatles flew to New York days after 'I Want To Hold Your Hand' reached Number One in the singles charts. They were greeted at Kennedy International Airport on February 7 by 3000 fans and immediately won over reporters and photographers at their first press conference: 'The Beatle wit was contagious … Photographers forgot about pictures they wanted to take. The show was on' (Gardner 1964a). The Beatles performed in the United States for the first time, before a studio audience and millions of viewers, as the featured guests of Ed Sullivan, host of America's most popular television variety show.[1]

The evening provided impressive statistics: 50 000 requests for the 728 seats in the CBS studio theatre (filled once for rehearsal and once for the television broadcast) (Davies 1996: 194); a Nielsen rating of 44.6 (73 900 000 viewers), indicating the largest audience in television history (Bowles 1980: 187);[2] and a reported drop-off in teenage crime as between 60 and 70 per cent of the American television audience (over 25 million homes) tuned in (Castleman and Podrazik 1980: 167).

Media coverage of the Beatles' visit was extensive. Popular news and entertainment magazines that had run stories on Beatlemania as a British phenomenon – including *Time* (November 15, 1963), *Newsweek* (November 18, 1963), the *New York Times Magazine* (December 1, 1963), *New Yorker* (December 28, 1963) and *Vogue* (January 1, 1964) – were now reporting on the American 'invasion'. *Life* followed up its January 31, 1964 piece 'Here Come Those Beatles' with 'Yeah-Yeah-Yeah! Beatlemania Becomes a Part of US History' on February 21. Even *Senior Scholastic* reported on February 21, 'Beatlemania Hits the US'. Popular music radio stations were dominated not only by Beatles' recordings but also by Beatle news, interview clips, quizzes and contests, and tips on the purchase of Beatle paraphernalia. The Beatles were discussed on late-night talk shows; religious leaders worried; social scientists hypothesized; celebrities wore Beatle wigs. In the street, it was all Beatles all the time.

By the time the Beatles left the US to return to England on February 21, after three concert performances and two more appearances on the Sullivan show,[3] most Americans living within range of television and radio had felt the impact of their visit. For millions of teenagers (this author included), life changed dramatically, permanently, as the Beatles became the central focus of existence, providing a source of joy and influencing not only musical taste but speech, fashion, romantic fantasies, friendships, books and magazines read, movies watched and overall world outlook. For the American generation entering its teens at the time of President Kennedy's assassination in 1963, change was already in the air. The civil rights movement commanded national attention, the war in Vietnam was entering our consciousness, and social and political upheaval around the world all suggested that something major was happening. The effect of the Beatles at this point in time was such that 'there is a tendency to think that the sixties, that is, the cultural era rather than the chronological decade, began in 1964, the year they [the Beatles] first hit the US pop charts' (Garofalo 1997: 200).

In this chapter I look back on the evening of February 9, 1964 from a distance of 40 years. I have two aims: first, to describe the Beatles' first live performance in North America on *The Ed Sullivan Show*. My description is based primarily on published footage of the show[4] (I saw it myself in 1964 but remember only its emotional impact) and on the observations of people who were present in the television studio that night. My second objective is to further explore the impact of February 9, 1964 by looking at the Beatles in the larger context of their performance career. This includes consideration of Brian Epstein's role – his discovery of the 'wild' Beatles in The Cavern and his invention and selling of the 'tame' Beatles – and the resulting tension between the two. I also address the phenomenon of Beatlemania and its exploitation by the Beatle 'industry', including broadcast and print journalists and critics, product manufacturers, and the psychologists and sociologists who explained it all to the American public at the time. More recent critiques of the role of gender in popular music performance and consumption suggest that while the Beatle industry capitalized on Beatlemania for its own ends, teenage fans may have been in the forefront of the movement for social change that developed in the late 1960s.

The Beatles on *The Ed Sullivan Show*, February 9, 1964

The phrase ' the British Invasion' started to appear in the American media with the arrival of the Beatles in New York – 'the Beatles invade, complete with long hair and screaming fans' wrote Paul Gardner in the *New York Times* (1964a) – and accelerated as more English pop artists made their way onto the record charts in 1964 and 1965. In fact, British culture was becoming increasingly fashionable and influential in the United States before the Beatles arrived in early 1964. The *New York Times* reported that the British 'have monopolized Broadway for two seasons' (Gardner 1964b). The American version of the English political satire television show, *That Was The Week That Was*, debuted on NBC with a one-hour special in late 1963 and then ran as a series through the 1964–65 season. Meanwhile, James Bond had become the suave hero of movie spy thrillers in *Dr No* (Terence Young, 1962) and *From Russia With Love* (Terence Young, 1963). And the first young British pop entertainer to appear on *The Ed Sullivan Show* during the 1963–64 season was not the Beatles, but Cliff Richard, who had been popular in Britain for five years, but was never successful in the US (Castleman and Podrazik 1980: 167).

Once he signed the Beatles for two live appearances on his show in February 1964, Ed Sullivan fully intended to be the first to introduce them to the American viewing public. However, on the evening of Friday, January 3, Sullivan was upstaged when *The Jack Paar Program* included film footage that Paar had purchased from the BBC, showing screaming English fans and the Beatles performing two songs. In Paar's introductory monologue he explained, 'I'm interested in the Beatles as a psychological-sociological phenomenon' (Spizer 2003: 88). Regarding the fans, he commented, 'These guys have these crazy hairdos and when they wiggle their heads and the hair goes, the girls go out of their minds. Does it bother you to realize that in a few years these girls will vote, raise children and drive cars?' Paar clearly had no interest in the Beatles as anything other than a joke, and by announcing their upcoming live appearance on the Sullivan show, he may have been commenting on the judgement of his old rival as much as the quality of the group (Spizer 2003: 89).

The promotion campaign set in motion by Capitol Records in early January 1964 has been described in detail elsewhere. Disc jockeys all over the country were caught up in the momentum, but in New York particularly the frenzy mounted as 'The Beatles are Coming' became the mantra of the day. By January 25, 'I Want to Hold Your Hand'/'I Saw Her Standing There' was Number One on the *Cash Box* Top 100, and two albums, Vee-Jay's *Introducing the Beatles* (1963) and Capitol's *Meet the Beatles!* (1964), were receiving extensive airplay.

The Beatles arrived in New York on February 7 to a tumultuous welcome and successfully faced the press for the first time. By the next day George Harrison was sick with tonsilitis and unable to attend the afternoon rehearsal at CBS-TV Studio 50 on Broadway and West 53rd Street. (Harrison was nursed by his sister

Louise, who had flown in from her home in St Louis to see him). Neil Aspinall stood in for George during the walk-through (Beatles 2000: 119). Dezo Hoffmann, a photographer travelling with the Beatles, reported:

> It was a happy occasion. Everyone was impressed and pleased with each other, the Beatles by the efficiency of the Sullivan people and the ingenuity of the original sets designed for them, and the CBS crew by the Beatles' professionalism (1985: 31).

Ringo Starr recalled:

> The main thing I was aware of when we did the first Ed Sullivan Show was that we rehearsed all afternoon. TV had such bad sound equipment … that we would tape our rehearsals and then go up and mess with the dials in the control booth. We got it all set with the engineer there, and then we went off for a break. The story has it that while we were out, the cleaner came in to clean the room and the console, thought, 'What are all those chalk marks?' and wiped them all off. So our plans just went out the window. We had a real hasty time trying to get the sound right (Beatles 2000: 119).

On Sunday, February 9 all four Beatles were present in Studio 50 for the dress rehearsal that preceded the taping of songs for another Sullivan show and the live broadcast that night. Harrison, still running a high temperature, was pumped full of medication in order to get through the day (Hoffmann 1985: 31). Many of those attending the afternoon rehearsal and the evening show were the teenage daughters of CBS or Capitol executives (Bowles 1980: 184). Among them were CBS News commentator Walter Cronkite's daughters Kathy and Nancy (Cameron 1964), Jack Paar's daughter Randy (who received one of the dedications from Sullivan after the Beatles' first set) and Randy Paar's guest Julie Nixon (Spizer 2003: 155).

Christopher Porterfield, covering the show for *Time*, recalled the event: 'To the reporters who were there … the noise was what seemed new. Surely these kids were louder, more frenzied, than Frank Sinatra's fans had ever been, or even Elvis Presley's. Sullivan made a pact with them before the show: Keep it down while other acts are on: otherwise you can do what you like' (2003). Shortly before the performance, Brian Epstein asked Sullivan, 'I would like to know the exact wording of your introduction.' Sullivan reportedly replied, 'I would like you to get lost' (Brown and Gaines 1983: 122).

The group's performance on *The Ed Sullivan Show* was actually a set of nested performances interrelated in a variety of ways. First was the musical performance of five songs before a live audience, in the context of a television broadcast whose cast included, in addition to the Beatles and the audience, the announcer George Fenniman, the host Ed Sullivan, the other performers on the show, the commercials and even Elvis Presley (in the form of a telegram).

The second was the performance by the studio audience, whose actions and reactions to what was happening both onstage and on the television monitors ran parallel to the stage performance. One (un-named) reviewer present in the studio for the rehearsal noted:

> the kids weren't actually looking at the Beatles themselves but at TV pictures of the Beatles that appeared on the nine or ten monitors scattered around the studio. I noticed this because the kids also began screaming louder every time a different Beatle appeared on the TV screen. The ones they screamed loudest for were Ringo, the drummer, and Paul, who was doing most of the singing (*New Yorker*, February 22, 1964: 22).

The television cameras frequently cut to this parallel performance, and it was the subject of much of the media coverage of the event. Castleman and Podrazik observed:

> Besides seeing and hearing the group perform, viewers were also exposed to their first direct dose of Beatlemania as the studio cameras focused on hundreds of teenage girls in the audience weeping, screaming, and even fainting (1980: 167).

The third performance layer was that of the television audience in the United States and Canada, who participated that night in what might be called a continent-wide communal ritual experience; we watched the show, mainly in family groups, and responded (depending, in part, on our age and gender) with excitement, joy, amusement, annoyance and/or revulsion.

> Parents didn't know whether to laugh at the group and the screaming fans or condemn them, but kids across the country drank it all in. In that one night, as television once again allowed millions to share an experience as one, the medium created a musical and cultural supergroup (Castleman and Podrazik 1980: 167).

A performance log

February 9, 1964, 8.00 p.m.
> *The Ed Sullivan Show* (broadcast in black and white) begins with the curtain rising on an empty stage and Ray Bloch's orchestral fanfare. The unseen announcer, George Fenniman, begins: 'Good evening, ladies and gentlemen. Tonight, live from New York, the Ed Sullivan Show!' Fenniman announced the evening's commercial sponsors, Anacin and Pillsbury. Then, a drum roll and Fenniman's 'And now, here he is, ED SULLIVAN!' (camera cuts to Sullivan at side of stage … applause, whistles, a few screams). Sullivan's opening:
> 'Thank you (very much). You know, something very nice happened, and the Beatles got a great kick out of it. Just received a wire, *they* did, from Elvis Presley and Colonel Tom Parker, wishing them a tremendous success

in our country, and I think that was very very nice' (audience applause ... in fact, according to Brown and Gaines, the telegram was sent by Colonel Parker without Presley's knowledge (1983: 122).

(Sullivan describes highlights of the season thus far) 'Now tonight the whole country is waiting to hear England's Beatles [a few screams] and you're gonna hear them, and they're tremendous ambassadors of goodwill, after this commercial' (commercial break).

'Now, yesterday and today our theatre's been jammed with newspapermen and hundreds of photographers from all over the nation, and these veterans agree with me, that the city never has witnessed the excitement stirred by these youngsters from Liverpool, who call themselves the Beatles. Now tonight, you're gonna twice be entertained by them, right now and again in the second half of our show. Ladies and gentlemen, the Beatles! Let's ... [drowned out by audience]'

00:00   Camera pans audience.
00:04   Camera dissolve to stage, moves in slowly; PM gives count-in '1 2 3 4 5'.
00:06   'All My Loving' begins (PM sings melody; GH and JL sing harmony).

The stage set is a circle of large, white arrows pointing to the band; in the centre is a low, round platform, on which a smaller platform holds the drum kit about four feet off the ground. At the start of the song, the other three are standing in a row, PM stage right, GH centre-stage and JL stage left; one vocal microphone is directly in front of PM; the second vocal mic is several feet in front of JL. The Beatles wear matching dark suits, ties, and black leather boots.

The first close-up shot is RS; the second is PM (2 angles, the second a close-up face shot); third is GH. GH and JL move to the second vocal mic to sing harmony.

Audience volume starts high, then drops; volume rises at the chorus, guitar break, last verse. Twice during the song the camera cuts to individual girls in the audience.

02:09   End of 'All My Loving' (audience volume high ... camera pans audience briefly, cuts back to stage).

The Beatles bow from the waist in unison and go right into next song.

02:14   'Till There Was You' begins; solo vocals by PM; the audience is nearly quiet until PM starts to sing and camera cuts to close-up face shot.

During this song, a camera close-up of each Beatle is shown as his first name is posted on the TV screen – 'Paul', then 'Ringo', then 'George' and finally 'John. Sorry girls, he's married'. Audience members are apparently watching the monitor, as there is screaming at each of these postings (there are also moments when there is no audible audience noise). There is a second close-up of PM, RS and GH (PM's, at the beginning of the last verse, is accompanied by screaming). The camera cuts once to a pair of girls in the audience.

04:21   End of 'Till There Was You' (audience volume high ... camera cuts to the very back of the hall facing the stage).

The Beatles bow as before and go right into next song.

04:25   'She Loves You' begins (PM gestures to start ... audience volume high) PM and JL sing melody; GH sings harmony at PM's mic. PM, RS, and JL each get a close-up. Audience volume rises on 'whoos'. The camera cuts twice to individual girls in the audience.

06:42   End of 'She Loves You' (audience volume high ... camera pans audience).

The Beatles bow as before.

06:47   Camera cuts away from the Beatles to Sullivan, clapping. He holds his hands up for quiet:

'Now! [one hand up] You promised! Now, those first three songs, those first three songs were dedicated to Johnny Carson, Randy Paar and Earl Wilson. Now, they'll be back in the second half of the show, after you've enjoyed Georgia Brown, the star of *Oliver*, Tessie O'Shea, one of the stars of *The Girl Who Came To Supper*, but right now, a word about Anacin.'

Following the Beatles, Sullivan presents Fred Kaps (comedian/magician); members of the cast of *Oliver* including Georgia Brown; Georgia Brown singing solo; Frank Gorshin (impressionist); (at this point Sullivan introduces Olympic gold medal winner Terry McDermott, in the audience); Tessie O'Shea (singer); and McCall & Brill (comedy team) who include a Beatles joke in their routine ('She used to be one of the Beatles.' 'What happened to her?' 'Somebody stepped on her.').

In his introduction to the Beatles' second set late in the show, Sullivan announces that they will be on his show again the next two Sundays. Then, 'Ladies and gentlemen, once again ... [drowned out by audience]'

00:00   PM's count-in '1 2 3 4'.

00:01   Camera cuts to Beatles onstage (new stage set) – 'I Saw Her Standing There' begins. PM sings melody, JL sings harmony. Close-ups of PM (4) and RS (2). Audience volume spikes at numerous points, including close-ups of PM and at 'whoo' at end of each verse; major spike between third verse and guitar break, when PM, GH and JL all shake heads and scream. Camera cuts to GH's right hand during guitar break. Camera cuts to an individual girl in the audience once during the song.

02:34   Camera pans the full audience (high audience volume).

02:39   'I Want To Hold Your Hand' starts immediately (audience volume peaks). PM and JL sing melody (harmonizing in the bridge). Close-ups of each Beatle (two each except JL, who gets three). The camera cuts to individual girls twice.

05:02   End of 'I Want To Hold Your Hand' (camera pans audience ... high audience volume). The Beatles put their instruments down and trot over to Sullivan, who shakes their hands, speaks to them briefly.

05:32   Beatles move offstage. Screaming continues, Sullivan gestures to stop.
Before introducing the last act, Sullivan speaks into the camera:
'All of us on the show want to express our deep appreciation to the New
York Police Department for its superb handling of thousands of youngsters
who cluttered Broadway at 53rd Street ready to greet the Beatles under the
command of deputy chief Sanford Garrell [?] and our deep appreciation to
the newspapermen, magazine writers, and photographers who've been so
darn kind to the Beatles and to us.'
Sullivan introduces 'a very fine novelty act', Wells and The Four Fays
(acrobatics). After a commercial break, Sullivan closes the show:
'First of all, I want to congratulate you – you've been a fine audience
despite severe provocation. Next week … [describes upcoming show to be
broadcast from Miami Beach]. Now, I'm delighted, all of us are delighted
and I know the Beatles on their first appearance here have been very
deeply thrilled by their reception here. You've been fine – now get home
safely – goodnight!'

The total onstage time for the Beatles was 12 minutes, 19 seconds. (The
breakdown of solo close-ups was ten for Paul McCartney, nine for Ringo Starr,
five for George Harrison and five for John Lennon).

The aftermath

Ed Sullivan's television variety show had been on the air since 1948, and by 1955
it consistently ranked in the top ten rated shows, attracting 44 million viewers
weekly. Despite his intuition that the Beatles would draw an audience, Sullivan's
decision to feature them for consecutive weeks had been a risk. However,
'whatever misgivings he might have had disappeared the next morning when
the preliminary ratings indicated that the show might have been of record
proportions. He decided then and there to use the taped appearance on February
23' (Bowles 1980: 185). When the Nielsen ratings were released, the February 9
show had received a score of 44.6 (translated to 73 900 000 viewers), the
largest audience in television history. 'Sullivan was beside himself with joy. It
was the first time in seven years that he had topped the ratings' (Bowles 1980:
187).[5]
    Critical responses to the Beatles' TV appearance tended to distinguish the
group's performance from the audience's. Very few commented on the quality of
the musical compositions or song performances (which did not vary from the
recorded versions). The exception was Theodore Strongin's report in the *New York
Times* in which he provided a technical explanation of the musical features that
made the Beatles' music interesting and appealing:

The Beatles are directly in the mainstream of Western tradition; that much may be immediately ascertained. Their harmony is unmistakably diatonic. A learned British colleague, writing on his home ground, has described it as pandiatonic, but I disagree.[6] The Beatles have a tendency to build phrases around unresolved leading tones. This precipitates the ear into a false modal frame that temporarily turns the fifth of the scale into the tonic, momentarily suggesting the Mixolydian mode. But everything always ends as plain diatonic all the same. Meanwhile, the result is the addition of a very, very slight touch of British countryside nostalgia, with a trace of Vaughan Williams, to the familiar elements of the rock'n'roll prototype (1964).

His comments were interspersed with those of 'a 15-year-old specialist' who nicely echoes his musicological insights in her own words: 'You can tell right away it's the Beatles and not anyone else.' Despite the bemused tone of Strongin's review and his description of the Beatles' vocal quality as 'hoarsely incoherent, with the minimal enunciation necessary to communicate the schematic texts' (1964), he was among the first to focus on the quality of the Beatles' music rather than their appearance and the behaviour of their fans.[7]

Strongin's column appeared directly below that of the newspaper's television critic Jack Gould, who dismissed the Beatles as musical performers: 'The pretext of a connection with the world of music ... was perfunctorily sustained by the Beatles'; his comments focused on the tameness of the performance in relation to the behaviour of the audience; he described 'the businesslike appearance of the Beatles'; he suggested that despite haircuts worn 'every morning on television by Captain Kangaroo' the quartet was 'composed of conservative conformists' (1964). He did however credit their skill in audience manipulation:

> There appeared to be a bemused awareness that they might qualify as the world's highest-paid recreation directors. In their sophisticated understanding that the life of a fad depends on the performance of the audience and not on the stage, the Beatles were decidedly effective. In their two sets of numbers, they allowed the healing effect of group therapy to run its course under the discipline of Mr Sullivan, the chaperone of the year (Gould 1964).

Gould summarized the performance as 'a fine, mass placebo' (1964). With Elvis Presley as the only possible standard of comparison for the fomenting of teenage hysteria, other observers were also surprised by the reserved behaviour of the musical performance: *Life* reported that 'on the whole, the Beatles' appearance on the Sullivan show seemed subdued, though the audience wasn't' (Cameron 1964) and in its front-page story the day after the TV show, the *Los Angeles Times* suggested that 'the seats ... were given more of a workout by jumping and squirming teen-age girls than were the fast-moving singers by their routine'.

Of the musical presentation, the critics had little to say; they found the appearance of the Beatles more interesting than their music and the behaviour of the fans the most interesting of all. The Beatles were apparently not satisfied with the performance either. Paul McCartney remembered, 'We weren't happy with the first Ed Sullivan appearance, because one of the mikes weren't working, John's, and it sounded weak on the air, we were told' (Badman 2000: 82). John Lennon's comments about the Beatles' performances on that first North American visit are more damning, and I include them as a transition to the next section:

> When the Beatles played in America for the first time, they played pure craftsmanship. Meaning they were already old hands. The jism had gone out of the performances a long time ago (Sheff 1981: 86).

The Beatles as performers: the 'wild' Beatles and the 'tame' Beatles

The Beatles, like most commercial performing artists, were intentionally packaged and marketed in order to be competitive and successful in the music business. Brian Epstein loved the rowdy, leather-clad Beatles he discovered at The Cavern, but to sell them, he conceived an image he believed would enhance their appeal beyond Liverpool, without violating the integrity of their music-making. Until early 1962 the Beatles were a dedicated but poorly organized bar band learning their craft and building their playlist. When Epstein became the Beatles' manager, he began exerting his influence on their way of dress and stage behaviour; he organized their bookings, raised their rates and promoted them tirelessly (Davies 1996: 128). The Beatles, eager for fame and success, gladly cooperated. Under Epstein's management, they performed constantly, gradually moving from bars and dance venues to concert halls. Meanwhile, Epstein devoted himself to securing the Beatles a recording contract, finally attracting the interest of producer George Martin at Parlophone, a small subsidiary of EMI. Between September 1962 and August 1966, the performing and recording careers of the Beatles coincided, with Epstein and Martin as full collaborators. During this period the Beatles not only achieved monumental popularity but became skilled professional performers; and increasingly, Lennon and McCartney were acknowledged as a major force in popular song composition.

The Beatles' performance at the Royal Variety Show on November 4, 1963, seen one week later by a British television viewing audience of 26 million, was arguably the peak of Epstein's 'tame' Beatles' performing career: the Beatles look professional in their matching suits and ties, tidy haircuts, bowing in unison; they are all smiles, enjoying themselves and the music, playing to the crowd, which included members of the royal family. Lennon makes his famous remark, accompanied by a shy bad-boy grin (mischievous but not cynical): 'For our last number, I'd like to ask your help. Would the people in the cheaper seats clap your hands, and the rest of you, if you'd just rattle your jewellery.'

But the tension between the 'wild' and the 'tame' Beatles remained. It may be seen as a positive force in their performances, in the contrast between carefully harmonized pop vocals and the momentary breaking loose at the end of a phrase, and in the insistence of the rock'n'roll groove in the cover tunes they continued to play throughout their performing years. The tension also manifested in disruptive ways for the Beatles; their popularity kept them almost literally caged, and their public image did not allow for deviation. Lennon in particular began to chafe at the confines of being a 'tame' Beatle. When the pressures and dangers of touring were removed after August 1966, even the relative freedom of the studio ultimately proved to have its own constraints. Following Epstein's death, a year after the Beatles' last concert, they began the process of re-inventing themselves, eventually conceiving the 'Get Back' project in an effort to reclaim the 'wild' Beatles and reconnect with the creative and personal unity of the early years of the group. Lennon's return of his MBE award in 1969, in a protest against the British government's foreign policies, signalled his rejection, at an official level, of the image Epstein had created for him and the other Beatles. By 1970, the group's centre could no longer hold, and the Beatles disbanded, entering a phase of individual re-invention.

Beatlemania

The Beatles were marketed to appeal to middle-class tastes and standards, and the majority, though certainly not all, of their American audience was white. Though popular AM radio audiences were increasingly racially mixed in many parts of the country, concert footage confirms that white teenagers, who could afford the ticket prices, made up the vast majority of those attending Beatle concerts. Contemporary commentaries about Beatlemania refer, then, to a teenage culture that, to a large extent, excluded blacks and other minorities.

The Beatles' first appearance on *The Ed Sullivan Show* gained them millions of fans, many of whom were not screaming teenage girls. The word 'Beatlemania', used first by a London headline writer to describe the pandemonium in the streets surrounding the Beatles' appearance at the London Palladium on October 13, 1963 (Lewisohn 1986: 154), applied specifically to the irrational behaviour of teenage girls and was equated with hysteria and a total loss of control in relation to the Beatles. American teenagers learned Beatlemania from local media coverage of their British counterparts, and the media immediately recognized the economic value of American Beatlemania. The rhetoric of a Beatles 'invasion' and 'conquest' was closely tied to the exploitation of female fans who were considered out of control and therefore susceptible to the manipulation of the popular music industry. It was vital that the image of irrationality be re-enforced. 'Hysteria was critical to the marketing of the Beatles' (Ehrenreich, Hess and Jacobs 1986: 30). After holding the match from which the blaze of Beatlemania was lit, the media then turned to psychologists, sociologists and religious leaders for guidance in interpreting the irrational behaviour of young female Beatles fans.

The teenager, both male and female, was under the microscope in the early 1960s, and subconscious motivations for teenage behaviour were the subject of much commentary. The simultaneous need to rebel against the adult world and to conform to one's peer group was scrutinized. The appeal, and danger, of rock'n'roll had been at the heart of the discussion since Elvis Presley's rise to popularity in the mid-1950s. 'By the late fifties, rock'n'roll was the organizing principle and premier theme of teen consumer culture' (Ehrenreich, Hess and Jacobs 1986: 29). Recurring themes were the need for teenagers to love music their parents hated and their embrace of one new music fad after another 'with the predictability of a plague of locusts' (Dempsey 1964: 15). 'Teen' became a market category, but also paved the way for 'an oppositional identity' (Ehrenreich, Hess and Jacobs 1986: 29) as a subculture.

Vance Packard, journalist and early 'pop' social critic, posited five 'vital ingredients' for a 'craze' like the Beatles, including the ability 'to fill some important subconscious need of teenagers. Youngsters see themselves as a subjugated people constantly exposed to arbitrary edicts from adult authorities ... rock'n'roll music, of course, annoys most parents, which is one of the main reasons why millions of youngsters love it' (1964). Rock'n'roll music does more than annoy parents, however; it also terrifies them with its power to mesmerize and loose the bonds of civilized behaviour, particularly that of their daughters:

> The subconscious need that they [the Beatles] fill most expertly is in taking adolescent girls clear out of this world. The youngsters in the darkened audiences can let go all inhibitions in a quite primitive sense when the Beatles cut loose. They can retreat from rationality and individuality. Mob pathology takes over, and they are momentarily freed of all of civilization's restraints (Packard 1964).

The notion of rock'n'roll as the road back to a primitive state of mindless hysteria was expressed in even more dramatic terms by David Dempsey:

> Today's music is a throwback, or tribal atavism, made endemic through mass communication. It is probably no coincidence that the Beatles, who provoke the most violent response among teenagers, resemble in manner the witch doctors who put their spell on hundreds of shuffling and stamping natives. Far-fetched? Not for some anthropologists. At any rate, it is a theory worth thinking about (1964: 15).

(Dempsey appears to be taking a shot at the various scholarly approaches used to analyse rock'n'roll culture as much as hysterical teenagers, but in doing so he may have been the first to use the term 'the anthropology of rock'n'roll').

Although rock'n'roll was considered the undoing of both male and female teenagers, Beatlemania was mainly a female affliction. The Beatles, unlike Presley, projected a cheerful innocence as performers, thus weakening the 'good girls like bad boys' theory. Psychologists had to look for other explanations for the fans' behaviour. The search for subconscious motivations encompassed the gamut of 'female' issues: the maternal instinct, the experience of childbirth, the fear of sexuality and the craving for love and connection. Packard recognized the genius of Epstein's creation:

> [The Beatles], under Mr. Epstein's tutelage … have put stress on filling other subconscious needs of teenagers. As restyled, they are no longer roughnecks but rather lovable, almost cuddly, imps. With their collarless jackets and boyish grins, they have succeeded in bringing out the mothering instinct in many adolescent girls (1964).

In fact, the Beatles were so 'lovable' that, given the need of teenagers to annoy their parents, Packard wondered whether the group's popularity would prove short-lived: 'they are not really offensive enough to grown-ups to inspire youngsters to cling to them' (1964).

A few days after the group's first appearance on *The Ed Sullivan Show*, psychologist Joyce Brothers ventured an explanation of the Beatles' appeal to young women: 'The Beatles display a few mannerisms which almost seem a shade on the feminine side, such as the tossing of their long manes of hair … these are exactly the mannerisms which very young female fans (in the 10 to 14 age group) appear to go wildest over' (cited in Hiram's Report 1964: 22). More than twenty years later, Ehrenreich, Hess and Jacobs re-assessed the behaviour of female Beatles fans in the early 1960s. Referring to that early interpretation offered by Brothers, they observed that it was the androgyny of the Beatles' appearance itself that was attractive.

> What was both shocking and deeply appealing about the Beatles was that they were, while not exactly effeminate, at least not easily classifiable in the rigid gender distinctions of middle-class American life … for girls, fandom offered a way not only to sublimate romantic and sexual yearnings but to carve out subversive versions of heterosexuality (1986: 32–4).

Their analysis introduced a post-Freudian, feminist perspective on Beatlemania that allowed for agency in the behaviour of teenage girls at the time. They suggested that Beatlemania was 'the first mass outburst of the sixties to feature women [and] the first and most dramatic uprising of *women's* sexual revolution' (1986: 11). The 'inhibitions' Packard referred to were sexual inhibitions, promoted by the sexual double standard of the time. The Beatles inspired a sexual attraction in which the young woman was the active player: 'The Beatles were the objects; the girls were their pursuers' (1986: 18). The fact that the objects of desire were unattainable only added to the intensity of feeling: 'Adulation of the male star was a way to express sexual yearning that would normally be pressed into the service of popularity or simply repressed' (1986: 27). The authors saw this behaviour as a protest against the social constraints surrounding the role of women at the time. It was, in fact, the young teenage girls of 1964 who became the feminists of the late

1960s and worked to redefine and expand women's roles in all areas of life. From this perspective, arguably 'the greatest contribution the Beatles made to youth culture may have been Beatlemania itself' (Muncie 2000: 42).

Conclusions

On February 9, 1964, Ed Sullivan introduced America to the Beatles. Whatever combination of factors came into play that night – the appealing appearance and sound of the Beatles, the campaign of Epstein and Capitol Records, the momentum of Beatlemania, the blessing of Sullivan's sponsorship – the evening is an established landmark in the cultural history of the United States. Like the Beatles themselves, the event has taken on mythic proportions.

Looking back in 1995, first-generation Beatles fan Frank Rich speculated that what attracted American teenagers like himself was 'an instinct that the Beatles were avatars of some change in our lives that we couldn't define but knew was on the way'; their arrival was an accident of history, but 'having been handed a historical moment ... the Beatles ran with it' (1995). It is no exaggeration to say that on February 9, 1964, Ed Sullivan also introduced a generation to its future.

Notes

1. An earlier appearance of the Beatles in film footage shown on American television (discussed later in this chapter) occurred on January 3, 1964 on *The Jack Paar Program*. Spizer (2003: 60) documents two earlier television news stories, the earliest on NBC's *Huntley-Brinkley Report* on November 18, 1963 and the second on the *CBS Evening News With Walter Cronkite* on December 10, 1963.
2. Four months before the Beatles' first appearance on *The Ed Sullivan Show*, 15 million British television viewers had seen the Beatles perform on *Sunday Night at the London Palladium*, broadcast on October 13, 1963 (Davies 1996: 180). Although the group had made numerous British TV appearances before that date, the impact of the performance was comparable to that of *The Ed Sullivan Show* in North America.
3. The Beatles performed their first US concert on February 11 at the Washington Coliseum in Washington, DC. The following day, February 12, they played two performances at Carnegie Hall in New York. Their second performance on the Sullivan show was part of a live broadcast from the Deauville Hotel in Miami Beach, Florida the following Sunday, February 16. The third performance, broadcast February 23, had been taped on February 9. The Beatles had already left the United States and returned to England on the evening of February 21.
4. I'm grateful for the timely publication of *The Four Complete Historic Ed Sullivan Shows Featuring the Beatles*, SOFA Entertainment 05-81575 (2 DVDs), 2003.
5. The second appearance of the Beatles on *The Ed Sullivan Show*, broadcast from Miami Beach, Florida on February 16, received a 43.2 rating (about 70 million viewers), but for the taped appearance on February 23, the ratings were 'only average' (Bowles 1980: 187).

6. The 'learned British colleague' to whom Strongin refers is William Mann, the apparent author of 'What Songs the Beatles Sang' which appeared in *The Times* on December 27, 1963 under the by-line, 'From Our Music Critic'. Mann was probably the first to look seriously at the compositions of Lennon–McCartney, which he found so interesting harmonically that he suspected they 'think simultaneously of harmony and melody'; he also noted the 'firm and purposeful bass line with a musical life of its own'. He praised the 'distinctive and exhilarating flavour' of the Beatles' recordings and noted with some pride that their songs are 'indigenous in character' (1963).

7. In addition to Mann (see above), see Alan Rinzler's 'No Soul in Beatlesville', in *The Nation*, March 2, 1964, in which the Beatles are condemned as 'derivative, a deliberate imitation of an American genre'.

Chapter 2

Bob Dylan: Newport Folk Festival, July 25, 1965[1]

Lee Marshall

> Bob Dylan: I did this very crazy thing. I didn't know what was going to happen, but they certainly booed, I'll tell you that. You could hear it all over the place (Press Conference, KQED-TV, San Francisco, December 3, 1965).

Newport 1965: preface and main set

On Sunday, July 25, 1965, Bob Dylan gave his first amplified public performance since leaving high school. The performance, alongside five other musicians, lasted just under 16 minutes and featured musicians who had coalesced as a collective less than 24 hours earlier. Musically, it was fairly ordinary. It is, however, one of the most written-about performances in the history of popular music, for the site of this performance was the main stage of the Newport Folk Festival, the bastion of folk authenticity, and it didn't go down too well.

It is not clear whether Dylan arrived at Newport with the intention of playing with a backing band: if he did, he had not told any intended accomplices. It may well have been the case that Dylan's belief in serendipity meant that he arrived with the intention of just bumping into his chosen musicians (Heylin 2000: 207) or it may be that his decision to play with a band was a direct result of events on the Saturday of the festival, July 24 (Sounes 2001: 218). Whatever the case, Dylan's first performance at the 1965 Newport festival was acoustic and unaccompanied, performing 'All I Really Want to Do' in a songwriters' workshop on the Saturday afternoon. Even at this, however, there were signs that Dylan's presence at the festival was causing problems, and his performance had to be curtailed because of the chaos precipitated by his appearance. Fans in the tent shouted for Dylan to be turned up because they could hear the banjos from the neighbouring workshop, which was hardly in keeping with the collective ethos of the event. The most significant performance of the day, however, was that of the Paul Butterfield Blues Band at a blues workshop. Their very presence at the festival had been a source of controversy, with organizing committee member and musicologist Alan Lomax unhappy at their urbanity, their amplification and their whiteness. It fell to Lomax to introduce the band at the workshop and his introduction was extremely condescending. The band was, however, well-received by listeners and after the set Dylan's manager, Albert Grossman – who had just agreed to manage the Butterfield Band – confronted Lomax, and these two rather portly men were soon rolling around in the dirt. As journalist Robert Shelton notes, 'while the scuffle [was] ... personal, it had some theoretical roots' (1986: 301). Lomax was the ultra-purist, scornful of white boys playing the blues, while Grossman was the corrupting commercial influence, managing some of the biggest names at the festival and thus the focus of a great deal of vitriol from the festival organizers.

How these events affected Dylan is unclear: whether he was prompted by Grossman to use the band as foil for his electric plans, whether he always intended to ask the band to support him, or even if he just saw the opportunity to get up the noses of people like Alan Lomax, events now moved at pace. Dylan already had some elements of his intended band: Michael Bloomfield, guitarist with the Butterfield Band, had been playing on the recording sessions for *Highway 61 Revisited* (1965) and was thus a clear choice; Al Kooper (also part of the *Highway 61* sessions) was to play the organ, and Barry Goldberg (a friend of Bloomfield and recruited at a Newport party) the piano. Dylan's need was for a rhythm section and he thus utilized the Butterfield Band's Jerome Arnold on bass and Sam Lay on drums. The hastily assembled group retreated to a Newport mansion and rehearsed until dawn, by which time Dylan was satisfied with the three songs that they had worked up.

Although he was by far the biggest name at the festival, Dylan's performance was scheduled to be the penultimate act of the first half of the evening set. Ironically, the assembled crowd gained a preview of the type of sound they would later hear from Dylan when, because of torrential rain earlier in the afternoon which delayed their set, the Paul Butterfield Blues Band was re-scheduled as the first act of the evening. Dylan received a long, eulogizing introduction from Peter Yarrow (of Peter, Paul & Mary, and a member of the festival's organizing committee), and he walked on stage in a 'matador-outlaw orange shirt' (Shelton 1986: 302) and a black leather jacket. With a cry of 'Let's go!' the band launched into 'Maggie's Farm'. Dylan shouted rather than sang the words – as if vocal range was irrelevant to his message, as if 'he's just discovered that as a singer he can stomp his foot through the boards' (Marcus 1997: 12). The sound is thin; nothing like the cathedral majesty that would be achieved on the 1966 world tour with The Band. Despite being a fairly straightforward fast blues, musical cracks are evident: Sam Lay turned the beat around on the opening song, so that he was playing on the upbeats (one and three) rather than the downbeats (two and four). The rhythm section finds the second song, 'Like a Rolling Stone', equally difficult to pin down and it quickly regressed to something much like its studio origins as a slow and stately waltz. The third and final song was 'Phantom Engineer' (later to develop into 'It Takes a Lot to Laugh, it Takes a Train to Cry') – a straight-up blues of the type the Butterfield Band played every night – and it is only here that the band finds some fluency, but 'for even the most ardent fan of the new music, the performance was unpersuasive' (Shelton 1986: 302). As the final notes of 'Phantom Engineer' rang out, Dylan called 'Let's go man, that's it!' and the band left the stage, less than 16 minutes from when they appeared.

The full extent of the audience reaction is, of course, difficult to gauge. No recording made by a member of the audience is circulating and the soundboard recording available barely picks up the audience response (this can be compared to an existent audience recording made at Dylan's next electric performance, at New York's Forest Hills Tennis Stadium on August 28, when the audience anger is astonishing in its intensity). However, as Dylan was to say at a San Francisco press conference later in the year 'they certainly booed!' According to some contemporary observers, the booing grew in intensity during the performance: a general disquiet when Dylan walked on stage grew into a flurry of boos during 'Maggie's Farm' which reached a crescendo by the end of 'Phantom Engineer' (Shelton 1986: 302). In addition to Dylan's use of an electric band, various other reasons have been suggested for the booing (Sounes 2001: 221). The most common story – used by Pete Seeger to later justify his reaction to the performance – is that fans were booing simply because the sound mix was so awful and no one could hear what Dylan was singing. It is certainly true that the most important thing about the performance for Dylan seemed to be volume, but the soundboard recording of the show does not support the argument that the sound was poor. An alternative argument – put forward by Al Kooper – is that the crowd booed because of the shortness of the set. However, while this could explain why the booing intensified at the end of 'Phantom Engineer', Kooper is an unreliable witness (he is the source of the popular myth that 'Like a Rolling Stone' was recorded in one take) and his view has not been endorsed by anyone else at the festival. It has even been suggested that people at the back of the crowd were booing merely to appear hip in response to booing from the front. However, even if these explanations contain an element of truth, none of them can fully explain the nature of the crowd's reaction to Dylan's performance nor, indeed, the reactions of certain of the festival's organizing committee (although, contrary to popular myth, Pete Seeger did not attempt to cut the power cables with an axe).

Dylan, individualism and folk authenticity

To understand the significance of Newport 1965 requires an understanding of how Dylan's performance consciously transgressed key facets of authenticity that were deeply held within the folk movement. Furthermore, the events at Newport can also be seen as a key moment in the transferral of these markers of folk authenticity into the emerging genre of rock. Because of this, the performance has taken on a mythological significance, as though it was this performance, and this performance alone that changed the course of popular music. Marcus, for example, states that 'within a year, Dylan's performance would have changed all the rules of folk music – or, rather, what had been understood as folk music would as a cultural force have all but ceased to exist' (1997: 13). The Newport performance is thus seen as a decisive act heralding a new musical world. However, while the events there were certainly dramatic, they cannot be understood as an individual act but only as the culmination of a process of estrangement which itself reflected the ever-present tensions in Dylan's relationship with the folk movement. This tension itself is the result of contradictions within the ideology of folk authenticity and, in the rest of this chapter, I will discuss the relationship between Dylan and the folk movement, which should highlight certain aspects of folk authenticity and make clear why the performance of 1965 was seen as an explicit rejection of the folk ideal.

If we take the Newport performance as a public proclamation of divorce it is a little surprising, given that this period accounts for less than 10 per cent of his career, that Dylan is still frequently characterized as a former folkie. It is even more ironic given that he was never fully integrated into the folk movement in the way that, for example, Joan Baez was. In particular, many of the old guard were suspicious of Dylan's motives, suspecting that he was merely using the popularity of the folk revival as a way of becoming famous. Dylan was similarly wary of the folk movement, and in his first recorded original song, he lampooned the response to his arrival on the scene in (the deliberately mispronounced) Green-wich Village:

> I walked down there and ended up
> On one of them coffee-houses on the block
> Got on the stage to sing and play
> Man there said 'Come back some other day,
> You sound like a Hillbilly,
> We want folk singers here'.

Why was this relationship so fraught? The main reasons, it seems to me, stem from notions of authenticity within the movement which emphasized specific formulations of folk music as authentic expressions of collective experience. Coming from this perspective, it is possible to understand how Dylan – the freewheeling, irreverent, genius-star – may be viewed with suspicion and as a threat to the authenticity of the movement and, equally, how Dylan may have been similarly circumspect of the folk movement.

The folksong revivals that occurred in Britain and America during the 1950s and 1960s reproduced the notions of authenticity that emerged during the first English folk song revival 40 years earlier. The father of this first revival was Cecil Sharp, a Cambridge graduate who, concerned at the effects that urbanization was having on English folk culture, set about recording folksong. However, rather than discovering what 'the folk' were singing, Sharp produced established criteria for what could be considered authentic folk songs and then set out to find them: no songs from towns of any size, no songs from factory workers and no songs from music halls were permitted. This carefully selected collection of songs was then watered down for consumption within polite society (Harker 1980: 147–9). However, the outcome of Sharp's activities, and the most influential flaw of the first revival, was a certain fetishizing of the 'folk song', which became an artefact, cast in stone, to be revered as the true representation of the folk. The folk song ceased to be a living thing – part of an ongoing dynamic culture – and became part of our cultural past – part of what Dylan would later describe as infinity up on trial.

The second English folksong revival, led by Ewan MacColl and Bert Lloyd, was understood as an attempt to take such songs back from the middle classes (Boyes 1993: 223–4) but the rigid definition of the folk song remained. This reached its nadir with the controversial 'policy rule' introduced by MacColl in the Ballads & Blues Club in London (later renamed the Singers Club). The rule basically stated that performers could only perform songs from the country of their origin so that, according to MacColl, 'you didn't have a bloke from Walthamstow pretending to be from China or from the Mississippi' (Denselow 1989: 26; see also Boyes 1993: 237–40). The key characteristic of this revival was thus authenticity (singers could not 'pretend' that they were part of the folk) and this fetishized form of folk music was by its very nature authentic and incorruptible.

It does not take too much imagination to work out why Bob Dylan would not appeal to someone who holds these ideals dear, nor why these ideals would not appeal to Bob Dylan. Dylan has never treated folk songs as too precious to touch, as his hijacking of the stately Scottish ballad 'Pretty Peggy-O' on his first album illustrates: 'I bin round this whole country, but I never yet found Fennario' (Lhamon 1990: 112). He parodied the folk world in 'Talkin' Hava Nageilah Blues', saying 'here's a foreign song I learned in Utah'. Dylan later commented upon the folk world in which he found himself during the lengthy interview which accompanied the release of *Biograph* (1986):

> It was just a clique you know. Folk music was a strict and rigid establishment. If you sang southern mountain blues, you didn't sing southern mountain ballads and you didn't sing city blues. If you sang Texas cowboy songs you didn't play English ballads. It was really pathetic (Crowe 1986: 8).

Dylan travelled to England in late 1962 and the trip had a large impact on his development as he soaked up a lot of traditional British ballads which would provide many of the sources for the songs on *The Times They are A-Changin'* (1964). While he was there, he performed at the Singers Club where Ewan MacColl asserts that Dylan was badly received. Anthea Joseph however, recalls that he was well liked, but that MacColl and his wife Peggy Seeger 'sat there in stony silence' (Heylin 1991: 36).[2]

This fetishization of the folk song reflected a similarly hypostasized conception of 'the folk' that has been embedded in succesive folk revivals. As Boyes claims, 'thanks to folksong collectors' preconceptions and judicious selectivity, artwork and life were found to be identical' (1993: 98). Folk songs were understood as a distillation of the lives of ordinary people but Marcus believes that what resulted was a breakdown of the relationship between art and life; rather than folk music being a form of popular art, a certain kind of life became art: 'the poor are art because they sing their lives without mediation and without reflection, without the false consciousness of capitalism and the false desires of advertising' (1997: 28). The outcome was a fetishization of all the good, the rural, the working class, creating what Jeff Nuttall has described as 'a patronising idolisation of the lumpen proletariat that only the repressed children of the middle classes could have contrived' (Harker 1980: 151).

Fetishized (authentic) folksong thus represented a fetishized people, and Marcus characterizes this collective ethos of the 1960s folk movement, and its attendant aesthetic and social ideals, thus:

> The country over the city, labour over capital, sincerity over education, the unspoiled nobility of the common man and woman over the businessman and the politician … a yearning for peace and home in the midst of noise and upheaval (1997: 21).

This kind of understanding was exemplified a couple of hours before Dylan took to the stage at Newport in July 1965. At the beginning of the final evening Pete Seeger, the personification of folk earnestness, played the audience a recording of a newborn baby. He said that the final night's programme was a message to this baby and asked the audience to sing to it, to tell it what sort of world it had been born into. According to contemporary Jim Rooney, Seeger already knew what it would be told: 'that it was a world of pollution, bombs, hunger and injustice, but that PEOPLE would OVERCOME' (Marcus 1997: 11).

In his early career, Dylan was certainly buying into at least some of this, and in his early work he locates goodness in the wild west and corruption in the urban east. His first two original recorded lines are 'Rambling outta the wild west/leavin' the towns I love the best' while in 'Let Me Die in My Footsteps' the glory of America is to be found in 'Nevada, New Mexico, Arizona, Idaho'. Whether Dylan was conscious of the ideological strands on which he was drawing at this time is debatable, but there is a big difference between his treatment of the subject matter at this point and his return to these themes on *John Wesley Harding* (1968). For example, the narrator of the early outlaw song 'Rambling Gambling Willie' maintains no reflexive distance from the outlaw and is carried along by Willie's personality, emphasizing his heart of gold in a manner reminiscent of earlier folk heroes such as Pretty Boy Floyd. This can be directly contrasted with the skilful and distanced manipulation of the narrator in 'John Wesley Harding' who merely tells us how the outlaw has been represented by others ('He was never known to hurt an honest man'), offering a more sceptical view of the Wild West mythology.

Similarly, Dylan's most protesty of protest albums, *The Times They are A-Changin'* contains much that adheres to the collective ethos of the folk movement (the title track, for example, was very consciously created as a folk-anthem); but in general, Dylan's work sits uneasily with the rest of the folk movement's canon because of the significance of individual experience, of feeling, of subjectivity within it. In the folk movement's fetishized folk and folk songs, by contrast, there is little room for individual subjectivity: 'Whether one hears them ringing true or false, they were pageants of righteousness, and while within these pageants there were armies and generations, heroes and villains, nightmares and dreams, there were almost no individuals' (Marcus 1997: 21). The folk movement was founded upon the importance of the collective – the folk, the 'people' – rather than the individual. If a certain type of life replaced art in the folk movement, the life was understood only structurally, as poverty, as oppression. The individual experiences of those in poverty, or those suffering racial discrimination, seemed not to matter. In Dylan's work, however, they did (and do) matter, and this emphasis upon subjectivity and individualism (both within his work and as an individual within the movement) created the key tension between Dylan and the folk movement that exploded at Newport.

When he was justifying his writing of more politically aware songs in 1963, Dylan wrote an open letter to his old friend Tony Glover. In it, he stated that he could not sing traditional folk songs such as 'Red Apple Juice' or 'Little Maggie' any more, but instead had to sing 'Masters of War' and 'Seven Curses'. He made clear his debt to his folk heritage, for 'the folk songs showed me ... that songs can say somethin' human' (Heylin 1991: 74). It is this 'somethin' human' that sets Dylan apart from his folk movement contemporaries, and it is worth noting that the first songs he wrote were not 'pageants of righteousness' but were, rather, stories of individual people caught in the machinery of everyday life – songs such as 'Man on the Street', 'Talking Bear Mountain Picnic Massacre Blues' or 'Ballad of Donald White'. These early considerations of social justice occur through an evocation of individual experience. It was only later that Dylan began to address issues as issues rather than experiences – songs such as 'Masters of War' and 'With God on Our Side' – and this can surely be attributed to his embeddedness in the folk movement.

One example of the kind of subjectivity in Dylan's work I am discussing here is 'Blowin' in the Wind' (which, coincidentally, uses the tune of 'No More Auction Block', an old folk song which considers slavery from the perspective of an escaped slave). 'Blowin' in the Wind' is a list of collective challenges that individuals face (Ricks 2003: 324). Thus, we are asked 'how many roads must *a* man walk down?' or 'how many ears must *one* man have?' Within this context, a significant line is 'how many years must some people exist before they're allowed to be free?' because here Dylan recognizes that 'a people', a collectivity, is merely made up of 'some people', a group of individuals. So while he asks the question 'how long until black Americans [a people] achieve freedom?' he does so in a manner that really asks 'how long until each individual black person is free?'

A song in which Dylan is more explicit about the relationship between causes, collectivities and individuals is 'The Lonesome Death of Hattie Carroll'. It tells the story of the murder of a bartender by William Zanzinger, the son of wealthy tobacco-farmers. The first verse details the murder, the second verse describes Zanzinger. The third verse describes Hattie, not exaggerating but describing her in a dignified and gentle way (Ricks 2003: 222). After each of these verses the same refrain is repeated:

Ah, but you who philosophise disgrace
And criticise all fears
Take the rag away from your face
Now ain't the time for your tears.

The final verse details the courtroom scene, where Zanzinger is given a six months sentence for murder. The refrain then changes to:

Ah, but you who philosophise disgrace
And criticise all fears
Bury the rag most deep in your face
Now's the time for your tears.

Here Dylan recognizes that the real tragedy of this song is in the death of an honest and good woman and not in the injustice of the courts. This last refrain chastizes those who cry crocodile tears over the woman when they are really crying over the sentence (Williams 1990: 93–4). Another way in which Dylan focuses upon individuals rather than causes is by the absence of any mention of race: there is no telling from the song whether Hattie Carroll is black or white. To those crying crocodile tears it is the crucial factor but to Dylan it misses the point. Similarly, 'Ballad Of Hollis Brown' is not primarily about poverty: it is about a farmer who, mad with hunger, shoots his wife and five children before turning the gun on himself. Only *then* is it about *poverty*.

It is easy to see how this important thread in Dylan's work would lead to his flirtations with existentialism in 1965 and 1966: the most important question that Dylan ever asked in his work is 'how does it feel?' In an interview in 1971, he said 'My thing has to do with *feeling*, not politics, organised religion or social activity. My thing is a feeling thing. Those other things will blow away. They'll not stand the test of time' (Scaduto 1996: 286). It is also easy to see how this 'thing' within his work would result in his strained relationship with the folk movement and its distrust of individual impulses and failings.

There is one further way in which individualism played a decisive role in the relationship between Dylan and the folk movement, and that is the individuality of Dylan himself. A crucial element of folk authenticity is that performers are understood to be part of the group they represent, part of the folk (this can practically be seen in MacColl's aforementioned policy rule). As such, the folk movement was essentially collective and each singer was merely one representative of the people. In this understanding, it is the song and not the singer (let alone the writer) that matters. However, particularly among the newer generation of folk singers, it was widely acknowledged that Dylan was far ahead of anyone else as a writer and a performer, and this elevation caused significant distrust towards Dylan by many in the movement. Such distrust was generated by an understanding that the elevation of an individual left the collective vulnerable to the whims and weaknesses of that individual (such an understanding was in a way correct, for Dylan's disavowal of the folk movement certainly diminished the movement's popularity).

One particular vulnerability that individuals had was to the temptations and trappings of fame and commercial success. Dylan's commercialism has often been a cause of criticism, particularly his relationship with Albert Grossman and it is this position of Dylan as an oxymoronic 'folk music star' that finally cracked at Newport in 1965, and signifies the importance of Dylan choosing to play with an electric guitar. Dylan was later to question what people had expected him to play; he had already released *Bringing it All Back Home* (1965) with its electric first side and his new single, 'Like a Rolling Stone', had entered the charts four days before the festival (Heylin 2000: 206). Furthermore, electricity had not been completely exorcised from earlier festivals: Muddy Waters had played amplified instruments the year before without a fuss (Shelton 1986: 301). However, Dylan's use of an electric guitar and his mode of dress were powerful symbolic gestures because they represented the elevation of the individual over the collective, the artificiality of the showbiz lifestyle and the victory of capitalism. As Oscar Brand stated, the electric guitar 'was the antithesis of what the festival was … the electric guitar represented capitalism' (Sounes 2001: 221); and when Robert Shelton offered support for Dylan's new music, the festival's technical director retorted, 'you've been brainwashed by the recording industry!' (1986: 303).

Dylan's split from the folk movement

The story of Dylan's drift away from folk thus signifies an increasing emphasis upon individualism, both in terms of Dylan's own experiences (an increasing interest in individual expressivism through fashion rather than a worker's uniform; increasing use of drugs; increasing criticism from within the folk movement of his adoption of the trappings of a pop star) and through his work (increasing introspection and existentialism; songs dominated less by causes). It reached its climax in July 1965 but two earlier performances are also significant: the Newport performance of 1964 and Dylan's acceptance speech for the Tom Paine Award in December 1963.

Before either of these occurred, however, there were two events that had a major impact upon Dylan and perhaps caused him to re-appraise his relationship with the folk movement. The first of these was the emergence of the Beatles in America in 1964. There is no doubt that, early on in their career, Dylan was blown away by the group: according to Eric Burdon of the Animals, the first time Dylan heard 'I Want to Hold Your Hand', he stopped the car to listen to it, got out and ran round the car five times shouting 'It's great! It's great!' (Heylin 1991: 92). It seems that this experience enabled Dylan to see the possibilities of transcending the popular music that had been dominating the charts while he was in the folk movement.

The second event that deeply affected Dylan was the assassination of John F. Kennedy which seemingly made Dylan realize two things: first, that he was only a folk singer, a position from which he could not change the world; second, that as long as he tried to write topical songs he would always be behind the times. Dylan later told his biographer Anthony Scaduto that the day after the assassination he played a show in New York and opened, as usual, with 'The Times They are A-Changin'. He admitted, 'that song was just too much for the day after the assassination ... I couldn't understand why I wrote that song, even' (Heylin 1991: 83). Even before it had been commercially released, the song was redundant.

The impact that this had on Dylan became public three weeks later; he had been chosen as the recipient of the Tom Paine Award by the Emergency Civil Liberties Committee. Dylan, always nervous in public, started drinking too early and, when he came to accept his award, unleashed a 'truth attack', telling the dignitaries in front of him that they should be on the beach, that it was a young person's world, and that he wanted to speak to an audience with hair on their heads. He questioned the validity of their issues and, towards the end of his speech, stated that he could identify with Lee Harvey Oswald. This caused uproar among the audience. As the dinner was a fundraiser for the ECLC, and thus had significant financial repercussions, Dylan was apologetic for his outburst (he did offer to cover any shortfall, but did not follow through on this offer). He wrote an open letter to apologize for his behaviour, but in it he merely revealed his increasingly individualistic direction:

> I am a writer and a singer of the words I write I am no speaker nor any politician/an
> my songs speak for me because I write them/in the confinement of my own mind an
> have t cope/with no one except my own self.

The focus on 'no one except my own self' was beginning to play more of a role in Dylan's songwriting. In June 1964, he recorded the songs that would make up his fourth studio album, the bluntly titled *Another Side of Bob Dylan* (1964). Some of these new songs received their public unveiling at that year's Newport Folk Festival the following month. At his first appearance of the weekend – a topical-song workshop on the Friday – Dylan began with a new song, 'It Ain't Me Babe', but no one seemed to recognize its statement of intent. At his main performance on the Sunday, he played three more songs from the album: 'All I Really Want to Do', 'To Ramona', 'Chimes of Freedom', and another new song, 'Mr Tambourine Man'. The latter two both feature an increasingly central individual in Dylan's work – the chimes of freedom were flashing for the 'countless confused, accused,

misused, strung out ones and worse/and for every hung up person in the whole
wide universe' while 'Mr Tambourine Man' is a highly introspective song on the
nature of songwriting (although its regularly reproduced misinterpretation – that it
is a 'drug song' – is equally individualistic). The change from the Newport Festival
of 1963 when, as a relative newcomer to the scene, Dylan was invited to sing with
both Pete Seeger and Joan Baez, and his 'Blowin' in the Wind' was sung by the
final, arm-linking, ensemble, was quite dramatic and many in the folk community
voiced their concerns (Allison 1987). Some were critical of Dylan's manner in
dealing with his stardom. For example, Irwin Silber (1964) wrote an open letter
in *Sing Out!* stating 'I saw at Newport how you had somehow lost contact with
people ... some of the paraphernalia of fame were getting in the way'. Others were
scornful of the new songs: Paul Wolfe in *Broadside* wrote that the performance
was the 'renunciation of topical music by its major prophet' and that the new songs
'degenerated into confusion and innocuousness' (Heylin 1991: 100–101). Dylan
offered no official response to the criticisms but wrote a scathing riposte called
'Advice for Geraldine on Her Miscellaneous Birthday'. This was published in the
programme for his Halloween concert in New York and began:

> do not create anything, it will be
> misinterpreted. it will not change.
> it will follow you the
> rest of your life.

Newport 1965: encore and aftermath

The celebrated events of July 1965 should therefore be seen both as the culmination
of a process and as the final implosion of the contradictory relationship between
Dylan's world view and that of the folk movement. His decision to perform with an
electric guitar and a band may not have been premeditated, but it was made with
the knowledge that it would upset a few people. Whether he expected the audience
to react as they did is another matter: he may have been intending to incite the
wrath of folk's inner core (such as Pete Seeger), but at his 1964 appearance, the
audience had been supportive of his new songs and it is plausible that he expected
1965's audience to follow suit. According to many backstage observers, Dylan
was visibly shocked by the reaction, with a number of accounts suggesting that
there were tears in his eyes. Shelton records that Dylan was stunned by the events
for all of the following week (1986: 304).

It also seems that Dylan had given no thought to playing any more than the three
songs rehearsed with the band, and the uncertainty and confusion of the aftermath
of the performance can clearly be heard on the recording: Peter Yarrow seems to be
trying to placate the crowd – telling them that Dylan had gone to get an acoustic
guitar – while at the same time coaxing him to return to the stage. Dylan eventually

did so, with a guitar supposedly lent to him by Johnny Cash. He played 'It's All Over Now, Baby Blue' as an appropriate adieu and, by the end of the song, he had recovered his performing wits: he began strumming the chords of 'Mr Tambourine Man' before pausing. 'Does anybody have an E harmonica?' he entreated the crowd, 'an E harmonica – anybody? – just throw them all up'. There followed a hail of harmonicas hitting the stage; Dylan picked one up, checked its tuning, and thanked the audience before commencing the song. 'Mr Tambourine Man' contained a two-sided irony: not only was it one of the songs that had caused controversy 12 months earlier, but it had only recently vacated the Number One slot in the Billboard pop charts through the electrified version by the Byrds (Heylin 2000: 213). These ironies were seemingly lost on the crowd who, having taught the recalcitrant singer the error of his ways, were merely glad to have the old Dylan back.

The relationship between Dylan and the folk movement had always been strained and by early 1965 he found its expectations too restrictive (this can quite clearly be seen in D.A. Pennebaker's documentary film *Don't Look Back* (1967) in which Dylan experiences a jump in time, leaving America in 1965-mode and arriving for a UK tour with everyone expecting him to be just like he was in 1963). After the British tour in May he had made the quite serious decision to quit the music scene altogether, a decision seemingly overturned by his excitement at writing 'Like a Rolling Stone'. The performance at Newport that year was thus a deliberate attempt to break free from these restrictions, a statement of artistic self-assertion. It also had far wider implications, however, for the controversy sapped the life from the folk revival: a fact apparent even in the immediate aftermath of Dylan's performance, when there suddenly seemed to have appeared an unbridgeable and irrevocable chasm between the new and the old, as festival organizer Joe Boyd clearly understood:

> After the interval for some reason the scheduling misfired and every washed-up, boring, old, folkie, left-wing fart you could imagine [performed] in a row, leading up to Peter, Paul & Mary in the final thing – Ronnie Gilbert, Oscar Brand, Josh White … Theodore Bikel – they all went on, one after another. It was like an object lesson in what was going on here. Like, all you guys are all washed-up. This is all finished (Heylin 2000: 213–14).

Notes

1. Some of the material here first appeared in Marshall (2000).
2. Still, it's nice to know that Bob wasn't bitter. In 1985, MacColl's daughter Kirsty wrote home, saying 'I was at a party with Bob Dylan last night. He's still one of your great fans in spite of the fact that you don't think much of him' (Denselow 1989: 29).

Chapter 3

When deep soul met the love crowd
Otis Redding: Monterey Pop Festival, June 17, 1967

Sarah Hill

The Monterey Pop Festival (June 16–18, 1967) was the first of its kind. As the first acknowledgement that pop music was building a history worthy of a three-day celebration, it provided the template for the festivals at Woodstock, the Isle of Wight and Glastonbury. As a time capsule of contemporary popular culture, Monterey Pop was the intersection of soul and psychedelia, of commercial pop and the rock underground, of Civil Rights and expanded consciousness, of southern California and northern California, of the southern states and the rest of the United States. It was a festival of amazing good will, of harmony between the city and its weekend visitors, between the police and the hippies, between the artists and the audience. It was the symbolic representation of the 'Summer of Love' and the realization of the countercultural ideology which gave the festival its remit of 'love and flowers and music'.

The roster at Monterey included unknown bands (Electric Flag, The Group With No Name), bands known mainly in the San Francisco Bay area (Quicksilver Messenger Service, Country Joe and the Fish, Big Brother and the Holding Company, the Grateful Dead) and bands whose reputations, if not their music, preceded them (The Who, the Jimi Hendrix Experience). Bands who had hits in the US Top Ten (the Byrds, the Mamas and the Papas, Jefferson Airplane) were there, as were the 'folk' contingent (Simon and Garfunkel, Laura Nyro) and the 'world' contingent (Hugh Masakela, Ravi Shankar). The spectrum of music on the main stage of Monterey Pop was a microcosm of the contemporary musical scene. Monterey Pop gave some performers (Beverly, the Paupers) their 15 minutes of fame, but others it catapulted into superstardom, to the extent that, over 30 years later, it is impossible to consider the career trajectory of Janis Joplin, Jimi Hendrix or Otis Redding without referring back to their crucial performances at Monterey.

Monterey Pop was based on the successful models of the Monterey Jazz Festival and the Monterey Folk Festival, themselves based on the established East

Coast festivals at Newport. The idea of a 'festival' – a celebration of a given type of music – was in the 1960s a challenge to genre conventions. The definitions of 'jazz' and 'folk', for example, were certainly undergoing constant re-assessment, with varying degrees of success. Jazz festivals in the 1950s and 1960s featured proponents of new musical directions alongside purveyors of the 'traditional'; the Newport Folk Festival of 1965, long protective of the legacy of Woody Guthrie and Pete Seeger, was the unwitting stage for a decisive shift from 'folk' to rock.[1] In both instances, the nature of the genre itself – jazz or folk – needed to be reinterpreted, and history needed to be reconciled with the natural processes of musical evolution. By contrast, 'pop' music was still rather young in the mid-1960s, with decades of evolution and reconciliation ahead of it, and in 1967 it was nothing if not disparate. As the first opportunity to showcase contemporary popular music, Monterey Pop was necessarily inclusive of folk, psychedelia, soul, blues and chart pop. The combination of acts on the festival bill demonstrated this enormous and natural diversity, made the 'pop festival' an unselfconsciously all-encompassing event, and allowed for musical dialogues to develop. The legacy of this inclusivity was foretold by Otis Redding's performance. As the climax of the festival's second night, it marked not only the inception of a dialogue between psychedelia and soul, but a key moment of transition for both genres.

The year 1967 was witness to many significant musical moments, both live and recorded. Perhaps the most significant event of the first half of the year was the release of the Beatles' *Sgt Pepper's Lonely Hearts Club Band*. Not only did it appeal to the widest conceivable audience, it united that audience in a kind of musical revolution which heralded the onset of the 'Summer of Love'.[2] The 'Summer of Love' was a hopeful term which had been invoked by the San Francisco City Council to mark a growing countercultural movement centred in the San Francisco Bay Area. It was propounded in part by a community of local musicians based in the Haight-Ashbury district of the city, and perpetuated by the media in a three-word summary of a much larger cultural construct. As the first 'official' congregation of pop fans and musicians in the summer of 1967, Monterey Pop might have symbolized outwardly the 'Summer of Love' to the media and the festival audience alike; it was not, however, the first major public event of the year. In fact, on the local level, the 'Summer of Love' had been in process for much longer. The year had begun in San Francisco with the Giant Freakout, featuring music by Jefferson Airplane, Quicksilver Messenger Service and the Grateful Dead; the Gathering of the Tribes (the Human Be-In), held two weeks later at Golden Gate Park, featured the same roster and more. Where hippies congregated in San Francisco, local bands were sure to be, and word would inevitably get around.

Those early 'happenings' of 1967 – the Giant Freakout, the Human Be-In – were the natural extensions of the hippie ideology. This was not restricted to San Francisco,[3] but San Francisco was its figurative home. The media focus on San Francisco as the home of the hippie was as attributable to the rise of local music as it was to a general predilection in that faction of the population for expanded consciousness. Contemporary reports began to circulate suggesting that there was a growing movement in the area buoyed by the consumption of lysergic acid, and focused on challenging the accepted norms of social behaviour. Most notably, music and LSD had coalesced at the 1965 Acid Tests, with the Grateful Dead acting as de facto house band. The community ethos of the Haight-Ashbury district of San Francisco was therefore as connected to the exploration of consciousness as it was to the soundtrack of the times. The music local bands were performing may not have been as mainstream or immediately accessible as *Sgt Pepper*, but the underlying message was the same: explore new realities, love one another.

These expressions of countercultural community could not remain underground, however, and the tension between mainstream and underground music is important to note, for reasons of socio-historical consequence and the ruptured seams of geography. Of particular importance here is the perceived division between northern and southern California. Monterey is much closer to San Francisco than to Los Angeles,[4] and as such, Monterey Pop was the first moment when the counterculture was exploited for the mainstream. This is not to suggest that Los Angeles was not party to the overall good vibes of the era, of course; merely to suggest that there was a fundamental difference inferred between the commercial industry in Los Angeles and the San Francisco underground music scene, which was enacted before, during and after Monterey Pop.

The local music industry can be a gauge of contemporary local character, and San Francisco and Los Angeles were decidedly distinct in the mid-1960s. The more successful bands of the time based in Los Angeles – the Beach Boys, the Monkees, the Doors, the Byrds, the Mamas and the Papas – were in part driven by financial reward, while some of the more prominent bands in San Francisco – the Grateful Dead, Big Brother and the Holding Company – were still operating without recording contracts.[5] 'Popularity' in this sense was gauged by local following and local critical support, not by record sales, and the audiences naturally perceived this distinction.

Given these differences of character, it is safe to say that Monterey Pop never would have happened had it been left to the San Francisco musicians to organize it. In the early part of 1967 the money for Monterey Pop was being raised by Los Angeles concert promoter Alan Pariser and booking agent Benny Shapiro. John Phillips, of the Mamas and the Papas, approached long-standing Los Angeles music industry insider Lou Adler with the loose idea of turning the festival into a charity event. The two ultimately assumed creative control of the festival, and Monterey Pop quickly became a forum for southern Californian business acumen. The main players of the San Francisco underground scene were by nature mistrustful of the Los Angeles music industry, and their experience staging local, large-scale outdoor events forced them to raise some concerns about the provisions in Monterey for camping, food and emergency services. In order to placate the San Francisco musicians, the manager of the Grateful Dead and a member of the

Diggers (the radical anarchist San Francisco 'organization') met with Monterey city officials and agreed to establish a camping site on the football field of Monterey Peninsula College, near to the festival fairgrounds. In order to placate the citizens of Monterey – and despite newspaper reports to the contrary – John Phillips promised that the money raised by the Festival would not benefit organizations such as the Diggers, but rather go to a scholarship fund for popular music education.[6] Both sides were agreed, and plans for booking the talent went ahead.

The participation of the San Francisco bands gave Monterey Pop a necessary countercultural cachet, but mainstream acts were somewhat more difficult to secure. In the absence of the Beach Boys or the Beatles,[7] the Mamas and the Papas became the top headlining act of the festival. They had had a number of Top Ten hits – 'Monday Monday', 'California Dreaming' – and were among the top-grossing acts of the period. Their inclusion on the programme lent credibility to the festival organization, and encouraged acts such as the Byrds and Simon and Garfunkel to participate; but it created an awkward tension between the goal of the festival – to provide a stage for a wide range of talent – and the possibility for monetary gain. Nobody embodied this tension more than John Phillips himself. Once he had assumed creative control of the festival, Papa John penned a song for Scott McKenzie intended to be the anthem of the summer. That song, 'San Francisco (Be Sure to Wear Flowers in Your Hair)',[8] did as much to perpetuate the myth of the Summer of Love as it did to draw music fans to Monterey for that June weekend. But it should be remembered that it was written in Los Angeles, and the San Francisco musicians who had been integral to the formation of the local hippie community heard it as a mainstream exploitation of their community ethos. To some extent the song reflected the general migration of young people into the Haight-Ashbury in search of that very community, but by the Summer of Love, many of the key figures in the San Francisco scene had already begun plotting their escape to the other side of the Golden Gate Bridge. 'San Francisco (Be Sure to Wear Flowers in Your Hair)' may have been the theme song of Monterey, but it was also unusually and immediately nostalgic.

The holistic approach to popular music in the 1960s did not mesh well with its commercial counterpart. Part of the musical ideology of the Bay area before the Summer of Love was that it was anti-*star*; the Los Angeles music scene was more commercially motivated and therefore difficult to separate from the industry which surrounded it. For these reasons, 'San Francisco (Be Sure to Wear Flowers in Your Hair)' was as antithetical to the actual Bay area musical aesthetic as it could possibly have been. And despite the success of the festival and the wide exposure that Bay area bands got through their performances there, when the festival closed on Sunday night with Scott McKenzie and the Mamas and the Papas performing 'San Francisco (Be Sure to Wear Flowers in Your Hair)', any overriding feeling of accomplishment their musicians might have felt was erased in one fell swoop.[9]

Nevertheless, Monterey Pop was at heart an international festival. Beyond the northern and southern California contributions, Monterey had a fairly comprehensive talent roster; there were, however, a few notable absences. Most surprisingly perhaps was the lack of representation from Motown, a label which by 1967 had sent an unprecedented number of 'crossover' singles to the top of the pop charts, both in the US and the UK.[10] Motown's enormous crossover success could have boosted the Top 40 quotient on the festival bill – the Supremes would have been an obvious inclusion, having earned their tenth Number One pop single in 1967 – and provided it with a greater racial balance. Given this missed opportunity, it is interesting to consider the acts that did appear, and the extent to which they reflected or fulfilled the potential for an R&B–pop intersection.

The three African-American frontmen at Monterey Pop – Lou Rawls, Otis Redding and Jimi Hendrix – represented different points on the continuum of black American popular music. There were going to be other black performers on the bill besides themselves:[11] Smokey Robinson was on the festival's board of governors, but did not perform; Dionne Warwick was scheduled to perform but could not be released from an extended San Francisco engagement; the Impressions were scheduled but cancelled their performance. Had these artists taken part, the impact that Redding and Hendrix in particular had on the festival crowd might have been different. Their performances would never have been considered anything less than momentous, but the fact that they were in the minority that weekend raises issues of representation, integration, and roots.

Lou Rawls appeared at Monterey on the Friday night bill, opening for Eric Burdon and the Animals and headliners Simon and Garfunkel. Rawls's roots lay in gospel; early experience of close-harmony singing with Sam Cooke prefaced his own crossover into secular music and allied his approach to that of Otis Redding.[12] Despite his mid-1960s shift into soul, Lou Rawls's Monterey set was an unusual combination of show tunes ('On a Clear Day You Can See Forever'), old standards ('Autumn Leaves') and songs highlighting his newer, more soulful direction ('Love is a Hurtin' Thing', 'Dead End Street', 'Tobacco Road'). These latter songs, though significant in their inclusion, got somewhat lost in the mix, and were not representative of the more dynamic soul that Otis Redding was to demonstrate the following night.

At the other end of the spectrum was Jimi Hendrix, who appeared in the Sunday night concert, sandwiched between the Grateful Dead and the Mamas and the Papas. Earlier opening act The Who, whose set-destroying performance of 'My Generation' shocked the crowd and the crew alike, were ultimately out-performed in the pyrotechnics and feedback stakes by Hendrix, who broke through to the Monterey audience on their own terms. His musical language – apparent in his performances of 'Killing Floor' and 'Wild Thing' – was akin to the blues-based psychedelic rock of other festival bands such as Big Brother and the Holding Company and the Grateful Dead, while his performance of 'Like a Rolling

Stone' allied the Jimi Hendrix Experience with the mainstream 'rock' audience. This likeness of approach to different musical styles, and the commonality of experience which it suggested to the different factions of the audience contributed to one of the more cathartic moments of the weekend, and set Hendrix on his trajectory to superstardom.

In many respects, Otis Redding serves as the actual and symbolic middle point between those two performances. Lou Rawls appeared on Friday night with his gospel-based new soul; Jimi Hendrix appeared on Sunday night with his hybrid psychedelic blues; Otis Redding appeared on Saturday night with a combination of deep soul and 'borrowed' pop hits. Lou Rawls represented the tradition from which Otis Redding came; Jimi Hendrix represented the embodiment of musical and social freedom for which Otis Redding and his integrated backing band, Booker T. and the MGs, provided the template.

To understand the significance of their contribution to 1960s popular music, it is important to consider the context within which Otis Redding and Booker T. and the MGs operated. Compared to contemporary 'soul' labels such as Detroit's Motown, the Memphis-based Stax record label was a small company,[13] but it exerted a wide and palpable influence on musicians in the US and the UK alike. The 'Stax Sound' was more raw, less polished, than Motown's.[14] Many of Motown's hits followed certain undeniably successful formulae, but Stax earned its reputation largely by the contributions of its regular and dedicated stable of artists. Booker T. and the MGs (Booker T. Jones, keyboards; Al Jackson, drums; Steve Cropper, guitar; Donald 'Duck' Dunn, bass) had gained a reputation from their hit single 'Green Onions'[15] but their work as Stax house band earned them their widest fame. Most significant, within the social climate of the southern United States in the 1960s, was the fact that Booker T. and the MGs were an integrated band. The management and musicians at Stax never made an issue of their ethnicity, but where 1960s R&B–pop 'crossovers' are concerned, it needs to be emphasized that Steve Cropper and Donald 'Duck' Dunn were two white musicians whose contributions to the soul canon were inestimable.

Perhaps because of their location, perhaps because of their recording schedules, perhaps because of the contemporary US music industry, the first real indication that anyone at Stax had of their success came from abroad. Otis Redding appeared before a national television audience on Britain's *Ready, Steady, Go!* in 1966. The resultant popularity of what the British press began to call 'Memphis Music' was obvious the following spring, when Stax launched a European tour of its rhythm and blues revue.[16] The success of that tour was an encouraging sign to the Stax musicians that popular recognition was possible back home as well, even in a still segregated music industry.

'Success' at home was both sporadic and limited. From the release of his first single 'These Arms of Mine' in 1963 until his appearance at Monterey, Redding had rarely made a dent in the US Top 40 pop chart, and never broke into the Top Ten, while seven of his singles reached the R&B Top Ten.[17] His albums fared much the same – *Otis Blue* (1965), which topped the R&B charts, only reached 75 on the pop charts, and two subsequent recordings, *King And Queen* (1967) and *Otis Redding Live In Europe* (1967) barely scratched the Top 40. Although his singles had sold well in the R&B market and his concerts had begun attracting larger numbers, Redding had not been considered a commercially viable player in the mainstream white American market. His inclusion on the bill at Monterey, perhaps surprising for these very reasons, was primarily the result of a mutual respect that he shared with Californian music industry insiders and local musicians in the larger urban areas of the state.

Otis Redding had begun to establish a relationship with the California audience in 1966, by playing the Whiskey-a-Go-Go in Los Angeles in April and San Francisco's Fillmore Auditorium that December. His Los Angeles shows were a clear marketing risk. The Whiskey-a-Go-Go was primarily a white rock venue, and few of the audience for his shows there were familiar with 'authentic' R&B, although remnants of the Stax sound had filtered through to them via the music of the British Invasion, if nothing else. But his Los Angeles concerts, so vastly different from any other long run at the Whiskey-a-Go-Go, were rapturously received and critically applauded, and the anticipation surrounding his San Francisco concerts was in part built on the success of those LA shows. While hardly a mainstream audience, the 1966 Fillmore crowd had wide and varied musical tastes, and local demand for a Redding concert was sufficient for Fillmore owner Bill Graham to book him for three nights.[18] That short run established his reputation with the local crowd, cemented his working relationship with Bill Graham, and presaged the success he would find at Monterey. His performance at Monterey Pop was therefore a natural progression from local to national acclaim; coupled with his success on the European tour, the summer of 1967 was the decisive turning-point in Otis Redding's career.

As noted earlier, Redding was one of a minority of two soul musicians at the Monterey Pop Festival. This may be interpreted as a halting motion towards music industry integration, but certain stylistic differences suggest otherwise. Redding headlined the Saturday night bill, which was largely devoted to the San Francisco sound, then just breaking through to the national audience. The act which immediately preceded him, Jefferson Airplane, had scored two Top Ten hits that year, 'Somebody to Love' and 'White Rabbit'; their album *Surrealistic Pillow* (1967) in part popularized San Franciscan psychedelic pop, and their appearance at Monterey was a particular triumph. Given their local roots and relative commercial success, they might have been the more obvious headliners. What they had in common musically with Otis Redding was certainly not immediately obvious. Following their set, the rain began to fall and the audience began to leave the fairgrounds. Booker T. and the MGs, along with the Mar-Key horns,[19] resplendent in their lime-green mohair suits, warmed up the crowd with an instrumental before Tom Smothers came on stage shortly after 1 a.m. to introduce the closing act. Redding then powered onto the stage for his first number, a manic version of Sam Cooke's 'Shake!',[20] and managed to get the audience back into (and out of) their seats for the rest of his 20-minute set.

From the moment he appeared on stage, the contrast between Otis Redding and the rest of that night's bill could not have been more obvious. His occasionally awkward patter and the altogether 'straight' appearance of everyone on stage showed just how far Memphis was from Monterey. The light show, so central a component of mid-1960s live performances on the West Coast and elsewhere, serves to underline this contrast between southern soul and western psychedelia. The entire performance, captured on film in *Monterey Pop* (D.A. Pennebaker, 1968)[21] while providing a somewhat limited perspective of the set, does offer the occasional tantalizing glimpse of the stage backdrop, all swirling colours and strobe effects. Otis Redding and Booker T. and the MGs may have looked anachronistic in their matching suits, but the sound of the crowd suggests a complete understanding of the musical ley lines being drawn that night between rock and deep soul.

There is certainly more audible crowd participation in Redding's set than in any of the others filmed by Pennebaker that weekend.[22] Given the more subjective nature of some of the performances – there was little room for call-and-response in Big Brother and the Holding Company's rendition of 'Ball and Chain', for example – he could have fallen flat trying to engage the audience in the interjections of 'Shake!'; the rather more straightforward structure and delivery of the song similarly might have sounded dated to the newly psychedelicized audience. What delivered the music home to the Monterey crowd was his exceptional stage presence. From the moment he appeared on stage he commanded their attention. He played with the audience; he teased them; he worked them up and took them down; in short, he gave them a visceral experience where other bands on stage that night had focused on the cerebral.

Redding did not always seem to know how to talk to the audience, however. Once 'Shake!' was over, he began to introduce the second number:

> This is another one of mine. A song we like to do for everybody. Love crowd. This little song is a song that a girl took away from me. Good friend of mine. This girl, she just took this song. But I'm still gonna do it anyway.

Aretha Franklin's recording of 'Respect' had reached the top of the pop charts two weeks earlier.[23] Whether the crowd was aware that Redding had written and also recorded 'Respect' is uncertain;[24] his performance of it at Monterey bore no resemblance to Franklin's recording, and was almost as manic as his rendition of 'Shake!'. The effect was undeniable; underneath his stomping and shouting, Booker T. and the MGs gave a spectacular performance of the song, an effortless display of groove and energy.

The pivotal moment of Redding's set was the third song 'I've Been Loving You Too Long'.[25] In an endearing attempt to bridge the cultural gap between the deep

South and the West Coast, he built on an idea planted in his head backstage and tested briefly before 'Respect':

> Right now we'd like to, we'd like for you to kinda, we're gonna slow it down this time and sing a soulful number. This song, this song is the song that, you know, we all oughtta sing some time. This is the love crowd, right? We all love each other, don't we? Am I right? Let me hear you say yeah, then!

On cue, the crowd erupted. That one moment, when Otis Redding, in his green suit, reached out to the sartorially free, expansive and adoring crowd, marked not only the moment of his decisive crossover, but also the moment at which the audience announced itself as a community, and accepted him into their fold.

'I've Been Loving You Too Long' was an extraordinary performance by any standard. The audio recording captures the raw emotion of Redding's delivery, but the film captures the playfulness behind it. Pennebaker was very careful to edit footage taken from the rear of the stage for this song, providing an intimate account of the dialogue between the singer and Booker T. and the MGs, and also between the singer and the audience. Just as significant an effect is the interference of the lighting, alternately obliterating Redding from view and embracing him in a warm halo of light.[26] It allowed the film audience to witness the union of Redding and his new community; the audio suggestions implicit in the performance – climaxing with sung declarations of 'Good God almighty, I love you' – are similarly suggestive of a personal motion toward communion.

The transition from 'I've Been Loving You Too Long' to the next song, 'Satisfaction',[27] was brief enough not to disrupt the energy or allow the audience to come down. A simple 'Jump again! Here we go!' introduced the main riff which, when paired with the Mar-Key horns, took the Rolling Stones' rock classic back to its soul roots. Listening to Redding's Monterey performance of 'Satisfaction', the directives the Rolling Stones had taken from southern soul music become clear. Mick Jagger's litany is transformed into a soulful entreaty; Keith Richards's distorted fuzz is embellished by the Mar-Key horns and transformed into a sharply punctuated aural dance. When the Rolling Stones' 'borrowed' R&B was 'borrowed back' by Otis Redding, it was one of many moments of mutual respect enacted at Monterey Pop, and it suggested very clearly to the audience that those soul–pop leylines were perceptible from both directions.

To close his set, he introduced a change in mood:

> Thank you so much. Right now. Thank you so much. We'd like to take time now and drop the tempo one more time. This is a song that I want to dedicate to all the mini skirts. You know, this song goes something like this, my favourite. Now dig.

'Try a Little Tenderness' was one of his signature tunes,[28] an old standard that he regularly used to end his concerts. The liberties Redding took with it at Monterey – changing the song's original reference to 'the same old shabby dress' into 'the same old mini skirt dress', as one example – placed this particular performance decisively in the late-1960s cultural aesthetic. Musically, it highlighted the ability of the Stax arsenal to transcend the limits of an otherwise simplistic idea and take the emotional power of Redding's interpretation to fever pitch. Many of the vocal tics for which he was famous – the typical interjections ('gotta gotta gotta'), his condensing of multi-syllabic words into their percussive components ('satisfaction' into 'fa-tion') – and the increasing hoarseness which suggested a straining at the limits of his range – coloured the final moments of his performance at Monterey. When he left the stage with a weary 'I got to go, y'all, I don't wanna go', it seemed all he could say after the workout he had given his larynx, his band and his audience. And there is one last performative point to note here. The false ending of Redding's arrangement of 'Try a Little Tenderness', which allowed him to leave the stage and return for an 'encore' chorus, was a dramatic device suited to the kind of multi-talent one-night stands of Redding's early career. Monterey Pop, formerly a pop music festival, had now been transformed from a three-day forum for mid-1960s psychedelic pop into a rhythm and blues revue.

To consider the US pop festivals which followed Monterey – Woodstock, Altamont – and to consider the larger political events of the time – the war in Vietnam, the assassinations of Martin Luther King Jr and Senator Robert Kennedy – is to see Monterey as the brief success of the hippie ideology. The open-mindedness which accepted the presence of the Mamas and the Papas alongside Ravi Shankar was accompanied by a certain cultural innocence. The consumption of the rather powerful acid being passed around the festival fairgrounds nonetheless resulted in no arrests that weekend; Monterey's Chief of Police announced his support of the hippies by suggesting that some of his new friends were going to show him around the Haight-Ashbury; some of the festival police, so overcome with good vibes, took to wearing flowers, if not in their hair, then in their uniform pockets.[29] Musically and culturally, Monterey Pop was a hopeful sign that popular music was capable of great things, and that youth culture might indeed be able to change the world.

Many of the Monterey acts – Country Joe McDonald, The Who, Janis Joplin, Jimi Hendrix – went on to play at Woodstock two years later. Based on documentary evidence, and cultural expectation, where their earlier performances belied inexperience, the latter showed a natural maturity, an even greater self-assurance. But significantly, the audience's expectations had also shifted. Monterey may have been the beginning of an ideological daydream, but Woodstock was its waking reality. There was a sense of innocence at Monterey which by Woodstock had turned into a world-weariness, not only because of the drug busts and race riots which marked the end of the Summer of Love, but for the period of international protests which extended into the 1970s, and the general ideological shift which accompanied the progression from LSD to harder drugs. Two bookended performances serve as a metaphor for this larger cultural development: Otis Redding at Monterey, singing 'Try a Little Tenderness', and Sly and the Family Stone at Woodstock, singing 'I Want to Take You Higher'. Between one performance and the other, soul merged decisively with psychedelia, and the result was both powerful and untouchable.

The impact that the Monterey Pop weekend had on Otis Redding also became clear. Redding wrote '(Sittin' on) the Dock of the Bay' while staying on a houseboat in Sausalito during his West Coast tour later in the summer of 1967.[30] It was a complete musical departure for him; it took him in a slower, more reflective, more 'pop' direction. It showed Redding re-interpreting the central trope of the American experience ('I left my home in Georgia, headed for the 'Frisco Bay') and aspiring to a much larger cultural resonance. The outward expression of soul, and of the Stax sound – Booker T. and the MGs' rhythmic drive, the Mar-Keys' horns, the fevered intensity of lyrical delivery – gave way to something much more considered, more introspective. Less than three weeks after recording the single, Otis Redding died in a plane crash while en route to a concert in Madison, Wisconsin. '(Sittin' on) the Dock of the Bay' was released within the month and was the first crossover success he had, reaching Number One on both the R&B and pop charts. This gentle song, a wistful masterpiece, is above all a love letter to a time and a place, and an enduring testament to the brief hope of the summer of 1967.

Notes

1. For a further exploration of this, see Lee Marshall's chapter on Bob Dylan's performance at Newport in this volume.
2. For more on the release of *Sgt Pepper* and its historical legacy see Taylor (1987) and Moore (1997).
3. In the first four months of 1967 there were also freakouts in Los Angeles and New York as well as a 'Love-In' in Detroit. On an international level, the founding of London's UFO club in December 1966 provided similar opportunities for the experience of contemporary music and psychedelic drugs in the UK.
4. Monterey is on the central coast of California, about 150 miles south of San Francisco.
5. Of course, there are exceptions. Moby Grape released their first, eponymous, recording, in 1967 on the San Francisco Sounds label; Jefferson Airplane, the most commercially successful contemporary San Francisco band, signed to RCA in 1966.
6. For more on the financial mysteries surrounding the festival, see Lydon (1967).
7. The Beatles had already retired from live performance, though they did contribute a hand-drawn poster for the Monterey Pop programme. Rumours that they were planning a surprise appearance at the Festival circulated nonetheless, right through the closing Sunday night performance.
8. 'San Francisco (Be Sure to Wear Flowers in Your Hair)', music and lyrics by John Phillips; released 1967, reached Number 4 on the pop charts that year.
9. In particular, Country Joe McDonald claimed that the inclusion of 'San Francisco (Be Sure to Wear Flowers in Your Hair)' at the close of the festival represented 'a total ethical sellout of everything that we had dreamed of' (Taylor 1987: 79).
10. For more information on the contemporary Motown output, see Fitzgerald (1995).

11. Hugh Masekela was also on the Saturday night bill, but as a black South African performer in the jazz tradition, he does not fit the categories African-American or American 'pop' music. This is in no way to discredit his performance; merely to suggest that he represented another tradition altogether. The reception of his music at the festival generally noted in contemporary accounts seems to have been less than rapturous, but that may be due to the fact that his set, at 55 minutes, was the longest of the weekend.

12. Indeed, Otis Redding's most significant influence was Sam Cooke; the single he released just before the festival – and with which he opened his Monterey set – was a cover of Sam Cooke's 'Shake!'.

13. Songs released by Stax in the years between its founding in 1960 and the Monterey Pop Festival included Carla Thomas, 'Gee Whiz' (1960), the Mar-Keys, 'Last Night' (1961), Sam and Dave, 'Hold On! I'm Coming' (1966) and Eddie Floyd, 'Knock On Wood' (1966). Each of these reached the Top Five on the R&B chart; only 'Gee Whiz' (Number 10) and 'Last Night' (Number 3) broke the pop Top 40. Motown singles might routinely sell more than one million copies each; by contrast, Otis Redding's 1965 releases combined sold fewer than 800 000.

14. For a comprehensive study of the Stax catalogue and the Stax style, see Bowman (1995).

15. 'Green Onions' reached Number 3 on the US pop charts in September 1962. The bassist on the recording was one of the original MGs, Lewie Steinberg, who was replaced by Donald 'Duck' Dunn in November 1964.

16. For more on the Stax European tour, see Guralnick (1986: 308–31).

17. 'I've Been Loving You Too Long' reached Number 21 on the pop charts and Number 2 on the R&B charts in 1965; 'Respect' (1965), 35 and 4; 'Satisfaction' (1966), 31 and 4; 'Knock On Wood' (1967), 30 and 8; 'Tramp' (1967), 26 and 2; 'Try A Little Tenderness' (1967), 25 and 4.

18. For the background on Graham's attempts to book Otis Redding and an account of Redding's first appearance at the Fillmore, see Graham and Greenfield (1992: 172–94).

19. Wayne Jackson, trumpet; Joe Arnold, tenor sax; Andrew Love, baritone sax.

20. Sam Cooke's 1965 recording of 'Shake!' reached Number 2 on the R&B charts and Number 7 on the pop charts. Otis Redding's recording was included on *Otis Blue/Otis Redding Sings Soul* (1965).

21. D. A. Pennebaker generally filmed only one song of each set at the festival. An edited selection of performances, *Monterey Pop*, was released in 1968, effectively setting the standard for the 'rock concert' film. Pennebaker and his crew filmed just two complete sets, releasing them in 1986 as short films: *Jimi Plays Monterey* and *Shake! Otis at Monterey*. All are included on *The Complete Monterey Pop* (2002).

22. The performance was also released on LP: *Historic Performances Recorded at the Monterey Pop Festival – Otis Redding/The Jimi Hendrix Experience* (1970).

23. Aretha Franklin's version of 'Respect' was recorded in February 1967 and released as a single. A landmark in its own right, it also helped make *I Never Loved a Man the Way I Love You* (1967) one of the most significant soul albums of the 1960s.

24. Otis Redding, 'Respect' (1965) reached Number 4 on the R&B charts and Number 35 on the pop charts.

25. 'I've Been Loving You Too Long' (Otis Redding/Jerry Butler), originally released on *Otis Blue/Otis Redding Sings Soul* and released as a single. It reached Number 2 on the R&B charts and Number 21 on the pop charts.

26. The edited versions of 'I've Been Loving You Too Long' included on *Monterey Pop* and *Shake! Otis At Monterey* are somewhat different. On the director's commentary

for the DVD re-release of *The Complete Monterey Pop*, Pennebaker mentions that he was editing the film when he heard the news that Otis Redding had died. His decision to show Redding in this halo of light was interpreted by some contemporary audiences as signifying a kind of foreshadowing of Redding's death.

27.   'Satisfaction' (Mick Jagger/Keith Richards), recorded by Otis Redding on September 7, 1965, released as a single in February 1966; it reached Number 4 on the R&B charts and Number 31 on the pop charts.

28.   'Try a Little Tenderness' (Harry Woods/Jimmy Campbell/Reg Connelly), recorded on September 13, 1966, released as a single on November 14, 1966; it reached Number 4 on the R&B charts and Number 25 on the pop charts.

29.   For more on the aftermath of the festival, see Selvin (1992).

30.   '(Sittin' on) the Dock of the Bay (Steve Cropper/Otis Redding), recorded on November 22, 1967, released as a single on January 8, 1968.

Chapter 4

The road not taken
Elvis Presley: *Comeback Special*,
NBC TV Studios, Hollywood,
December 3, 1968

Ian Inglis

The career of Elvis Presley embodies both the glorious optimism of the American dream and the desperate tragedy of the American nightmare. Born to an impoverished family in Tupelo, Mississippi, the Memphis truck-driver became the world's most celebrated entertainer and one of the iconic figures of the twentieth century; his irresistible ascendancy through the 1950s and early 1960s provided a ringing endorsement of the belief that in the land of opportunity, nothing was impossible for those with talent, hard work and a degree of good luck. When he died in 1977, drug-damaged, bloated and obese, face down in a pool of vomit on the floor of his bathroom, his death seemed a conclusive demonstration of the corrupting and poisonous repercussions of a life in which the barriers to any forms of material excess had been removed.

Indeed, the regular 'sightings' of Elvis Presley – even today, some 30 years after his death, there are hundreds of reports each year – testify to the significance that his story continues to hold for the personal component of American political life. To admit the circumstances of his death is to undermine the legitimacy of a national ideology that promotes ambition, possession and wealth – for what good are such attributes if they lead to a miserable and lonely death? To deny his death and to continue 'the liberatory celebration of his life' (Gottdiener 1997: 200) – as so many have sought to do – is to re-affirm that ideology.

In fact, many of the biographical details included in analyses of Presley's career only become meaningful when they are seen as indices of the wider social and cultural contexts in which they were embedded, and/or as signposts to the consequences which followed. For example, the censorship of his television appearances in 1956 reflected the widespread alarm over the sexual, racial and behavioural implications of styles of music and performance that he refused to modify; his induction into the US army in 1958 and his two-year stint as a GI demonstrated a mutual awareness of the benefits for military propaganda and personal publicity afforded by his celebrity status; his relocation to Hollywood on his release from the army in 1960 served to effectively contain the potential disruptions of rock'n'roll within a familiar occupational and ideological framework; and his offers to President Richard Nixon and FBI Director J. Edgar Hoover in 1970 to act as an undercover agent on behalf of the Bureau of Narcotics and Dangerous Drugs exposed the tensions and contradictions created by the growth of the counterculture in America.

None of these actions were inevitable; they were selections from a variety of alternative trajectories. Added together, however, they serve to provide the narrative of Elvis Presley's career – a career that can be divided into three periods, each of which is separated by a significant transitional moment of choice.

1. The rock'n'roll years 1954–57
                    The army years 1958–60
2. The Hollywood years 1960–68
                    The comeback year 1968
3. The Las Vegas years 1969–77

In 1968, the intervening moment of choice between the Hollywood years and the Las Vegas years was provided by an hour-long NBC TV show. Sponsored by the sewing machine manufacturer, it is correctly titled *Singer Presents ELVIS*. However, it has come to be known as the *Comeback Special*.

During his rock'n'roll years in the 1950s, Elvis took part in many hundreds of live performances. In the eight years from his army release until the *Comeback Special*, he made just three. The first was an eight-minute appearance on ABC TV's *Frank Sinatra Show* in May 1960. In February 1961, he starred in two charity concerts at Memphis's Ellis Auditorium. And in March of that year, he appeared in another benefit concert at the Bloch Arena in Hawaii, where he sang 19 songs (his longest-ever show) in a performance characterized by 'a sheer joyousness, a general exuberance of expression that refuses to be denied' (Guralnick 1999: 102).

Consequently, the decision to withdraw from live performance had nothing to do with musical disenchantment, but was a purely commercial tactic, instigated by Elvis's manager, Colonel Tom Parker, who saw movies as a cost-effective way of satisfying the global demand for his singer. Although the 23 films he made over the next eight years were financially rewarding (typically, Elvis received a $1 million dollar salary per film, plus 50 per cent of the profits, plus soundtrack album royalties), very few of them attracted any positive critical responses.

> His films settled into predictable, pallid productions … Requiring little intellectual participation, they adhered to a strict code, avoiding excessive violence and sexual suggestiveness, and the story lines showed life as simple and optimistic … Most of the songs were inane numbers written to suit a part of the film, and were hopelessly dull if heard outside that context (Hammontree 1985: 43–4).

In addition, Elvis's prolonged sabbatical coincided with a number of musical developments unforeseen at the start of the decade. They included the studio innovations of Phil Spector and the 'wall of sound', the success of Motown, the growing chart presence of soul music, the influence of Bob Dylan and the cult of the singer-songwriter, the rise of the guitar hero, the emergence of West Coast, folk-rock and psychedelic musics, and the enormous impact of the Beatles and the subsequent British Invasion of America. Throughout most of this period, Elvis was substantively excluded from the increasingly serious discourse that surrounded popular music; his record sales waned, and he was widely regarded as either a historical relic or a kitsch curiosity. John Lennon's description of the Beatles' meeting with Elvis in his Bel Air mansion in August 1965 – 'it was just like meeting Engelbert Humperdinck' (Coleman 1984: 212) – is a concise summation of the status of the singer's reputation in the mid-1960s.

Ironically, Elvis's return to live performance was similarly prompted by financial considerations. In the light of his decreasing popularity and the dwindling profits generated by his recent films, Parker was forced to propose a deal whereby NBC would only guarantee the required (and prestigious) $1 million fee in return for a movie – *Change of Habit* (William A. Graham, 1969) – *and* a TV special. At the first discussions with NBC in October 1967, Parker insisted that the TV special should take the form of a Christmas show, an idea he clung to throughout the negotiations, despite muted opposition from Elvis himself, and more overt arguments from the show's personnel, including executive producer Bob Finkel, producer/director Steve Binder, musical supervisor Bones Howe and musical director/arranger Billy Goldenberg. Whereas Parker might have seen the TV show as an unavoidable and minor component of a movie deal, Binder was more aware of its significance:

> I felt very, very strongly that the television special was Elvis's moment of truth. If he did another MGM movie on the special, he would wipe out his career … if he could do a special and prove he was still number one, he could have a whole rejuvenation thing going (Hopkins 1971: 271).

Eventually, the concept of a Christmas show was abandoned, and rehearsals and pre-recording began in June 1968 at NBC's Burbank studios. Taping of the actual performances took place in the last week of the month. In addition to two lavishly choreographed production numbers, and separate opening and closing sequences, all of which were recorded without an audience, there were two live segments performed in front of an audience. One presented Elvis and four musicians, sitting on stools on a small, informal stage in the middle of the audience of 200; the other featured a stand-up Elvis on the same stage, accompanied by an unseen orchestra. The show was broadcast nationwide on the evening of Tuesday, December 3, by which time the four hours of film had been edited down to 50 minutes.

As Elvis's highlighted face appears on an otherwise darkened stage, the immediate comparison it provokes is not to the cheerful, bland persona of his movies, but to the sullen truculence of his earlier years. Significantly, the singer issues a challenge: 'If you're lookin' for trouble, you came to the right place. If you're lookin' for trouble, just look right in my face.' The camera pulls back to show a black-suited Elvis in front of studio scaffolding, peopled by several dozen silhouetted figures, which freely recalls the celebrated sequence from *Jailhouse Rock* (Richard Thorpe, 1957). Although the song he sings, 'Guitar Man', is a recent hit record, the intent of the show is clear – to revisit the Elvis Presley of the 1950s. Furthermore, his vocal performance offers a more powerful, rougher version of the song, in which the niceties of the record are replaced by a frankly aggressive and uninhibited delivery. A closing long shot frames him in front of 20-foot high red neon letters that spell ELVIS.

The shot fades to be replaced by the first appearance of Elvis and his fellow musicians seated casually in an inward-facing circle on the studio stage. The singer is flanked by guitarists Scotty Moore and Charlie Hodge, and drummer D.J. Fontana – all performers with whom Elvis recorded and performed in the 1950s. In addition, Elvis's friend Alan Fortas sits with them – ostensibly as a member of the band, but in reality as an informal support – and another friend, actor and musician Lance LeGault, is just off stage, close to Elvis. The combination of familiar musicians and close friends evokes, as is intended, the informal spontaneity of an unscheduled jam session. While the other musicians wear simple maroon jackets, Elvis is clothed from head to foot in black leather; the high-collared jacket, designed by Bill Belew, identifies him, unequivocally, as the leader. This position is emphasized during the performance of 'Lawdy Miss Clawdy' and 'Baby What You Want Me to Do', as the group members shout encouragements at him. In a pre-scripted sequence, Elvis refers, haltingly, to the stereotype of his curled lip and recalls a performance in Florida, when he was ordered to reduce his body movements on stage. However, the anecdotes are recited rather than remembered, and leave the viewer uncertain who he is speaking to – to the band, to the audience, to himself. Instead of an endearing example of self-deprecation, it is an unconvincing and self-conscious interlude that contrasts oddly with the playfulness of the previous songs.

The next segment of the show has Elvis alone on the stage, singing a 'greatest hits' sequence – 'Heartbreak Hotel', 'Hound Dog', 'All Shook Up', 'Can't Help Falling in Love', 'Jailhouse Rock' and 'Love Me Tender'. Although his timing is not perfect and there are a couple of occasions when he gets a word wrong, it is an impressive and confident performance. He chats with the audience –'It's been a long time, baby' – borrows a handkerchief to mop his forehead, paces around the stage, kneels and stretches. This may be the first time in years that any audience has seen an Elvis Presley who perspires and whose hair falls down over his eyes, rather than a film star whose appearance is constantly monitored by a make-up team and whose movements are blocked in advance by the demands of a movie director. He is clearly at ease, although some of the dramatic gestures and poses with which he chooses to end each song have little in common with the unrestrained *jouissance* of his on-stage dancing in the 1950s.

Seated again with the band, he pauses to say that he wishes to talk a little about music; immediately his assurance is again replaced by hesitation and uncertainty. The opportunity to hear unscripted observations about the state of popular music from the person who, more than anyone, shaped and influenced that music, is squandered. As in the previous spoken interlude, there is little authoritative or authentic comment; instead, there are glimpses of the 'awkward small talk ... perfunctory nods and stammered little asides' (Guralnick 1994: 92) that characterized the nervous teenager who was invited back to the Sun studios for his first full recording sessions in July 1954. He concedes that much has improved over the past ten years and admits, without obvious enthusiasm, that he likes the music of the Beatles, but maintains that much of rock'n'roll evolved, and continues to evolve, from the traditions of gospel and rhythm'n'blues.

This leads in to the first of the show's two production numbers – an extended gospel sequence, in which a finger-snapping, hand-clapping Elvis, in maroon suit, white shirt and black scarf, is supported by the Blossoms (three black female session singers). They perform 'Where Could I Go But to The Lord', 'Up Above My Head' and 'Saved'. More than 30 dancers are also featured in a set of energetic routines that provide continuity from one song to the next. In contrast to the impulsive exuberance of the previous rock'n'roll numbers, the segment follows, in production and performance, the conventions of the Broadway musical.

On the live stage again, the band and Elvis reprise 'Baby What You Want Me to Do', plus 'Blue Christmas' and 'One Night'. For the latter number, Elvis requests a shoulder strap for his guitar so that he can stand; when one fails to appear, he again seems impatient and distracted, but responds to the shouts of encouragement and screams of the (largely female) audience to stand anyway. In fact, just before the taping of the show, Colonel Parker had persuaded the more attractive women in the audience to come forward to crowd around the stage, where they would appear most prominently in camera-shot. As the applause diminishes, Elvis sits on the edge of the stage, a pretty woman strategically placed on each side of him, to sing the first of the evening's two new songs – 'Memories', written for the show by Mac Davis. Presumably planned to cement the experience of the contemporary Elvis remembering and revisiting his own musical memories, it clearly fails. Not only are its lyrics and melody far less memorable than the songs that have preceded it, but in style and delivery it has more in common with the recent movie soundtrack tunes from which Elvis was so keen to distance himself.

The show's second production number was, at one time, planned to provide the rationale for the entire special. It relates, musically, the tale of a young man (the guitar man) who journeys far away from home, in the course of which he is able to recognize his true self. The notion of self-discovery and a person's return to his roots were, of course, the principle themes underpinning the TV show. A disillusioned Elvis is shown, guitar on back, on a stylized highway, deciding to leave the 'Nothingville' of the song title. He arrives on the crowded midway at a carnival whose neon lights advertise 'Girls', 'Shooting' and 'Photos'. While befriending a woman, he is challenged by the local villain. Elvis sings 'Big Boss Man'; his karate fails to deter the villain, but a punch to the stomach does. Leaving the carnival and moving on through streams of human and automobile traffic (in a meticulously choreographed dance routine) he sings 'Guitar Man' and is invited to join the resident band at a club; here he performs, in a gold lamé jacket, 'Little Egypt'. A performance of 'Trouble' repeats the show's opening couplet and is continued in several settings – the club, a nightspot and, finally, the studio stage again. Adapting the lyrics of 'Guitar Man', Elvis avows that this, above all, is what he wishes to be. As he walks away, we are left in little doubt that in coming back to the live stage, the real Elvis has, indeed, rediscovered his own true self. The entire number is replete with references to the career of Elvis – the young musician in search of fame, the gold lamé suit designed for him in the 1950s by Nudie's of Hollywood, his interest in karate.

The special closes with the second of the two new songs. Against the backdrop of the neon ELVIS, wearing a white suit, and with a microphone in his left hand, Elvis sings, to an orchestral accompaniment, 'If I Can Dream', written for him by the show's vocal arranger, Earl Brown. Although its plea for peace, love and understanding may seem unremarkable to today's audiences, it was at the time a bold and unpredictable step by a singer who had previously eschewed any references, however slight, to 'social comment' in his songs. As significant as the content was the delivery. Elvis gives an impassioned performance, appearing to be genuinely moved by the music. With his right hand flailing wildly through the air, and a tone of desperation in his voice, he seems to articulate the outrage and frustration that had engulfed much of America in the wake of the assassinations of Robert Kennedy earlier in June and of Martin Luther King Jr in April. His final address to the camera is a brief 'Thank you. Good night'. While the closing credits roll, he is pictured once more against the red neon ELVIS, the guitar man playing rock'n'roll music, just as he had promised in song.

Media reaction to the special was generally positive; equally important were the viewing figures, which gave the show a 42 per cent share of the audience. Immediately after the TV special, Elvis himself announced: 'I want to tour again. I want to go out and work with a live audience' (Guralnick 1999: 317). By January 1969, 'If I Can Dream' had climbed to Number 12 in the *Billboard* singles charts, giving him his biggest hit since 'Crying in the Chapel' in 1965. Jon Landau's assessment that 'there is something magical about watching a man who has lost himself find his way back home' (Hopkins 1971: 279) illustrated the excitement that the show had generated and the anticipation about what might follow.

Sudden and dramatic comebacks of the kind that the TV special seemed to presage occur infrequently within the entertainment industry. The transformation of the career of Frank Sinatra following his Oscar-winning role in *From Here To*

Eternity (Fred Zinnemann, 1953) and the return to Hollywood stardom enjoyed by John Travolta after his appearance in *Pulp Fiction* (Quentin Tarantino, 1994) may be among the best known examples. But these two differ from the situation faced by Elvis Presley in late 1968/early 1969, in that Sinatra and Travolta were merely re-admitted to a movie industry that had existed for several decades, and in which they were simply players. By contrast, Elvis had, in many ways, created the popular music industry – or, at least, the particular part of it that now awaited his return. Even during those years in which he had not performed, and in which his records had attracted less and less acclaim, he had continued to command an iconic or talismanic significance for many of the decade's leading musicians.

Frith has referred to the distinction that exists within popular music between 'rock' and 'showbiz' (1988: 161). The former is perceived to be characterized by qualities of creativity, authenticity and distinction; the latter may be dismissed as commercial, synthetic, predictable. Like the traveller forced to choose between two divergent roads in the Robert Frost poem from which this chapter takes its title, Elvis was now confronted by two quite different career trajectories – a return to rock or a move into showbiz. The impact of the live rock'n'roll components of the show and the favourable response to the sentiments of 'If I Can Dream', which mirrored the capacity of many contemporary singer-songwriters to employ popular song as a tool with which to engage in political debate, seemed to indicate a ready association with the developing themes of rock. On the other hand, the intricate and polished production numbers displayed a preference for the routines and conventions of mainstream stage entertainment. So too did the constant costume changes throughout the TV show, which left open the question of who Elvis was, by allowing him to adopt, at different times, the personae of family entertainer, leather-jacketed rocker and nightclub singer. However, unlike the later dress strategies of, for example, David Bowie and Madonna, Elvis's changes had little sense of artifice or irony, and revealed instead a confusion *about* identity, rather than a play *with* identity.

Initially, he seemed to favour the opportunity the TV special had given him to consolidate his musical re-invention. In January–February 1969, he recorded at Chips Moman's American studio in Memphis. Moman, a former producer with Stax Records, had recently produced hits for Wilson Pickett, Dusty Springfield, the Box Tops and Joe Tex. Backed by the studio's house band of Memphis session musicians, Elvis recorded more than 30 tracks. In contrast to the trite, formulaic pop songs featured in his recent films – *Spinout* (Norman Taurog, 1966), *Double Trouble* (Norman Taurog, 1967), *Clambake* (Ladislav Smocek and Arthur H. Nadel, 1967), *Speedway* (Norman Taurog, 1968) – the songs drew on the traditions of rhythm'n'blues he had identified in the TV show, and the contemporary soul for which American was renowned. Indeed, many of the songs were soul standards that Elvis was keen to cover; they included Clyde McPhatter's 'Without Love', Chuck Jackson's 'Any Day Now' and Jerry Butler's 'Only the Strong Survive'. In addition, he recorded several new songs that would re-affirm his presence in the charts through the rest of the year – 'In the Ghetto' (a million-seller and his first Top Ten hit since 1965), 'Suspicious Minds' (his first Number One single since 1962), 'Don't Cry Daddy' and 'Kentucky Rain'.

The producer's admiration for Elvis – 'one of the hardest-working artists I have ever been associated with … what energy and enthusiasm he has' (Guralnick 1999: 336) – was matched by the critical reception given to the Memphis recordings:

> It was, flatly and unequivocally, Elvis's most productive recording session ever. It also made it abundantly clear that the days of the 'Fort Lauderdale Chamber Of Commerce' and 'No Room To Rhumba In A Sports Car' movie soundtrack songs were over (Hopkins 1971: 283).

However, at the same time that these recordings were taking place, Colonel Parker was in negotiation with the International Hotel, Las Vegas, whose 2000-capacity showroom would be the resort's largest when the hotel opened in July. Resisting the offer to open the showroom (that was eventually left to Barbra Streisand), Elvis duly contracted to play a four-week season from July 31 to August 28 for a $1 million fee. In promotional terms, the deal was exceptionally kind to Elvis. By seizing the opportunity to star at the most prestigious new venue in the entertainment/gambling capital of America, he would benefit from a press and publicity campaign of a scale unseen since the Beatles landed at New York's Kennedy Airport in February 1964. However, the choice of a cabaret season in Las Vegas through which to confirm his return to live performance, made other, equally powerful, statements that were less attractive.

Whereas Elvis's collaboration with Chips Moman recalled the circumstances of his very first recordings, at another small independent studio in Memphis – Sam Phillips's Sun studio – the decision to appear in the sumptuous surroundings of Kirk Kerkorian's International Hotel was a symbolic rejection of the challenges to age, race and social position which, for many, defined the production and consumption of rock'n'roll, and an overt endorsement of the corporate world of show business, just as his enthusiastic entry into Hollywood had been, years earlier. In addition, the commercial inclusion of popular music alongside the organized crime, prostitution and gambling that lay at the heart of Las Vegas effectively distanced such musicians from rock'n'roll's romanticized ideology of youthful rebellion – an ideology, of course, which Elvis, above all others, had helped to construct. Furthermore, the peers with whom he was now symbolically and substantively associated were some of those who had been most vehement in their condemnation of rock'n'roll, or those whose own output had little to do with its style and content; among the opening night's invited guests were Pat Boone, Carol Channing, Dick Clark, Shirley Bassey, Cary Grant, Dean Martin and Zsa Zsa Gabor. Yet perhaps the most revealing aspect of Elvis's season in Las Vegas was its coincidence with another, equally significant, musical event. While 500 000 young Americans were celebrating in the mud of Woodstock their fusion of music, drugs, opposition to the country's involvement in Vietnam, sexual liberation and political confrontation, Elvis, from the comfort and security of his penthouse suite at the International Hotel, was happy to allow himself to be identified as the definitive symbol of affluent middle America; his award of Entertainer of the Year at Las Vegas merely confirmed that position.

In the light of the spectacular success of his 1969 season in Las Vegas, there was no doubt about which road a resurgent Elvis would take. From 1970 to 1976, he returned for 13 seasons to Las Vegas and five seasons to Lake Tahoe; and extensive nationwide tours across America satisfied the 'broad-based, middle-American family audience' (Guralnick 1999: 453) unable to visit either of the two resorts. While the chart successes of 1969 were unrepeated, the financial rewards of the concerts more than compensated for the disappointment felt by many at their form and content:

> The gaudiness of the show, the camp aspects of some of its Vegas glitz, the lush showbiz sentiments and orchestrations of much of the music, the bizarreness of some of the spoken interludes, all these elements led critics to begin comparing Elvis to Liberace or Zsa Zsa Gabor (Guralnick 1999: 533).

There is, within the human and social sciences, a device known as counterfactual analysis, whereby the practitioner is encouraged to imagine a changed history in which alternative courses of events have come to pass. Often dismissed as a form of science fiction better suited to Hollywood than to serious academic enquiry, counterfactualism occupies only a small place in historical investigations: 'whether by posing implausible questions or by providing implausible answers, counterfactual history has tended to discredit itself' (Ferguson 1997: 19). Within social psychology, however, there has been a greater readiness to recognize that 'reactions to events often not only require knowledge of what happened but also require a sense of what failed to happen' (Dunning and Madey 1995: 103).

If counterfactual thought is applied to the history of Elvis Presley after 1968, it can therefore provide comparative scenarios against which the real course of events may be contrasted, and also increase an understanding of the particular time and place in which those alternatives existed as plausible options.

What if Elvis Presley had appeared at Woodstock instead of Las Vegas in August 1969? What if he had gone back on the road with a small backing band and a support act, rather than toured with a large orchestra, dancers and comedians? What if he had chosen to perform and record with other contemporary musicians, as was commonplace in the early 1970s? What if he had rejected the extravagant caped and belted stage outfits in favour of jeans and a T-shirt? What if he had turned up at Bill Graham's Fillmore West rather than the Sahara Tahoe in the summer of 1971? In considering these alternatives, we may come to see that for Elvis Presley, his life after 1968 was not defined by the history he experienced, but rather by the history he rejected.

However, the assurance with which such speculations may be approached is hindered by the lack of any overall consensus about the circumstances of his career. While I, and many others, have characterized the years from 1960 to 1968 as largely unproductive and unsatisfactory (in a musical sense) there are others who fiercely denounce such a reading as a fiction:

> The myth ... inevitably depicts the years between his discharge from the army and his 'comeback' as a period of stagnation and decline where Elvis made music that was bad and movies that were worse. The most obvious problem with this myth, however, is that millions of Elvis's fans ... eagerly bought these 'bad' records and attended these 'bad' films (Rodman 1996: 59).

Of course, the centrality of the subjective in assessments of popular music is not surprising and, indeed, may be crucial if adequate accounts of the relationship between audience and star are ever to be presented. In the case of Elvis Presley, that recognition is multiplied: as I suggested earlier, his story, and our responses to it, rest upon an unbreakable link between the personal and the political. For audiences in his own country, not only did his rags-to-riches progress illustrate the American dream, but his regular personal appearances in the 1950s and 1970s allowed them to claim him as one of their own. Yet elsewhere in the world, that perception of Elvis is absent. His steadfast refusal (for whatever reasons) to appear outside America, either before or after 1968, worked to confer on him a *genuinely* legendary status. Rather like Robin Hood or the Knights of the Round Table – figures generally believed in, but whose existence might be difficult to guarantee – Elvis was regarded by many as a supernatural being, whose life possessed all the mysteries, symbolic powers and myths typically granted to such figures. For those audiences, the *Comeback Special* was simply one of many reported episodes in a fabulous and distant life, which made little actual difference to the nature of their relationship with him or their knowledge of him. Indeed, any personification of Elvis rests, in part, on the romantic symbolism with which his history has been invested:

> Elvis was not a phenomenon. He was not a craze. He was not even, or at least not only, a singer, or an artist. He was that perfect American symbol ... and the idea was that he would outlive us all – or live for as long as it took both him and his audience to reach the limits of what that symbol had to say (Marcus 1991: 5).

The significance of the *Comeback Special* is therefore twofold. First, it gave Elvis-as-performer the unexpected opportunity to re-assert his musical abilities, which subsequently allowed him to choose one of two roads along which he might travel as a performing musician. Second, it gave Elvis-as-myth the opportunity to continue to speak to his audiences, and for those audiences to continue in their (varied) responses to his messages.

It has been noted that 'it has always been the prime function of mythology and rite to supply the symbols that carry the human spirit forward, in counteraction to those other constant human fantasies that tend to tie it back' (Campbell 1949: 11). For many millions of people, Elvis Presley existed, and continues to exist, as one of those symbols. Just as the impact of his entry into popular music in the mid-1950s was achieved against a background of institutional hostility and personal vilification, so too his re-entry in the late 1960s to a musical world that had largely discarded him was immediate and unexpected. In the first case, he was feared as a dangerous rebel; in the second, he was regarded as an outdated and predictable entertainer. While the contexts and consequences were very different, both events thus attested to the ability of music and musicians to confront and overcome, personally and professionally, the dominant order of the day.

The *Comeback Special* thus stands as one of the pivotal moments in the life and career of Elvis Presley, in the narrative of rock'n'roll, and in the cultural history of popular music. While the central core of its live segments sought to reproduce the small, informal shows in and around Memphis from which Elvis's performing career had evolved, its production numbers looked forward to the calculated routines of the Las Vegas years and his touring shows. The nostalgic celebration of his old hits indicated how newer forms of popular music had, over the last few years, supplanted rock'n'roll in the public catalogue of disruptive or subversive entertainment. And the topography of an improvisational, acoustic-based set provided a template that would be adopted 25 years later by MTV's *Unplugged* series.

The *Comeback Special* provided an early and clear illustration of the observation that in contemporary cultural life, the only certainty is that there are no longer any certainties. Situated at a decisive moment in Elvis's own musical and personal history, it presented the singer with a choice whose outcomes could not be foreseen but whose repercussions are still felt. The road he took, and the places to which it led him, are well known. The road not taken, and the Elvis who might have travelled along it, we can only imagine.

Chapter 5

Land of the free
Jimi Hendrix: Woodstock
Festival, August 18, 1969

Mike Daley

Many of the first histories of rock (Gillett 1971; Belz 1972) were written in the late 1960s, at a time when rock journalism was in its first full flowering (the first issue of *Rolling Stone* had been published in November 1967) and the music itself was widely perceived as having entered a period of consolidation. Rock, for better or worse, had reached its first stages of maturity. The development of the album as an artistic unit and endorsements from the likes of Leonard Bernstein and British musicologist Wilfrid Mellers were lending a certain legitimacy to the work of those performers and songwriters in the vanguard of mainstream popular music making. The time was ripe for rock literati to bestow rock with a historical narrative; rock needed a historical thread to make sense of its unprecedented popular success and its rapidly splintering stylistic branches.

But histories can never be innocent of the human need to mythologize, and these (and other) early accounts set in motion a process whereby the short history of this music would be understood in terms of a creation myth and a linear trajectory (derived from Renaissance-era historiography) of style development in a tripartite model made up of primordial beginnings, classic flowering and a final period of decadence and decay. Gillett and Belz both saw this period of decadence stemming from the stylistic fragmentation and increasing commercialism of late 1960s rock, the period in which they were writing. The urge to see the present as the denouement of the narrative is common among writers of contemporary histories of any artistic movements and, perhaps predictably, this model has been somewhat stretched in later histories of rock, in which the final part of the model has been dragged along closer to the writers' present.

This brings us to the historical moment that is the subject of this chapter – Jimi Hendrix's appearance at the Woodstock Music & Arts Fair (commonly referred to as the Woodstock Festival or, simply, Woodstock) on August 18, 1969 at Bethel, New York. Hendrix's set has come to synecdochally represent the Woodstock Festival's mythos as a cultural signpost in rock history. This assessment of Hendrix's impact *qua* Woodstock, is, I will argue, a relatively recent formulation, fuelled by the pervasiveness of the documentary movie *Woodstock* (Michael

Wadleigh, 1970) and by retrospective judgements about Hendrix's overall artistic importance in the grand scheme of rock history. More specifically, Hendrix's symbolic impact has come to be focused on one particular song from his set, 'The Star-Spangled Banner'.

The story behind the Woodstock Festival has been told and retold, and so I summarize it only briefly here. Michael Lang, a 24-year-old former head shop proprietor, had organized the successful Miami Pop Festival in December 1968 which, over two days, had successfully presented 35 acts on two stages to an audience of around 100 000. Featured performers included the Mothers Of Invention, John Lee Hooker, Joni Mitchell, the Grateful Dead, Steppenwolf, Chuck Berry, Procol Harum, Fleetwood Mac and the Jimi Hendrix Experience. Spurred on initially by the triumphant Monterey Pop Festival of 1967 – where Hendrix had made his American debut after forming his trio and recording his first album *Are You Experienced?* (1967) in England – large-scale rock festivals had become big business by 1969. Lang, after re-locating to Woodstock, had conceived of an alternative recording retreat based on the 'Recording Farm' and 'Operation Brown Rice' collectives in California. Woodstock, long established as an artists' colony, was home to a strange admixture of moneyed rock stars, struggling musicians and conservative farmers. After meeting with investors Joel Rosenmann and John Roberts, Lang decided to launch the recording facility with a gala concert in the area. This concert idea was soon to expand into a plan for a large-scale festival.

By the summer of 1969, the Jimi Hendrix Experience had completed what would be its last American tour. Bassist Noel Redding marked the occasion by resigning from the band and Hendrix began to formulate plans to put together a new band. His evolving 'Electric Church' concept was freer and more experimental, more communal, than the tight Experience power-trio had been. Disappointed by his clashes with Redding, Hendrix sought to create a supportive, fluid backdrop for his music, hopefully unmarred by ego clashes. He was concerned to surround himself with trustworthy compatriots, which meant for him musicians that he had known pre-fame. Manager Mike Jeffrey was somewhat distrustful of Hendrix's new direction, but nonetheless rented an eight-bedroom house for him near Woodstock, at the end of Tavor Hollow Road close by the villages of Shokan and Boiceville. Hendrix, in turn, put his old army buddy Billy Cox on notice to step in on bass, and he, at Hendrix's request, looked up another old friend, guitarist Larry Lee. Jerry Velez, a Puerto-Rican born, Bronx raised percussionist whom Hendrix had met at the Scene Club in New York, was one of the first to be invited to stay at the Shokan retreat. Another percussionist, much respected for his work around Woodstock, was Juma Sultan, and he too was quickly pulled into the fray. The new group, to be dubbed Gypsy Suns and Rainbows, was almost complete.

While Hendrix vacationed in Morocco, his newly minted band tentatively rehearsed at the Shokan house. Following Hendrix's return, the line-up was consolidated, after some argument over the choice between Mitch Mitchell (of the Experience) and Buddy Miles on drums (eventually resolved in favour of Mitch Mitchell). By all reports, rehearsals proceeded fitfully; Hendrix's road manager, Gerry Stickells, recalled:

> Rehearsals, as I remember they called them, consisted of getting stoned and talking about how great it was going to be. The fact that they kept adding people to the line-up proved to me that it wasn't together. They went along because someone else was paying the bills (Black 1999: 42).

As the Woodstock gig drew closer, Hendrix taught the band to play some of his old hits – 'Purple Haze', 'Fire', 'Foxy Lady' – as well as working up some newer songs and some jam-based instrumentals.

With the August 15 opening day approaching, the organizers of the Woodstock Festival found matters rapidly reeling out of control. The venue changed twice and was only eventually confirmed when a local dairy farmer, Max Yasgur, offered to rent 600 acres of his prime farmland to the organizers for $75 000. The site was 100 miles north of New York City and 70 miles west of Woodstock, the original projected home of the festival. On August 7 the promotion company held a pre-festival concert for the workers preparing the site. One of the performers, the Earthlight Theatre, stripped naked for their set, which prompted 800 local residents to sign a petition to stop the festival. But by then, the mass pilgrimage to Bethel was under way. An estimated 30 000 people were on site before security, food service or medical aid were in place. The Woodstock Festival had begun. With little in the way of security or fencing, most of the concert-goers simply walked in, and soon enough it was declared a free festival. Only around 60 000 of the 400 000 who attended Woodstock paid to get in.

The roster of musical talent at Woodstock was one of the most impressive ever assembled. Beginning with Richie Havens, the Friday (August 15) show included Country Joe McDonald, John Sebastian, the Incredible String Band, Sweetwater, Tim Hardin, Bert Sommer, Ravi Shankar, Melanie, Arlo Guthrie and Joan Baez. Saturday (August 16) brought Quill, the Keef Hartley Band, Santana, Mountain, Canned Heat, Creedence Clearwater Revival, the Grateful Dead, Janis Joplin, Sly and the Family Stone, The Who and Jefferson Airplane. Sunday's (August 17) line-up featured Joe Cocker, Country Joe and the Fish, Ten Years After, The Band, Blood, Sweat & Tears, Johnny Winter, Crosby, Stills, Nash & Young, the Paul Butterfield Blues Band and Sha-Na-Na; Hendrix was scheduled to perform the final slot.

By the time the concert was underway, the site was virtually impossible to reach by car, and many performers flew to the site by helicopter. Hendrix and his band ended up making the trip in two station wagons. He was unhappy about the media reports of the size of the gathering, and by four o'clock on Sunday afternoon was refusing to play. The fee ($18 000) was small by his standards, although he was, in fact, the highest-paid performer at the festival. Mike Jeffrey intervened and persuaded Hendrix to play on the basis of the prestige of the engagement.

Rain delays and poor organization combined to prevent Hendrix and his group from taking the stage for their festival-closing set until eight o'clock on the Monday (August 18) morning. By then, fewer than 30 000 audience members remained. The *Woodstock* movie depicts well the haggard hordes, the scattered garbage, the hard morning air, the grey skies. The camera focuses on Hendrix's guitar with an astringent clarity, his guitar notes sharp and clear.

> One of the abiding images of the place and time of Woodstock is Jimi, in white-beaded leather jacket, blue jeans, gold chains and a red head-scarf standing centre-stage alone sending out 'The Star-Spangled Banner' as a series of shock waves across the audience in the early-morning light (Shapiro 1991: 385).

The performance was – to put it lightly – loose and somewhat confused, the band showing its lack of rehearsal and perhaps the unreadiness of some of the musicians. The contributions of the two percussionists are inaudible to this listener, at least in the released mixes of the concert. Larry Lee's guitar, when it is discernible, is usually horribly out of tune, and his abilities are clearly not equal to the task of trading licks with Jimi Hendrix. Even Mitch Mitchell, Hendrix's long-time cohort, sounds confused and unfocused – perhaps due to the non-existent stage monitoring more than anything. Hendrix seems to be struggling himself, although still playing at a level that few have equalled. Others have been decidedly more damning in their assessments:

> Never in his two and a half years with the Experience had Hendrix exhibited such disregard for professionalism, not even during that band's formative weeks when, with a paucity of original material, cover versions of songs had been performed with as much enthusiasm as could be mustered. On stage at Woodstock, the same Jimi Hendrix who had refused Noel Redding the opportunity to perform 'She's So Fine' – even when fans had shouted requests for the number – allowed guitarist Larry Lee to traipse off-key through two songs, 'Mastermind' and the Impressions' 'Gypsy Woman' (Marcus 1969: 54).

Listening to the *Jimi Hendrix: Woodstock* (1994) recording, which is more complete than previous releases – but which does not include Larry Lee's two vocal turns, the encore of 'Hey Joe' and other elements, and has been partially re-ordered – there are some sublime moments: 'Voodoo Chile', 'Villanova Junction' and 'Izabella' stand out. But the undoubted highlight of the set, and the portion that has come to symbolize Hendrix-at-Woodstock, as well as many other things, is 'The Star-Spangled Banner'.

Coming out of 'Voodoo Chile (Slight Return)/Stepping Stone', Hendrix plays the opening salvo of 'The Star-Spangled Banner' in the lowest position on the neck, using open strings where possible, and with his new Univibe rotating-speaker effect pedal warbling the pitches. In the background, Mitch Mitchell is filling in with tom and cymbals builds in free rhythm. The crowd, roused to its greatest excitement of the set, cheers wildly. Hendrix adorns the simple anthemic melody with scoops and articulations like a lone gospel singer. This vocal interpretation continues through the first two stanzas, with some trumpet-like trills appearing later on. With feedback beginning to encroach on the held notes, Hendrix engages the wah pedal to emphasize the treble. He follows the B section line 'and the rockets' red glare …' with the wail of a falling bomb and its subsequent explosion, manipulating his Stratocaster's vibrato bar to its lowest position. Some rolling confusion follows, screaming voices, machine gun rat-a-tats, unearthly strangled cries, a mother's futile wails. Then the line 'the bombs bursting in air', followed by a low-toned siren, some unplaceable sounds of unreality, another bomb assault, twisted metal and bodies, a trickle of blood. 'Our flag was still there' leaps up to a keening, pure-toned quotation of 'Taps'. The final stanza, beginning 'Oh say, does that star spangled banner yet wave', is given a straight treatment but is filtered through ululating pickup toggle switch effects, with the word 'wave' held through successions of fed-back harmonic overtones. With a strangled stop, Hendrix resumes with 'o'er the land of the free', with the final note of the line again left for dead, to have its fundamental pitch leeched out by the feedback decay, and a final bomb's fall to earth. After a short series of portentous, incongruous chords, Hendrix segues into a perfunctory 'Purple Haze'.

In early journalistic accounts of the Woodstock Festival, little attention was given to Hendrix's appearance. Gillett (1971) failed to mention him at all and Marcus (1969) merely name-checked him in his eyewitness account, preferring to focus on Country Joe McDonald and Crosby, Stills, Nash & Young. As late as the mid-1980s, Ward, Stokes and Tucker referred to his presence at Woodstock only to report his performance fee (1986: 497). It seems that in the several years immediately following the festival, the music was dwarfed by the perceived social importance of the event. But in the late 1980s, as the twentieth anniversary of Woodstock was reached, and re-assessments of the festival and the ensuing years of rock history were placed under some journalistic scrutiny, Hendrix's appearance began to take on a new profundity. In particular, the re-release in 1989 of the *Woodstock* and *Woodstock II* concert compilations on CD led some critics to see Hendrix's performance and its symbolic importance in a new light:

> The best of all the participants captured here is Jimi Hendrix, whose 'Star-Spangled Banner', bleeding into 'Purple Haze' is among the most staggering of the live excursions he left to posterity. While his stuff on *Woodstock II* is mainly pedestrian by his blinding standards, 'Star-Spangled Banner' blasts the American Dream to tatters and his 'Haze' falls like nuclear confetti, both bitter and celebratory (Sutherland 1989).

Hendrix biographer Harry Shapiro has offered a cogent analysis of the 'meaning' of 'The Star-Spangled Banner', relating it to the revolutionary spirit of the times. Commenting on the mainly white, affluent, audience demographic, he contends that 'just being at Woodstock was as close to an act of revolution as most of the audience ever came' (1991: 385). In addition, he notes that Hendrix's own attitude towards the war in Vietnam was rather ambivalent; he had served as a paratrooper some years earlier, and in interviews had expressed some worries about the encroaching 'yellow danger' in South East Asia:

> Did you send the Americans away when they landed in Normandy? That was also interference ... but that was concerning your own skin. The Americans are fighting in Vietnam for a completely free world. As soon as they move out, they [the Vietnamese] will be at the mercy of the communists. For that matter the yellow danger [China] should not be underestimated. Of course, war is horrible, but at present it's still the only guarantee of peace (Shapiro 1991: 387).

Evidently, Hendrix had a more conflicted view of the war in Vietnam than would be suggested by many of those who have offered interpretations of his performance of 'The Star-Spangled Banner'. Indeed, it has been argued that his performance acknowledged and articulated the complexities of the Vietnam problem more acutely than any other artistic expression:

> 'The Star-Spangled Banner' is probably the most complex and powerful work of American art to deal with the Vietnam war and its corrupting, distorting effect on successive generations of the American psyche. One man with one guitar said more in three and a half minutes about that peculiarly disgusting war and its reverberations than all the novels, memoirs and movies put together. It is an interpretation of history which permits no space for either the gung-ho revisionism of Sylvester Stallone and Chuck Norris or the solipsistic angst of Coppola and Oliver Stone; it depicts, as graphically as a piece of music can possibly do, both what the Americans did to the Vietnamese and what they did to themselves (Murray 1989: 24).

However it is assessed, it is clear that Hendrix's rendition of the anthem pushed some powerful buttons in the years following Woodstock, as that festival increasingly came to symbolize the last hurrah of the love and peace era. The Altamont festival later that same year, with its air of dread, filmed by Albert and David Maysles and released as *Gimme Shelter* (1970), came complete with an on-camera murder. It provided a bitter bookend to the idealism and naivety of the 1960s. Woodstock has come to represent a unique moment of community, and Hendrix's appearance in particular symbolizes the freewheeling spirit of the era as well as the troubled heart of the anti-war movement.

Chapter 6

If anything, blame Woodstock The Rolling Stones: Altamont, December 6, 1969

Norma Coates

Perhaps Ralph J. Gleason was responsible for Altamont. Or Mick Jagger? Sonny Barger? Woodstock? All or none of the above? After all, one could, based on the evidence, argue that it was the venerable *San Francisco Chronicle* music critic – the spiritual godfather to Jann Wenner and the writers at *Rolling Stone* magazine in the late 1960s – who goaded the Rolling Stones into performing a free concert at the Altamont Speedway in the bleak hills, 50 miles outside Oakland on Saturday, December 6, 1969. As the story goes, the Stones danced a little too close to the devil, in the form of the Hell's Angels, that fateful day. The Angels beat up a lot of people and then killed a young black man, while Mick Jagger callously sang and danced along to 'Sympathy for the Devil'. Thus, the 1960s ended, along with the utopian promise of that decade and the youth counterculture.

As time progressed, the 'countermyth' of Altamont, as Ellen Willis (1999: 155) has described it, has itself become a myth, in the sense theorized by Roland Barthes (1972). The event is now drained of historicity, except in relation to its role as 'the end of the sixties' – a dubious claim given the many other contenders for that title.[1] Instead, it stands in for the outlaw ethos inherent in the popular conception of rock'n'roll. Altamont is now part and parcel of that indefinable quality still used to create an aura of exceptionality around rock music and to artificially separate it from the pop mundane: authenticity. Gone is the outrage among the discursive gatekeepers of rock music – rock critics – that accompanied the actual event.

A lengthy report in *Rolling Stone* entitled 'Let It Bleed' (not coincidentally the name of the album that the Rolling Stones had completed and released during their 1969 US tour that culminated at Altamont) gave birth to the myth of Altamont even as it attempted to deflect responsibility for the debacle away from its writers and associates and the communal, outsider version of rock culture that they celebrated. The version of Altamont that entered popular memory and rock mythology, though, is not all that was reported in *Rolling Stone* as its writers sought to allocate blame. Also implicit in the 'disaster', maybe more so than the Hell's Angels, was the presence of a film crew headed by documentarists Albert and David Maysles, who were making a movie based on the Rolling Stones' tour. Gleason had accused the group of 'hating their audience' because of the high ticket prices; *Rolling Stone*, and other commentators, continued this theme, with their condemnation of the idea that Altamont's violence would be exploited for financial gain upon release of the movie filmed that day.

Of course, Gleason was not responsible for Altamont; he was about as complicit as any of the other principals involved. This chapter suggests that the vision of rock music and the promise of the counterculture constructed and reiterated on the pages of *Rolling Stone* and other 'alternative' journals and newspapers, was wilfully blind to the practical realities of rock music, rock performers and stars, rock audiences, rock festivals – indeed, the whole apparatus of 'rock culture'. What was at stake was an unwillingness on the behalf of anyone involved – from the Rolling Stones to the promoters to the press to the audience – to accept that the counterculture, especially its rock star representatives, was rarely counter-anything, especially that long-standing villain, capitalism. Compounding that, the actual event of Altamont tore the scales from the eyes of the rock public, revealing the violence, economic and spiritual as well as physical, that lay as much at the root of 'rock culture' as at that of mainstream culture. It may seem a stretch to describe the economic needs of musicians and the music industry as violent, but business, as the old cliché has it, is war, and someone is always going to pay.

This chapter also argues that Altamont was employed by critics to deny their complicity in the tragic outcome of the rock festival.[2] Expectations of behaviour by artists, audiences and even security (or lack thereof) were set by the vision of the counterculture constructed on the pages of alternative and rock journalism, and then lifted and repeated by the mainstream press. Rock festivals, and the 'peace and love' spirit associated with them in the wake of Woodstock, became mass-mediated fantasies divorced from the actual realities of events. Moreover, the demand for free concerts by journalists after Woodstock made it difficult for the Rolling Stones, given their status as the world's leading rock group at the time, to refuse to give one. Rock performers, especially the Rolling Stones, were elevated to the position of avatars and spokesmen of the counterculture. The 'rock star' was a creation of the rock press as much as of the rock audience. The problem for rock critics and rock audiences arose when the objects of their worship proved to be 'in it for the money'. In the past, the promoters were the target of venom (Lydon 1967). Now, it was the performers themselves. To save their constructed image of rock culture, critics had to figuratively slay the monster they created.

That Altamont happened is not surprising; that it did not occur earlier is. In popular American memory, the Altamont concert is the evil twin of Woodstock, 'a three-day festival of peace, love, and music'. Woodstock was held a few scant months before Altamont, with nary a Hell's Angel in sight. That festival did not erupt into violence (at least none that was circulated publicly, or defined as 'violence' in the received sense of people getting physically hurt, just one of many available definitions of the term). Woodstock was the exception to the festival rule, not the norm. In a front-page article written just a month before the start of the Woodstock Festival, *Variety* considered incidences of violence at music festivals. Gatecrashers were seen as a major part of the problem. The article went on to describe three festivals, including the Newport Jazz Festival, that erupted into violence. According to reporter Marty Bennett, 'each of these blow-trading shows "featured" fence-breaking, rocks, bottle, and fist-throwing' and police had used tear-gas to quell the violence at a festival at Mile High Stadium in Denver (1969: 1). Within the *Variety* article, production technician Chip Monck, who managed logistics and construction at both Woodstock and Altamont, asserted that the presence of uniformed cops inspired violence and suggested that their presence at rock festivals be lightened; and Michael Goldstein (described as a New York music publicist) suggested that promoters make it unofficially possible for some people to sneak into the fairgrounds without paying, reasoning that by letting 'troublemakers' in for free, their less aggressive 'followers' would pay the ticket price without incident. Bennett wrote that 'the biggest problem facing promoters in this booming new entertainment area is in fashioning a delicate balance between the "freedom" angle that sells tickets and the suppression of rowdies who are tagging along without paying their tab' (1969: 73).

Violence, not just peace and love, was apparently endemic at rock festivals. Rowdies will appear in any crowd, of course, but a major part of the problem could be traced to the contradictions inherent in the rock festival itself, especially its discursive positioning as a 'coming together of the tribes', identified by Willis as

> the utopian moment of the rock'n'roll crowd … [in which] the live crowd, and especially the arena or festival crowd, functioned largely as a confirmation of the existence of the community, and a kind of convention of the community's representatives who were empowered to act out its myths and fantasies; these events and the symbols they produced then got recycled by the media back into the collective consciousness of the crowd as a whole (1999: 155).

Many of the discursive gatekeepers of the community got caught up in the recycled symbolism in the media. Lost in the utopian dream was the grimmer reality of rock festivals, which was (is) that they brought lots of potentially volatile young people, often under the influence of some mind-altering substance of dubious quality, into a media event – all at the mercy of the ever-fickle weather. For example, warm summer rain, albeit lots of it, fell on Woodstock; whereas the chilly December day and night of Altamont is held by many as among the negative influences upon behaviour and mood at the event.[3]

Rock festivals, rock journalism and the emergence of the youth counterculture were among the many things that had changed or emerged since the Rolling Stones had last toured the US in 1966. One of the more significant changes was the new importance of the rock star. The rock and alternative press published interviews with rock performers which sought their attitudes about social/political issues and life in general, not just about music.[4] Tours of major groups like the Rolling Stones also received great attention in the mainstream press. In addition, by 1969, with Bob Dylan in semi-reclusion and the Beatles close to their break-up and long off the live stage, they were arguably the world's most important rock performers. That they were making some of the best music of their career added to the attention they received in all forms of media.

This is also the period during which a satanic dimension was accorded the Rolling Stones by the media, aided by the group itself. Always the 'bad boys of rock', compared to the Beatles, they took this persona further. Like the blues artists who inspired them, they seemed to have made a mythical pact with the devil, a perception reinforced by the release of *Their Satanic Majesties Request* (1967), their recording of 'Sympathy for the Devil' and Jagger's compositions for two Kenneth Anger films, *Invocation Of My Demon Brother* (1969) and *Lucifer Rising* (1970–80). Moreover, Brian Jones had recently been found dead at the bottom of his swimming pool, in mysterious circumstances. The rock press took the devil pose and ran with it. Never shy of controversy, the group ran with it too, as one of its public personae, thus moving rock into a hitherto unexplored, deeper and darker dimension with – until Altamont – no great complaints from the media.[5]

Much was made of the group's arrival on US soil, especially in the alternative and rock press. The *Los Angeles Free Press* was particularly interested as the Rolling Stones took up residence in the Hollywood Hills for a month before the tour began, in order to complete recording of *Let It Bleed* (1969) in Los Angeles. But the reception was not entirely uncritical, especially in San Francisco, still (at least in the popular imagination) a crucial centre of the US rock scene. The whole San Francisco Bay area continued to bask in a countercultural credibility, left over from the days of student protest in Berkeley and the heyday of the Haight-Ashbury district two years before. The San Francisco rock press, predominantly through Ralph Gleason's contributions to the *San Francisco Chronicle* and *Rolling Stone*, still wielded an enormous amount of discursive power and influence over American rock journalism. Gleason himself enjoyed a considerable moral authority, in part because of his unofficial role as *Rolling Stone*'s mentor.

The power of Gleason and *Rolling Stone* soon came to bear on the Rolling Stones after the announcement of ticket prices. Tickets for this tour, the prototype for the large arena rock tours that would soon follow, were priced from $5.50 to $8.50; one of the Los Angeles shows featured a VIP section at $12.50 a seat. The magazine compared those charges to those of other leading groups – Blind Faith charged a top price of $7.50, and the Doors just $6.50 – and found the Stones wanting (Hopkins 1969a: 16). In these days of ticket prices soaring up to $300 (often for groups like the Rolling Stones), complaints about having to pay $8.50 to see a top rock group seem amusing. But in 1969, such prices signalled a rupture between the countercultural and commercial ethos, and proved false the implicit belief that rock performers were above crass economic gain. This was especially important because of the growing split between rock 'authenticity' and mainstream/pop fakery playing out in many areas of rock discourse. Money was often seen as the differentiating element between the two.

Gleason expressed these sentiments in a scathing article published in the *San Francisco Chronicle* and excerpted throughout the rock press, including *Rolling Stone*:

> Can the Rolling Stones actually need all that money? If they really dig the black musicians as much as every note they play and every syllable they utter indicate, is it possible to take out a show with, say, Ike and Tina and some of the older men like Howlin' Wolf and let them share the loot? How much can the Stones take back to Merrie England after taxes, anyway? Paying five, six and seven dollars for a Stones concert at the Oakland Coliseum for, say, an hour of the Stones seen a quarter of a mile away because the artists demand such outrageous fees that they can only be obtained under these circumstances, says a very bad thing to me about the artists' attitude towards the public. It says they despise their own audience (Hopkins 1969a: 16).

The idea that rock performers owed something more to their audience, not vice versa, bears interrogation. That the performer merely owed what any performer owed the audience, an evening of entertainment delivered well, is in Gleason's view insufficient. His comments belie an expectation that rock stars behave differently and be less concerned with worldly rewards than other performers, as well as the denial that rock, and rock stardom, are ultimately business enterprises. Deena Weinstein has noted that rock criticism was founded on an art–commerce binary, consistent with a 'myth of romantic ideology' that promoted

> will, feeling, passion, intuition, and imagination against regulation by intellectual and practical disciplines ... the myth of the irreconcilable opposition between art-authenticity and commerce was established: henceforth musical discourse had a literary discourse to police it, indeed, to normalize it (1999: 58–9).

In this case, the 'practical discipline' is literally commerce, the desire of the rock band to support itself – and to do so *in a manner expected of them by the rock press as well as rock fans*. What is problematic, then, is not the Rolling Stones' desire to reap money from their adoring fans, but the critical expectation that they and other rock stars would act any differently, given the pedestal that critics helped to place them on. Arguably, it is this expectation that pushed the Stones into going ahead with the free concert at Altamont.

The criticism of ticket prices, led by Gleason and reprised in other alternative and rock magazines, continued to hound the group, especially Mick Jagger, as they made their way through their US tour. For example, in late November, an anonymous *Rolling Stone* writer in a piece entitled 'The Stones and the Gathering Madness' complained that those who paid $7.50 to see the Stones 'wouldn't even be within screaming distance'. The reporter went on to quote one of the people working for Concert Associates, promoters of the Los Angeles show, as saying that it was the group itself who set the prices. The article concluded by subtly critiquing the group as being 'larger than life' while asserting that they remain 'the best rock and roll group in the world'. It is as if the writer, on behalf of the magazine, cannot grasp that the Rolling Stones are merely acting as expected (Rolling Stone 1969).

Rolling Stone continued to criticize the group (if not in so many words) for acting like rock stars – a role the magazine helped to construct and reiterate. For example, its front-page review of the group's first Los Angeles concert was entitled 'Kiss Kiss Flutter Flutter Thank You Thank You' with the second 'flutter' interrupted by Jagger's long scarf dangling out of the frame of the picture just above it.[6] The article was peppered with references to the money the Rolling Stones were making from the tour, its ticket prices and a sponsorship deal with Chrysler Corporation to supply the group, and its entourage, with cars and station wagons throughout the tour. Disgruntled accounts of invitation-only press conferences, restricted photography and large bodyguards provided colour. Jagger's stage demeanour, a refinement of his dancing three years before and a harbinger of the on-stage athleticism that continues to mark his performances even in his sixties (as opposed to 'the sixties'), was also subtly taken to task, as was his costume, complete with Uncle Sam hat. It is not that rock stars were above preening and adorning themselves in outrageous clothing; what appears to be objectionable was that Jagger's costume and stage presence was perceived as contrived rather than organic. Jagger acted like the rock star he was supposed to be, and was duly chastized for it (Hopkins 1969b).

Into this combustible discursive environment entered Altamont. Rock writer David Dalton claims that the idea of a free concert in the US was initially bandied about in Keith Richards's living room in exclusive Cheyne Walk, on the banks of the Thames, in London's Chelsea neighbourhood, earlier that summer. It was, he believes, Grateful Dead manager Rock Scully who planted the seeds of an idea for a concert in San Francisco: 'Soon, overweening plans were afoot. We expect nothing less from the combined forces of the two most delusional and drug-drenched bands on the planet' (Dalton 1999). If true, this story lends credence to the notion that the rock crowd suffered from a mass delusion about their own powers and capabilities. Following this (il)logic, the original plan was that the event should take place in San Francisco's Golden Gate Park, at the edge of Haight-Ashbury and the site of the hippie exemplar, the 1966 Human Be-In. This was not to be, after Keith Richards prematurely revealed the site to the *Los Angeles Free Press* and, consequently, the San Francisco city authorities refused permission for the concert.

Some writers have made much of the festival's poor planning, blaming it, in part, for the disastrous results. Possibly to deflect criticism, *Rolling Stone* began to distance itself from the event, writing about 'the big free concert they [the Rolling Stones] had vaguely promised since they arrived in this country' and disavowing the crucial role the magazine itself had played, by referring to a quote in which Mick Jagger insisted that the group had decided to do it 'when we first fucking got to Los Angeles' (Burks and Alterman 1969). The reasons behind the group's decision were not given, but in one account of the tour, the Rolling Stones were haunted by Gleason's criticisms from the moment they arrived in the country; at their first press conference in Los Angeles, Jagger mentioned the possibility of 'fixing something up for the people', causing someone to ask, 'A free concert?'(Booth 1984: 29).

Once the Rolling Stones let the free concert Pandora out of the box, there was no putting it back. Negotiations were left in the hands of their management and crew, while the group completed its tour and recorded tracks for the next album, *Sticky Fingers* (1971), at the renowned Muscle Shoals Sound Studio in Alabama. By the time that the concept of a free concert was taking shape, another wrinkle had entered the picture. According to Albert Maysles, the Rolling Stones – under the influence of the Bob Dylan documentary *Don't Look Back* (D.A. Pennebaker, 1967) and other *cinéma-vérité* accounts of the rock scene – were interested in making a film of their 1969 US tour. Talks with director Haskell Wexler did not work out, but Wexler suggested to the Maysles brothers that they make the film. The tour was well underway by the time the Maysles met with the group and arranged to work together. The brothers filmed the last two arena shows of the tour at New York's Madison Square Garden, then travelled with the group to Muscle Shoals, and to San Francisco, where they were able to film the negotiations conducted by attorney Melvin Belli to arrange the Altamont show. Film critic Michael Sragow (2000) reports that the group paid the Maysles Brothers $14 000 to shoot the Madison Square Garden concerts, and $129 000 to film the Altamont festival. The second fee was set only after the free concert had been announced, indicating that the concert was not arranged in order to accommodate the movie. The resultant film, *Gimme Shelter* (Albert and David Maysles, 1970), provided much of the means through which *Rolling Stone*, Ralph Gleason and other counterculture critics bounced the 'blame' for Altamont away from themselves.

The outcome of the Altamont free festival is familiar to all who have seen *Gimme Shelter* or have heard or read about the event over the years, so it is not belaboured here. *Gimme Shelter*, especially, captures the sense of dread regnant at the festival – as well as a powerful and exciting performance by the Rolling Stones. Articles written contemporaneously provide some of the narrative for the popular version of the Altamont story.[7] Somehow the idea gets started – perhaps over a drug-fuelled conversation in London, perhaps because the group was trying to eliminate any bad feelings about its ticket prices. The concert has to be in or near San Francisco, as a homage to that city's importance as the psychic home of the American counterculture, as well as to its music scene. But then the group's money men enter the picture and things begin to get complicated. The first site picked is the Sears Point Raceway near Novato, California. It works on many levels – it has an amphitheatre, good fencing and a good layout. Pending approval from neighbouring towns, the stage and light towers are built. Then Filmways, the film distribution company that owns Sears Point, realizes that a movie is being filmed.

It demands a share of the proceeds from the film. Negotiations collapse and everything is moved at the last minute to the Altamont Speedway, a desolate site in the scrub desert outside Livermore, California.

Dick Carter, the race track's owner, had recently allowed a Stanford University class in small business administration to use his business as a case study. One of its students calls Carter when he hears that the planned concert at Sears Point has fallen through, urging Carter to step in and offer Altamont to the Rolling Stones. *Gimme Shelter* documents Carter's offer, as well as acrimony-free negotiations between Carter and Belli. Carter wants the publicity, nothing more, and a free Rolling Stones concert at his drag strip will surely get him that. Wary of having uniformed police officers present, and on the recommendation of Rock Scully, the Rolling Stones hire the San Francisco Hell's Angels as a security force at Altamont in exchange for $500 worth of beer. This misguided move is what puts the blame for the debacle on the group.

The nature of the ongoing dalliance between the San Francisco hippie community and the Hell's Angels was overwhelmingly ignored by the alternative and rock press in the wake of Altamont. While some in the San Francisco hippie and rock community had concerns about the cosy relationship between 'freaks and Angels' in Haight-Ashbury during the 1967 Summer of Love, inaugurated by Merry Prankster/countercultural novelist Ken Kesey, they did not voice them for fear of being thought uncool (Echols 1999: 158). The problem, according to Gleason's post-mortem on Altamont, which throws all blame on Mick Jagger and the Rolling Stones, was that the group put the Angels in a position of authority – they sold their souls to the real devils for 'a truckload of beer' (1970: 89). Missing is any sense that the Rolling Stones were, naively, just doing as they were told. In fact, Booth reports an 'angry and bewildered' Jagger, immediately after the concert, asking 'how could anybody think those people are good, think they're people you should have around?' (1984: 373). Jagger ignores his own complicity in events, but it is still a good question to ask.

While Jagger tried to distance himself from Altamont, *Rolling Stone* went into full denial-of-complicity mode with its collectively written article 'The Rolling Stones Disaster at Altamont: Let It Bleed', published in its January 21, 1970 edition, and whose title alone immediately casts blame for the 'disaster' upon the group. The article deserves scrutiny because of its role in turning Altamont into mythology, its arrogant moralizing and its placing the entire blame for the Altamont debacle on Jagger, the Rolling Stones and their associates, and none on the magazine itself. Why was Jagger, until recently so lionized by the rock press, now so scapegoated? Indeed, the caption under the singer's picture reads 'Is Mick responsible for the killing?'

In fact, the article is quite remarkable for the collective amnesia about the crucial role played by the rock media in the Altamont debacle. The authors stated that 'Altamont was the product of diabolical egotism, hype, ineptitude, money manipulation, and at base, a fundamental lack of concern for humanity' (Bangs et al. 1970: 20) The writers also provided a 'checklist for disaster' allegedly followed by the concert's organizers: it included the promise of a free concert; the announcement of the location just a few days in advance; the change of location; the insufficient provision of sanitation and other services; insufficient warnings to neighbours; the construction of a poor sound system; and the hiring of Hell's Angels as security guards. The Hell's Angels apart, most of these accusations could have been thrown at Woodstock's organizers, too; and while its changes of venue were not as extreme or peremptory, in many ways Woodstock was a fluke, and possibly only an 'act of God' saved it from becoming its own special Altamont. Grace Slick of the Jefferson Airplane (who played at both events) commented that 'Woodstock was a bunch of *stupid* slobs in the mud and Altamont was a bunch of *angry* slobs in the mud' (Echols 1999: 264). Who gathered the slobs to the Altamont mud? Jagger? The rock press? Or a symbiotic, if not parasitic, merging of the two?

It is clear from the start that *Rolling Stone* wants to position itself as an objective observer, although objectivity is quickly lost as the opening, eye-witness account of Meredith Hunter's murder plays out in painful detail over a number of pages. Then comes the recipe for disaster, and the finger-pointing continues from there. Jagger is portrayed variously as callous or naive. His comments about the Hell's Angels are left without commentary, the commentary being implicit in the lack of commentary:

> I think we expected probably something like the Hell's Angels that were our security force at Hyde Park, but of course they're not the real Hell's Angels, they're completely phony. These guys in California are the real thing – they're very violent. I had expected a nice sort of peaceful concert. I didn't expect anything like that in San Francisco because they are so used to having nice things there. That's where free concerts started; and I thought that a society like San Francisco could have done much better (Bangs et al. 1970: 20).

Quickly, Jagger goes from the press hanging on his every word to the press letting his words hang him. Lacking is any consciousness that Jagger may not have said anything truly important in the years before Altamont, when his every pronouncement was deemed newsworthy, and interesting, and subject to analysis in the rock press. The article itself is a masterpiece of rock mythmaking, through its writing style and its imagery. Again, attention is directed at the group's 'diabolical' mien:

> The 300,000 anonymous bodies huddled together on the little dirt hills were indeed an instant city – a decaying urban slum complete with its own air pollution. By the time the Stones finally came on, dozens of garbage fires had been set all over the place. Flickering silhouettes of people trying to find warmth around the blazing trash reminded one of the medieval paintings of tortured souls in the Dance of Death … It was in this atmosphere that Mick sang his song about how groovy it is to be Satan. Never has it been sung in a more appropriate setting (Bangs et al. 1970: 20).

This is an especially telling passage since it shows the authors trying to play both sides off the middle. They make erudite comments about medieval art, linking rock all the way back to exalted images of high culture, thereby conflating the two, while simultaneously tearing down the idol of their creation. Nowhere is their implicit pre-Altamont support of Jagger's Satan act acknowledged. They create a surreal, appropriate background for Mick's message while trying to kill the messenger.

Indeed, Altamont turned into rock'n'roll mythology exactly because of an inaccuracy in the article, which, like the fabled Sam Phillips quote about Elvis Presley, became 'reality' through dint of repetition. Six pages in, after the murder has been described in detail, the Stones accused of crimes against humanity and Satan brought into the picture, the article states that Meredith Hunter was killed during the performance of 'Sympathy for the Devil'. It fits *Rolling Stone*'s narrative and, consequently, rock mythology, very well … but it is wrong. Those who were there, plus the Maysles Brothers' camera crew, confirm that the murder occurred during 'Under My Thumb'. Given that Hunter was a black man in a sea of white faces, listening to music arguably stolen from blacks by whites (remember that the Rolling Stones' version of 'Love in Vain' on *Let It Bleed* was originally credited not to Robert Johnson but to 'Payne'), there is poetic justice there, but to have him murdered during 'Sympathy for the Devil' is so much more fitting with rock narratives and its constructed outsider mystique. To this day, this inaccuracy is repeated in countless articles and lodged in the popular memory of events.[8] It may not have been intentional, but little move was ever made by the magazine to correct its original inaccuracy. As *Rolling Stone* established itself as the voice of rock culture and the 'go to' source for mainstream journalists and writers wanting the 'inside story' about youth culture, it became difficult to substitute the truth for the better story. The repetition of its version of what took place at Altamont has enabled that account to become the myth that it is today, articulating the event to other rock myths while obscuring the many implications and causes of the very real murder and mayhem that happened there.

In fact, even the Hell's Angels receive less blame than Jagger and the Stones. It was suggested that the problems emanated from the fact that Hell's Angels' pledges were on duty that day, while their leaders were at a district meeting. Eager to earn their way in, and without older members to temper them, the pledges went overboard with violence. Chapter head Sonny Barger defended the actions of Angels who wanted to protect their motor-cycles, and the *Rolling Stone* writers appear sympathetic to this, quoting Barger's explicit denunciation of the 'flower children'. Thus, the inherent violence in the festival crowd was glossed over by its surrogates, the writers for the counterculture press.

Eventually, the article identifies the real villain of the piece – money, particularly that to be made upon the release of the movie being filmed by the Maysles Brothers, a point also emphasized by Gleason (1970).[9] *Rolling Stone* concluded that 'to understand the chain of events that finally put the Stones on Dick Carter's patch of land, it is necessary to understand the big-money negotiations that were going on concerning the movie the Stones were making of their tour' (Bangs et al. 1970: 26). By implying that the concert and the movie were co-planned, *Rolling Stone* suggested that Altamont had to go ahead (despite the obstacles); the (financial) need to shoot the film thus 'caused' the 'disaster'.

What is most notable throughout *Rolling Stone*'s assessment of events is the 'absent presence' of the role of rock criticism in setting the stage for what took place. By 1969, rock criticism had become as much about hagiography as about music, in great part because of *Rolling Stone* itself. From its outset, the magazine focused more on rock culture than on rock music, and on rock stars as generational spokespersons whose words were highly significant. *Rolling Stone* may have spurred Jagger and the Rolling Stones to produce an ill-conceived free festival as much through its writers' enthronement of the group as the kings of rock as through their criticism of the US tour ticket prices.

But rock critics alone did not 'cause' Altamont. A number of things 'caused' it. If anything, the spirit of the times and the concomitant burden placed upon the counterculture by the mainstream media as well as its own scribes was responsible for Altamont. Enormous pressure was placed upon 'rock' and rock artists to conform to a vision of rock as a space somewhat outside or, more accurately, above, the sway of crass commercialism. Rock festivals, from this perspective, represented a new type of community, one in which conventional mores were cast aside for a new spirit of peace and love. Altamont proved the poverty of that belief, and the inability of good intentions to fly in the face of human nature. If anything, the events of December 6, 1969 proved that peaceful Woodstock, not violent Altamont, was the true anomaly of the era.

Notes

1. For example, that claim could be attributed to any of the events of 1968, such as the assassinations of Martin Luther King and Robert Kennedy, or the violence at the Democratic National Convention. Or, one could attach that title to the Tate/LaBianca murders in Los Angeles in August 1969. Or to the Woodstock Festival.
2. I focus primarily on one article here, as I believe that *Rolling Stone* had the most influence on the version of the story that filtered out into mainstream consciousness, but see, for example, Gleason (1970) and Lydon (1970).
3. See, for example, Tamarkin (2003).
4. For example, an interview with Mick Jagger published in the November 21, 1969 edition of the *Los Angeles Free Press* is prefaced with this remark from its writer John Carpenter: 'Though the interview is not all that one would wish, I think it is interesting, if for no other reason than because the subject, Mick Jagger, is' (1969: 33).
5. Indeed, the rock press seemed to take Jagger's Satan pose for granted, as illustrated in this *Cashbox* review: 'Jagger was on his whole Satanic trip, if you can imagine a bitchily dancing Lucifer who never stopped snapping his body or twirling his long red scarf which he alternately manipulated like a gay El Cordobes and a crazed Isadora

Duncan. He climaxed the show by turning on the house lights so that the Stones could dig the crowd and the crowd could dig each other, then calling out to "Come on, San Francisco, let me see you shake your ass!" He brought them down the aisles for a frenzied finale of "Little Queenie", "Honky Tonk Women" and "Street Fighting Man". The Stones make you happy all the way. Their rhythmic gut appeal has no competition. They remain the greatest rock and roll performing act in the world' (Donahue 1969).

6. This issue was printed while *Rolling Stone* was still produced on newsprint, before it became a glossy magazine.
7. The chronology of events here is taken from Gleason (1970).
8. For example, in the introduction to her 1998 candidacy statement arguing for inclusion of *Gimme Shelter* in the US National Film Registry, film archivist Karen Lund repeats the sensational details first recounted in *Rolling Stone*'s article, including the claim that Meredith Hunter was killed as the Rolling Stones performed 'Sympathy For The Devil'.
9. Space does not permit me to discuss *Gimme Shelter* and its reception by rock and, especially, film critics here, much as I would like to. That issue is worthy of a full study in itself.

Chapter 7

Watch that man
David Bowie: Hammersmith
Odeon, London, July 3, 1973

Philip Auslander

London, July 4, 1973. Based on what happened last night, everyone is convinced that David Bowie has ended his career or, at least, will never perform live again. 'Rock'n'Roll Suicide' declares one newspaper headline; 'Bowie Kills Concert Career' insists another.[1]

London, July 3, 1973. Near the end of his concert at the Hammersmith Odeon, the last stop on a tour of the United Kingdom, Bowie asked for the crowd's attention. His expression of appreciation began conventionally enough, then drew anguished protests from the fans: 'Of all the shows on this tour, this particular show will remain with us the longest. Because not only is it the last show of the tour, it's the last show that we'll ever do. Thank you'.

This gesture transformed the concert into a landmark moment in rock history that has been interpreted in a variety of ways: as a symptom of mental and physical exhaustion on Bowie's part, as a crass publicity stunt and as a shrewd business move calculated to generate demand for Bowie by creating an artificial scarcity (Sandford 1998). There is undoubtedly some truth to each of these interpretations. Bowie had been working intensely for the previous 20 months, during which time he had released two albums, *The Rise and Fall of Ziggy Stardust and the Spiders From Mars* (1972) and *Aladdin Sane* (1973) which went immediately to Number One on the strength of advance sales; placed five singles on the British charts, all but one in the Top Ten; appeared on television numerous times; and toured the United Kingdom (twice), the United States (twice) and Japan. Although Bowie had reached the Top Ten before (with 'Space Oddity' in 1969) and had made four previous albums, he was enjoying his first taste of large-scale success. The aggressive Tony DeFries, Bowie's manager since 1970, had engineered much of that success; in 1973, DeFries was engaged in cut-throat negotiations with RCA, Bowie's American record label. The publicity garnered by the apparent retirement announcement could only make Bowie's stock rise, especially when he returned to touring in the spring of 1974.

There can be no doubt that Bowie's announcement was the tip of an iceberg built of personal difficulties and business manoeuvrings. But there is also a sense in which Bowie's retirement announcement was integral to the concept of rock performance he developed during his engagement with the musical subgenre of glam rock, of which his performances as Ziggy Stardust were the apotheosis. Textbook definitions of glam emphasize the androgyny and implied homo- or bi-sexuality of glam rockers' performance personae and I shall discuss those aspects of Bowie's performance here.[2] But I shall also argue that for glam rockers in general, and Bowie in particular, ambiguous gender and sexuality were means rather than ends: the larger message of glam rock was to posit identity as something entirely malleable and open to radical re-definition, a principle on which Bowie has built his entire career.

That the music classified as glam rock ranges from the sophisticated, self-conscious deployment of rock and pop styles by such artists as Bowie and Roxy Music, to the straightforward hard rock of Kiss, to the simplistic, minimalist pop of Gary Glitter indicates that, like most rock subgenres, glam rock cannot be defined purely in terms of musical style. Glam was defined primarily not by a sound but by the appearances adopted by the performers, by the poses they struck rather than the music they played.

While the origins of many rock subgenres are difficult to pinpoint, the beginnings of glam rock are easy to trace. Two British rock musicians, Marc Bolan and David Bowie, were instrumental in bringing glam rock into being as the 1960s became the 1970s. Both men entered the rock music scene in the mid-1960s. Bowie was a member of various groups and a solo artist; Bolan was a member of a Mod rock group called John's Children before forming his own group in 1967, an acoustic duo named Tyrannosaurus Rex that became a mainstay of London's underground music scene. By 1970, both sensed the exhaustion of the hippie counterculture that had had a strong influence on the direction of rock and chose to pursue a direction representing a specific repudiation of the counterculture. 'What Bowie and Bolan both saw was that "glamour" was the antithesis of hippiedom: for long-hair puritans, glamour symbolized affluence, capitalism, "show business"' (Hoskyns 1998: 23). In defiance of the audience with which they had previously aligned themselves, both Bowie and Bolan embraced glamour. In February 1970, Bowie, who would appear on the cover of his album *The Man Who Sold the World* (1970) wearing a dress, experimented with a flashy new theatrical look for a London concert at which his group opened for 1960s stalwart and Woodstock veteran Country Joe McDonald. By the end of that year, Bolan had begun dressing in women's clothing, swapped his folk guitar for an electric guitar, transformed his group into an electric quartet and renamed it T. Rex. When Bolan appeared on television's *Top of the Pops* with glitter on his cheeks in 1971, the glam rock phenomenon was fully launched in the United Kingdom.[3] As Street wittily observes, the countercultural 'injunction to "feed your head"' had been replaced by 'the exhortation to paint your face' (1986: 172).

In adopting androgynous looks that hinted at queer proclivities, Bolan and Bowie prodded the counterculture at an ideologically vulnerable spot, for the counterculture's approach to sex and sexuality was complex and self-contradictory. Although parts of the movement made a point of flouting sexual convention as a way of antagonizing the dominant culture and conceptualizing a new sexual politics (Bailey 1994), countercultural representations of women and sex often revealed a conservative heterosexual male imperative that sometimes spilled over into misogyny, as Beth Bailey (2002) has shown in her analysis of the underground comics of the 1960s. The relationship of women to this brand of 'liberation' was therefore frequently ambivalent and gay people often felt even more excluded. Although the counterculture professed openness about sexuality and some gay people were attracted to its centres (especially San Francisco), the fact remained that the counterculture's 'privileging of masculinity through an emphasis on "groovy" heterosexual performance meant that the counterculture was often homophobic as well as sexist' (McRuer 2002: 217). If this was true of the counterculture at large, it was particularly pronounced in the realm of rock music. It is no exaggeration to say that the rock imaginary was (and largely still is) a white, heterosexual, male imaginary. During the 1960s, the number of prominent rock performers who were female or of colour was observably very small and no rock performer publicly claimed a homosexual identity.

Any number of British groups and performers followed the lead established by Bowie and Bolan: Sweet, Slade, Mott the Hoople, Mud, Alvin Stardust and Gary Glitter were but some of the more prominent to put on make-up and glittering costumes.[4] Even popular music artists not specifically identified as glam rockers, such as Rod Stewart and Elton John, took on some of the visual aspects of glam, whether in costume, make-up or hairstyle. The height of 'T. Rextasy' and the year Bowie launched the Ziggy Stardust persona, 1972 was probably the peak year of the glam era. By July 1973, when Bowie gave his concert at the Hammersmith Odeon, the innovative phase of glam was over. Nevertheless, glam persisted as a viable rock style for a little longer, attracting new adherents – Suzi Quatro, Roy Wood and Wizzard, Sparks et al. – whose work constituted a second wave of glam that held sway from 1973 through 1975.

Glam's valorization of style and pose over authenticity may have been its most profound challenge to the counterculture. The ideology of authenticity with which both the international underground and psychedelic rock were imbued insisted that the musician's performance persona and true self be presented and perceived as identical – it had to be possible to see the musician's songs and performances as authentic manifestations of his or her individuality.[5] (I hasten to emphasize the words 'presented' and 'perceived' – it is not the case that the rock musician's performance persona and self really must be identical, only that a credible illusion of identity be created and maintained.) The underground was therefore deeply suspicious of theatrics in rock performance. Coming onto the scene at the end of this countercultural moment, glam rockers specifically refused this equation. By insisting that the figure performing the music was fabricated from make-up, costume and pose, all of which were subject to change at any moment, glam rockers foregrounded the constructedness of their performing identities and implicitly denied their authenticity.

Bowie understood his iconic glam performance persona, the bisexual space alien Ziggy Stardust, in specifically *theatrical* terms. Bowie often described himself as an actor; in the summer of 1971, for instance, he announced his plans for the near future by saying 'I'm going to play a character called Ziggy Stardust. We're going to do it as a stage show. We may even do it in the West End. When I'm tired of playing Ziggy I can step out and someone else can take over for me' (Harvey 2002). In an interview published in July 1972, a year before Bowie announced the end of Ziggy Stardust, he told the *New Musical Express* that he planned to spend 'another few months getting [Ziggy] entirely out of my system, and then we'll don another mask' (Murray 1972). Although this way of thinking about performance clearly makes sense from the point of view of an actor, it also clearly flies in the face of rock's ideology of authenticity.

Bowie-as-Ziggy's androgynous appearance and ostensible bisexuality, showcased not only onstage but in all of his public appearances, garnered a great deal of attention, both positive and negative. One fan reported 'my parents didn't like him at all – and since they spoke about him as though he was some sort of monster I began to think of him as something really evil!' (Vermorel and Vermorel 1985: 73). A pair of sociologists accused him of having 'emasculated' rock music (Taylor and Wall 1976: 116). On the other hand, many of his fans clearly appreciated his androgynous appearance and intimations of queer sexuality; one fan of unidentified sex wrote in a letter: 'Dear beautiful David I could make love to you, beautiful wo-man me too honey I'm a wo-man myself you ought to see me dressed up I'm sexier than you beautiful goddess' (Vermorel and Vermorel 1985: 25). A *Gay News* review of Bowie's concert at the Royal Festival Hall in July 1972, entitled 'Gay Rock', concluded with this laud: 'David Bowie is the best rock musician in Britain now. One day he'll be as popular as he deserves to be. And that'll give gay rock a potent spokesman' (Holmes 1996: 78).

In a now-legendary interview with Michael Watts published in *Melody Maker* in January 1972, at the very beginning of the Ziggy phase, Bowie declared: 'I'm gay ... and always have been.' The crucial thing about this and related episodes is not what was said but the way it was said. In his article, Watts clearly implied that he did not take Bowie's declaration at face value:

> David's present image is to come on like a swishy queen, a gorgeously effeminate boy. He's as camp as a row of tents, with his limp hand and trolling vocabulary. 'I'm gay', he says, 'and always have been, even when I was David Jones' [Bowie's real name]. But there's a sly jollity about how he says it, a secret smile at the corners of his mouth ... The expression of sexual ambivalence establishes a fascinating game: is he, or isn't he? (1996: 49).

In discussing the constitution of gender identities, Judith Butler argues that 'gender attributes ... are not expressive but performative', meaning that 'these

attributes effectively constitute the identity they are said to express or reveal'
(1990: 141). Extending her analysis to sexual identities, I argue that Bowie's
presentation of his sexuality on these occasions suggests a perception of such
identities as performative, not expressive. His performance of a gay or bisexual
identity did not express some essential quality of his person; it was, rather, a
performance of signs that are socially legible as constituting a gay identity. In
Butler's terms, the question 'is he, or isn't he?' is the wrong question because it
cannot be answered: 'If gender attributes and acts [or, here, attributes and acts
associated with sexuality], the various ways in which a body shows or produces its
cultural signification, are performative, then there is no pre-existing identity by
which an act or attribute might be measured' (1990: 141).

Bowie's performance of gay sexuality thus was multiply subversive. On the one
hand, it flew in the face of rock culture's traditional heterosexual imperative. On
the other hand, it did so without simply asserting Gay Rock as an equal alternative
– just as Bowie challenged rock's ideology of authenticity through his insistence
on rock performance as theatrical role-playing, he did not perform 'authentic'
homosexuality, either. Rather than raising questions about his own sexuality,
Bowie threw the sexuality of rock into question not only by performing a sexual
identity previously excluded from rock but also by performing that identity in such
a way that it was clearly revealed *as a performance* for which there was no
underlying referent. As Butler suggests, Bowie's pointing to the performativity of
queer identity brought 'into relief the utterly constructed status of the so-called
heterosexual original' (1990: 31) to imply that the heterosexuality considered
normative in rock culture is no more foundational than any other sexual identity.

Like his public appearances, Bowie's concerts from this era raised issues of
gender and sexuality in a way unprecedented in rock culture. Drawing on a
semiotics of gender performance developed by Goffman, I shall argue that
Bowie's performance as Ziggy Stardust at the Hammersmith Odeon, as captured
by documentarian D.A. Pennebaker in *Ziggy Stardust and the Spiders From Mars:
The Motion Picture* (1983) reflected a complex interplay of masculine and
feminine gender codes enacted by male performers. Part of this complexity
derived from Bowie's individual performance, in which he frequently performed
femininely coded gestures and poses, yet sometimes reverted to more masculine
ones. This complexity also derived from a clearly identifiable, though not
altogether stable, gendered division of labour between Bowie and lead guitarist
Mick Ronson, with whom he shared the stage and interacted extensively during
the concert. Even though Bowie sometimes exhibited masculine coding in his
performance and there were ways in which Ronson was feminized, the primary
staged relationship between them was one in which Bowie embodied femininity
and Ronson masculinity, a relationship made very explicit at some of the more
overtly erotic moments of the performance.

The opening song of the concert, a rendition of 'Hang on to Yourself',
established these images and relationships immediately. Bowie appeared in a long

glittery tunic and sang while smiling ingratiatingly at the audience. Goffman identifies this kind of smile as a 'ritualistic mollifier' and 'more the offering of an inferior than a superior'. This kind of smile is also coded as a feminine expression, inasmuch as 'women [are represented as] smil[ing] more, and more expansively, than men' (1979: 48). In and of itself, Bowie's smile might not be interpreted specifically as feminine, but I will argue that in the context of his staged relationship with guitarist Ronson, it should be. Bowie ceded the stage, retiring to the back, while Ronson played a guitar solo. Although Ronson was thoroughly 'glammed up' in glittering costume, blonde shag haircut, eye make-up and lipstick, his position in the gender economy of the performance was clearly the masculine one. Although Bowie plays several instruments, he appeared initially only as a singer, a feminine position in rock since women have participated in the music far more frequently as singers than instrumentalists (Bayton 1998). As lead guitarist, Ronson occupied a position that is coded as masculine within rock culture. Ronson made a great show of his guitar solo, strutting about the stage, showing off his instrumental virtuosity by playing the guitar with one hand, stalking across the stage with his body in a wide-open stance that contrasted sharply with Bowie's more feminine, closed stance as he sang at the microphone.

Bowie's feminized deference to his guitarist carried over from his absenting himself during Ronson's solos into the moments at which they interacted, frequently in overtly erotic ways. During the song 'Moonage Daydream', when Bowie and Ronson shared a microphone while singing, Bowie gazed fondly and smilingly at the guitarist, and gave him an affectionate kiss. (The song itself is a space-age love song, including romantic lyrics like 'press your space face close to mine, love' and the more phallic and sexual 'put your raygun to my head'). This flirtation was consummated during the song 'Time'.

At this point in the concert Bowie wore a feather boa and adopted a Marlene Dietrich-like persona appropriate to the cabaret-style song. After sashaying around the stage while manipulating his boa and singing, Bowie turned toward Ronson, breathing heavily. The guitarist literally leapt toward the singer, who fell submissively to the floor in a prone position suggesting sexual rear entry of either the heterosexual or homosexual variety. Ronson straddled Bowie while playing his guitar solo, thrusting his guitar toward Bowie in an unmistakably phallic fashion. They rose and fell together in a copulatory rhythm just prior to a blackout.

At one level, this scene can be understood as a dramatization of the often sexually charged relationship between male singers and guitarists in rock groups. Fellow contributor Susan Fast, discussing Led Zeppelin, proposes that Robert Plant, the group's singer, performed 'a feminine musical *persona* to guitarist Jimmy Page's masculine *persona*' (2001: 44). In her analysis of the musical and verbal interplay between the two musicians, Fast points to moments at which Plant was cast 'in the role of receiver of sexual pleasure during intercourse, the "woman" who is asking for more, thus strengthening his role as feminine other to Page' (2001: 45). Clearly, Bowie and Ronson's performance made literal and visible that which is generally only implied in the interactions between rock singers and guitarists; in doing so, they transgressed the carefully policed border between homosociality and homosexuality (Sedgwick 1985: 15).

But the scene is also ambiguous on a dramatic level: what exactly was being represented? Ronson and his guitar performed sexual aggression. But on whom was he aggressing? Was Bowie, in his cabaret singer guise, to be understood as a straight woman or a gay man? The simulated sex act provided no suggestion of a physiological answer to this question. The polyvalence of Bowie's and Ronson's performances of gender and sexuality created the 'hyperbole, dissonance, internal confusion, and proliferation' Butler identifies as strategies for destabilizing normative representations (1990: 31). There was also ambiguity as to whether Ronson's sexual aggression towards Bowie was that of a lover or a rapist. Although Ronson's tackling Bowie at the start of this sequence could be read as a sexual assault, the final image of this sequence suggested more that his aggression was welcome. The song ended with another blackout; when the lights came back up, Bowie and Ronson were posed in a tableau, with Bowie behind and above Ronson, head turned passionately to the right, his left hand reaching down to touch the strings of Ronson's guitar right over the guitarist's genitals.

At the end of 'Hang on to Yourself', Bowie had the first of many costume changes. This one occurred onstage: after the spotlights came back on from a blackout, hands darted out from both sides of the darkness surrounding Bowie's circle of light and snatched away an outer layer of clothing, revealing a different costume beneath. This routine – which Bowie used again at the beginning of his *1980 Floor Show* (1973) television special, his last performance in the Ziggy persona – clearly positions Bowie himself as an object of display. In the course of a two-hour performance, he wore five different costumes that actually seemed to be seven because two of them featured a cape or tunic that was removed to reveal the outfit beneath. All of these costumes, designed either by Bowie's friend and collaborator Freddi Burretti or the Japanese designer Kansai, were feminine in one sense or another. They featured oversized earrings and bracelets, a see-through top, hot pants, leotards and so on. The performance was almost as much a fashion show, with Bowie posing and parading in different outfits, as it was a concert. This concept, too, re-appeared in the *1980 Floor Show*, in which Bowie-as-Ziggy wore a different costume for each song he performed.

Bowie's performance persona changed along (though not necessarily in synch) with his costumes from rocker to folkie balladeer to torchy cabaret singer to his incarnation as a Mick Jagger-type figure who stalked back and forth across the stage during 'Let's Spend the Night Together' while wearing a decidedly feminine see-through sheer black top. (Bowie dedicated his performance of the Rolling Stones' song to Jagger, the original icon of sexual ambiguity in rock and a recurrent figure in Bowie's career.[6]) Like the costumes themselves, these changes of outfit and persona are coded as feminine, according to Goffman:

Men are displayed in formal, business, and informal gear, and although it seems understood that the same individual will at different times appear in all these guises, each guise seems to afford him something he is totally serious about, and deeply identified with, as though wearing a skin, not a costume ... Women in ads seem to have a different relationship to their clothing and to the gestures worn with it. Within each broad category (formal, business, informal) there are choices which are considerably different from one another, and the sense is that one may as well try out various possibilities to see what comes of it – as though life were a series of costume balls. Thus, one can occasionally mock one's own appearance, for identification is not deep (1979: 51).

This observation sheds important light on Bowie's performance. Not only were Bowie's costumes feminine, but his frequent changes of costume read as the feminine lack of commitment to a single identity Goffman describes. While Ronson remained onstage for the entire concert, working hard and unsmilingly in his role as rock guitar hero, the feminine Bowie had the freedom to leave the stage and re-appear in new outfits and new guises. (These moments revealed a fundamental difference between Bowie's performances and those of the psychedelic rock to which he was reacting. The fact that Ronson had to play for long enough to allow Bowie to change costumes indicates that the music served the spectacle rather than the other way around.)

Goffman's point is important for another reason, too, for it suggests that the very strategies by which Bowie coded himself as feminine simultaneously allowed him to assert the artificiality of that coding. His frequent changes of costume suggest a feminine lack of identification with any particular outfit or persona. The fact that the outfits and personae he passed through were themselves coded as feminine further suggests that he did not identify deeply with a feminine image of himself and did not expect his feminine representations to be taken as expressing an underlying identity. Rather, Bowie took aspects of feminine gender display and used them in what Goffman calls 'a quotative way' (1979: 3). Bowie treated gender identity in the same way he treated sexual identity: as performative and, therefore, lacking in foundation.

When Bowie announced from the stage of the Hammersmith Odeon that the performance he and his band had just completed was 'the last one we'll ever do', he was trying to communicate the relatively unremarkable actuality that he intended to disband that particular group and retire the Ziggy Stardust character, an intention that should have come as no surprise to his audience since he had announced it as much as a year earlier and often referred to Ziggy Stardust specifically as a character he was playing. But because the discourse of authenticity is paradigmatic in rock, his audience could not hear Bowie repeating his actor's intention to play other characters. Because they perceived Ziggy Stardust as equivalent to Bowie, what they heard was his announcing an intention never to perform again. Ross identified this tension between Bowie's theatrical conception of his work and the rock audience's expectations nearly a year earlier in an article for *Phonograph Record* when he described Bowie as 'assum[ing] an understanding of the nature of theatre which a rock audience denies almost by definition' (1972). Laing summarizes clearly the implications of these conflicting frames of reference for an artist who tried to bridge theatre and rock:

> In contrast to musical theatre, much popular singing is heard within the space of the autobiographical: the skill of a singer or songwriter is judged by how far the audience is convinced of the authenticity of the emotion portrayed ... Hence, the ambiguity of Bowie's portrayal of Ziggy allowed the slide into autobiography for much of his audience. For them, he *was* Ziggy (1985a: 24).

At first blush, then, it would seem that Bowie's challenge to rock's ideology of authenticity failed because he did not create a new frame within which his audiences could understand his actions. He was hardly the first rock artist to change his persona: compare, for example, the Beatles in 1963, when they were basically a very talented boy band, to the Beatles in 1967, when they were considered musical innovators, adepts of psychedelia and avatars of countercultural politics. But whereas the Beatles undertook this transformation gradually and seemingly organically, Bowie-as-Ziggy came out of nowhere and returned there at the end of his run. Bowie's rock audiences had no experience with this kind of abrupt transformation of performance persona and no context in which to comprehend it. When Bowie reappeared in the spring of 1974 to publicize his new album, *Diamond Dogs*, and, even more decisively, in 'soul boy' guise that winter performing material from *Young Americans* (1975), his strategy of moving from role to role became clear and apprehensible.

Bowie's transformations throughout the 1970s and into the 1980s were radical, frequent and extreme: from the boy in the dress to Ziggy Stardust to Aladdin Sane to the Thin White Duke and beyond. More important than his particular transformations was his implicit assertion of the conventionality and performativity of all his personae. Bowie's summary statement of this point is the final Ziggy album, *Pin Ups* (1973), on which he performs songs by groups he admired during the mid-1960s. The photographs accompanying the record feature Bowie in a number of personae, including the spaced-out Ziggy Stardust and a much cooler musician wearing a suit and holding a saxophone. The cover shows Bowie in highly stylized make-up, which suggests that his face is a mask. On the recording itself, Bowie sings in a number of styles in different voices, including different accents, a vocal version of masking which suggests that, contra rock's romantic ideology of self-expression, the singer's 'self' is determined by the song, not vice versa.

Although Bowie was the single most successful glam rock artist, his tactic of constructing an overtly performative (in the sense of not being anchored in a prior reality) persona was taken up by a great many artists, including Gary Glitter, Suzi Quatro, Roy Wood, Alvin Stardust, Sweet, Kiss (whose kabuki-cum-comic book attire somewhat resembled Ziggy's science fiction overtones and Japanese wardrobe) and others. Glam rock pointed the way for several rock and pop genres of the 1970s and 1980s.[7] Most immediately, glam's emphasis on constructed personae paved the way for punk, as Laing suggests in his discussion of stage names (it is worth remembering here that neither David Bowie nor Marc Bolan was a birth name):

> In 1972, former singer Paul Raven re-emerged as Gary Glitter, followed a year later by Alvin Stardust (former stage name Shane Fenton, original name Bernard Jewry). These names clearly could not be easily 'domesticated'. They announced themselves as artifice, even in their show business referents. 'Glitter' could not easily be seen as a character trait of the singer as 'real person' ... It was more like a description of his *persona*, his adopted pose in his work. Enter Johnny Rotten, Sid Vicious, Rat Scabies, Joe Strummer, Ari Upp, Poly Styrene *et al.* As chosen names these were clearly ranged on the side of explicitly artificial (in the manner of Glitter and Stardust) (1985a: 50–51).

There are, of course, important differences between the ways that glam rockers and punk rockers created and named their respective personae, but it is clear that glam innovated the idea of the rock performance persona as a self-declared construct. This aspect of glam remained influential beyond punk to the New Romantics such as Billy Idol and Adam Ant, whose sartorial choices were directly influenced by Bolan, and beyond them to the New Wave glitter of Blondie (whose frequent producer Mike Chapman had co-produced many of the most commercial British glam acts with Nicky Chinn) and the overt theatricality of Talking Heads.

The aspects of glam that alluded to androgyny and queer identity, most especially Bowie's performance as Ziggy Stardust, created a broad ripple effect as well. Boy George, for example, was directly inspired by Bowie: 'For me, Bowie was a life-changer ... If you're a kid living in an environment where you feel alien most of the time, and you suddenly see this guy on telly in a catsuit with no eyebrows putting his arm around another man, it's incredible' (Sweeting 2003). Arguably, glam was a significant factor in opening the door for such overtly gay acts of the 1980s as Frankie Goes To Hollywood, Culture Club, Flock Of Seagulls, Bronski Beat and others. In addition to extending itself into Brit Pop and dance music, glam also formed an alliance with hard rock, producing the so-called glam metal bands of the 1980s, including Motley Crüe, Twisted Sister and Poison (Walser 1993: 24–36).

David Bowie neither single-handedly created glam rock nor ended it with his announcement from the stage of the Hammersmith Odeon. But that announcement, itself a performative utterance (Austin 2003) that both declared and enacted the disposability and performativity of identity, was the quintessential glam rock gesture.

Notes

1. These headlines are reproduced in the cover notes to the 2003 video re-release of D.A. Pennebaker's *Ziggy Stardust and the Spiders From Mars: The Motion Picture*.
2. For textbook definitions of glam rock, see Charlton (2003: 255–65) and Shuker (1998: 151–2).
3. There is some debate as to whether Bolan or Bowie should be seen as the true father of glam rock. Bowie seems to have a degree of chronological priority, though Bolan probably did more to publicize and popularize glam, at least initially. My purposes here do not require resolution of this issue. Bowie and Bolan grew up in the same London neighbourhood and were friends at this period; each seems to have influenced the other.
4. In the United States, glam rock was often called glitter rock. There was an American branch of the glam family tree that included such performers as Alice Cooper, Iggy Pop, Lou Reed, the New York Dolls and Jobriath. There were several centres of glam activity in the United States during the early 1970s, including New York City, Detroit, and Los Angeles. Although cosmetically similar, American glitter differed from British glam in sensibility. Whereas much of British glam was relatively innocent and playful in ways that allowed it to become mainstream entertainment, American glam artists like Pop, Reed and the New York Dolls performed music that reflected an American urban *demi-monde* of drug addicts, prostitutes and transvestites. Even more purely theatrical artists like Alice Cooper presented a harsher outlook than their British counterparts.
5. For a discussion of the ideological importance of authenticity to rock, see Auslander (1999: 65–111).
6. Duncan describes Mick Jagger as glitter rock's grandfather: 'before Alice Cooper and David Bowie and the New York Dolls … there was Mick Jagger, rock'n'roll's foremost androgyne, Woodstock nation's leading homo-hetero' (1984: 105). Bowie referred frequently to Jagger in interviews; in 1985, they recorded 'Dancing In The Street' together and made a video to go along with the record.
7. Hoskyns sees the legacy of glam in the work of flamboyant African-American artists ranging from Labelle and Parliament-Funkadelic to Prince and Michael Jackson (1998: 108–9). Although there are surface similarities, it is not at all clear that any of these artists was directly influenced by glam rock (with the obvious exception of Prince). There are traditions of glamour and spectacle within African-American music itself that would need to be taken into consideration in assessing the relationship of these performers to glam rock. Here, I will simply suggest that their penchant for spectacle be seen as a phenomenon that is parallel to glam rock rather than derivative of it.

Chapter 8

Patti Smith: *The Old Grey Whistle Test*, BBC-2 TV, May 11, 1976

Sheila Whiteley

> The image is a vital resource that forms complex propositions from simple and
> isolated elements. Each time an image relays desire, this image thinks, with
> unsuspected vitality, the drift of meaning. So it is that images penetrate the solid
> matter of our ideas without our knowledge (Brossard 1991: 196).

It is 30 years since the release of Patti Smith's first album *Horses* (1975), which
contained the track 'Land'.[1] Remembered most for the 'Horses' refrain, which
situated the disruptive potential of avant-garde poetry within a punk idiom, its
lyrics juxtaposed the matter-of-fact with the poetic and rhythmic dimensions of
the heroin experience. As a long-time fan, I know the song well, but it was the
initial impact of seeing it in live performance, on the BBC-2 TV series *The Old
Grey Whistle Test*, that galvanized my love for a woman whose image embodied
androgyneity, and who re-defined women's role in rock. Her persona, arguably
defined by Robert Mapplethorpe in his 1975 photograph for the album sleeve of
Horses, is both self-assured and ambiguous, heavily posed and confrontational –
in essence, a stylish asexual who refuses to be complicit in her female identity.
Variously, she has projected herself as a lesbian ('Gloria', 'Redonda'), an
androgyne (*Horses*), a priestess and female God (*Easter*).[2] In essence, she is both
Sappho and Sibyl, and for her many admirers the allure of Patti Smith remains
potent.

My discussion of Smith's televised performance of 'Horses' explores three
separate, yet related, ideas. The first is concerned with disruption and subversion:
the subject matter, high-energy vocals and aggressive stance that marked Smith as
a progenitor of punk. The second explores the disturbing androgyneity of her
image and its relation to female desire. The third notes the conflation of the cultural
with the historical that marks this performance as topical, moving between the real
and the unreal.

Disruption

> Pierre Klossowski: Words, not bodies, strike a pose; words, not garments, are woven; words, not armors, sparkle (Deleuze and Boundas 1990: 286).

For those who are unfamiliar with Patti Smith's debut album, *Horses*, its title is an allusion to heroin, so linking it with CBGBs and the New York punk scene of the early 1970s to Andy Warhol, John Cale and Lou Reed. The close relation between the high cultural discourse of poetry, the angry rock style of Lou Reed (a former student of the poet Delmore Schwartz at Syracuse University) and Bob Dylan's self-conscious poetry were formative influences on Smith. However, there is little doubt that the underlying feeling of menace that pervades *Horses* owes much to the influence of John Cale (who produced the album) and the Velvet Underground. Championed by Andy Warhol, the Velvet Underground's discordant, throbbing cadences, pulsating tempos and theatricality were routinely enhanced by graphic lyrics that focused on street culture, drugs ('I'm Waiting for the Man', 'Heroin'), and an amorality that bordered on voyeurism ('Venus in Furs'). Combined with Smith's 'personal love affairs' with the nineteenth-century French poet Rimbaud, political novelist and activist Jean Genet,[3] novelist William Burroughs, artist Jackson Pollock and such rock icons as Bob Dylan, Jim Morrison, Jimi Hendrix and Keith Richards, it was scarcely surprising that her writing was largely concerned with both a radicalization of form and political and cultural revolution:

> sonic klein man its me my shape burnt in the sky its me the memoire of me racing thru the eye of the mer thru the eye of the sea thru the arm of the needle and jacking new filaments new risks etched forever in a cold system of wax … horses groping for a sign of breath …

The seeming babble that characterized Smith's writing on the sleeve-notes to *Horses* is but one indication of her use of rhythm, sound, colour and ungrammatical and disjointed syntax that situate her within the avant-garde. The effect is one of discomfort. The dialectical flow is continually interrupted and, far from being neutral, her language reveals the operation of power relations as it constantly negates the confines of language through an unrepressed irrationality. At the same time, it situates the breathless ecstasy of the heroin experience, the altered state of consciousness, the euphoria that flows from 'jacking new elements', and the risk – 'horses groping for a sign of breath'.

In essence 'Land' explores the fate of Johnny, a heroin addict, from the initial fix through to his death. There are two principal moods. The first is almost a monotonal exposition of events, seen and interpreted through the eye of the narrator. The second is more upbeat, primal, a cocaine-induced interlude ('I fill my nose with snow') where the narrator escapes momentarily into the euphoria of dance before returning to Johnny and the nightmare of the final fix ('his vocal chords shot up … like mad pituitary glands [as] he felt himself disintegrate').

While the subject matter is disturbing, its effectiveness as a sound-poem lies primarily in the fragmentation and manipulation of words which juxtapose the mundane ('the boy was in the hallway drinking a glass of tea') with the poetic and rhythmic dimensions of the heroin experience ('he picked up the blade and he pressed it against his smooth throat (the spoon) and let it deep in (the veins) dip into the sea, to the sea of possibilities'). Contextualization ('I put my hand inside his cranium') is extended by word play ('we had such a brainiac amour') and driven by assonance ('shined open coiled snakes white and shiny twirling and encircling'), by repetition ('I feel it, I feel it, I feel it, I feel it') and by association ('go Rimbaud go', 'go Johnny go') that relates the drug-addict to the outsider, the marginalized misfit in society.

Although the song is long (9.26 minutes) and complex in its imagery, the heightening experiences of the 'fix' are charged by a rhythmic intensity which impels the movement from a starkly simple and unaccompanied statement of fact ('he merged perfectly with the hallway'), through to a pulsating echo that is underpinned by the throb of Lenny Kaye's guitar ('he drove it in, he drove it in, he drove it deep in Johnny') which, in turn, informs the pulse of the second stanza as the heroin starts to hit ('he saw horses, horses, horses, horses, horses, horses, horses, horses').

Smith's colouring of the vocal line is marked by her rhythmic use of phrases which impel the narrative of events ('started crashing his head against the locker, started crashing his head against the locker'), assonance and sibilance ('white shining silver studs'), exaggerated vowels ('do you know how to pony like Bony Moronie'), phonetic resemblances and aural puns ('do the sweet pea, do the sweet pee-pee'), sounds that 'babble' and 'battle', going beyond the full stop (the ultimate sign of closure) through an often incoherent speech that privileges confusion ('at the Tower of Babel they knew what they were after').

While the words are familiar today, the impact of seeing it in live performance – Patti Smith, dressed in white shirt and leathers, wearing dark glasses – remains nothing short of electrifying. The snarl of her vocal delivery is focused by her body language. Her gestures mimic the words to effect 'a double "transgression" – of language by the flesh and of the flesh by language' (Deleuze and Boundas 1990: 286) as she continually disrupts the syntax in imitation of the conflicting experiences of heroin-induced euphoria. Initially, Kaye's guitar is superimposed over her face ('the boy took Johnny, he pushed him against the locker'), before the camera cuts to a profiled image, with the ecstatic 'he saw horses, horses, horses, horses, horses, horses, horses, horses', and given a sense of visual immediacy as she removes her dark glasses, to adopt a heavily posed rock-hero position, sullen, with the camera exploring her lips, teeth, mouth against an evocation of dance crazes, past and present: 'Do you know how to twist? Well, it goes like this. Then you mashed potato. Do the alligator, do the alligator …'

Changes of mood, the shift from the dynamic of 'got to lose control' and 'you like it like that' to the ecstatic of 'do the watusi, do the watusi' are intensified by the camera angles and the theatrics of the performance. Initially focusing on her left shoulder, which pulsates to the underlying beat, the camera pans to her almost-frontal face which is superimposed over her profiled image, her hair covering her face, before the sudden drop to her knees and the cut to her mouth, orally caressing the microphone in a semblance of fellatio – 'do you like it like that' – before the enticement of 'do the watusi', where she shrugs over her shoulder in a semblance of indifference, and the blank gaze that accompanies the shift to the reflective 'life is filled with holes, Johnny's lying there, his sperm coffin', the metaphor 'sperm coffin' providing a stark reminder of the effect of heroin on virility ('life is filled with holes').

The 'in yer face' performance that characterizes Patti Smith's interaction with the camera/viewer is quintessential punk, but the play on words that drives the underlying dynamic of 'Horses' also provides an insight into New York underground culture, so playing on the listener's desire for meaning. References to dance crazes – the watusi, the twist, the mashed potato, the pony – collide against the imagery of addiction, the tracks that trace the needle-marks of the syringe ('there's a little place, a place called space … it's across the tracks'), the knives and switchblades (used to heat the heroin), the snow of cocaine, and the transition from euphoria to nightmare withdrawal symptoms that converge in a stream-of-consciousness babble that ends with 'a scream … so high (my heart) pitched that nobody heard, no-one heard that cry'.

While the play on meaning, the cutting up of words and syntax can be considered as embodying the bricolage of punk, Patti Smith's live performance of 'Horses' identifies her as 'the original punk rocker'. Accompanied by lead guitarist/rock writer Lenny Kaye, Richard Sohl (piano), Ivan Kral (guitar, bass) and Jay Dee Daugherty (drums), the sound is raw and primitive, a reminder that punk rock was essentially about confrontation, 'dramatising the last days as daily life and ramming all emotions into the narrow gap between a blank stare and a sardonic grin' (Marcus 1992: 595). The date of the album's release is also significant in that it preceded the Sex Pistols' first gig, at St Martin's College of Art, London in November 1975, and the subsequent release of their first single, 'Anarchy in the UK', in November 1976. It is also evident that whilst punk was ostensibly pitched against the excesses of progressive rock, the Number One singles in the UK at the time included 'If' (Telly Savalas), 'Bye Bye Baby' (the Bay City Rollers), 'Whispering Grass' (Windsor Davies and Don Estelle), 'Tears on My Pillow' (Johnny Nash), 'Sailing' (Rod Stewart) and 'Hold Me Close' (David Essex). The year of Smith's *The Old Grey Whistle Test* performance – 1976 – was dominated by Abba ('Mama Mia', 'Fernando', 'Dancing Queen') and included such Number One singles as 'Combine Harvester' (the Wurzels) and 'The Roussos Experience' (Demis Roussos). The overall impression is one of a conforming mainstream, broken only by glimpses of 'what might be' in a re-release of David Bowie's 1969 single 'Space Oddity'.

The dramatic intrusion of 'Horses' into this otherwise docile scene was both timely and shocking in its impact. Clearly, the recording studio setting was small-scale, and the double-tracking on the album – that informs the play of conscious/subconscious reactions to Johnny's escalating paranoia – is missing. The impact, however, remains. It is raw, stripped-down rock that pulsates with menace, with Smith radiating both intelligence and subversion in a theatrical performance that is primitive and violent, flying in the face of all that was considered popular, tasteful and commercial.

Androgyny

'… the space of possibilities'

Patti Smith's performance of 'Horses' is also a reminder that while punk 'offered women permission to explore gender boundaries, to investigate their own power, anger, aggression – even nastiness' (O'Brien 1995: 113) she was the instigator, the sexy androgyne whose extraordinary stare and lithe, sensual body challenged the sexual certainties of mainstream femininity.

It is relevant, here, to return briefly to the formative influences on Patti Smith, her identification with the poetic communities of 1950s New York and the New York Pop Art scene of the 1960s.

Patti Smith's determination 'to be bad … to be a star … never to return to burn out in this Piss Factory'[4] resonates with her move to New York in 1967. As an epicentre for the thriving poetic communities of the 1950s, it was built around existential values, nihilism, jazz, poetry, drugs and literature. Popularized by Jack Kerouac, Gregory Corso, Gary Snyder and Allen Ginsberg, influenced by such French intelligentsia as Sartre and de Beauvoir and the renegades of high culture, Celine, Rimbaud and Yeats, the heady mixture of bohemian culture spread across the US in the 1960s, initially centring on Greenwich Village, New York. The importance of Greenwich Village to the emerging rock scene of the 1960s is reflected in Bob Dylan's disavowal of his past on the album *Another Side of Bob Dylan* (1964). Disenchanted by the petty politics surrounding folk, he had expanded his own poetic consciousness by reading the poetry of John Keats and French symbolist Arthur Rimbaud, and his 1965–66 albums (*Bringing It All Back Home, Highway 61 Revisited, Blonde on Blonde*) are characterized by lyrical complexity and literary sophistication. It is also evident that the Beat generation influenced Patti Smith's other heroes: Jim Morrison, the 'lizard king' of rock, ruled by the dictum 'death and my cock', whose non-conventional lyrics, allied to hallucinogenic experience, subverted the distinction between poetry and popular music; and Jimi Hendrix, whose poetic language stressed the chaos of sounds and rhythms, disorientation and a radicalization of form. Both had died at the age of 27, so instigating the association of death with the heroic.[5]

The Beat philosophy of anarchy and individualism was also reflected in the curious figure of Andy Warhol, the most prominent figure of the New York Pop

Art scene. His mass-produced and recurring visual images are now recognized as symbols of 1960s gay culture: 'the silkscreens of Elvis and Troy Donahue (1962–1964); the New York World's Fair mural of "Thirteen Most Wanted Men" (1964); the films *Sleep* (1963), *Blow-Job* (1963), *My Hustler* (1965), *Lonesome Cowboys* (1967) and *Flesh* (1968)' (Cresap 1999: 52). More specifically, Warhol's endless promotion of camp taste and drag culture at The Factory,[6] and his personal involvement with the Velvet Underground (he designed the infamous peel-off banana screen-print for the *Velvet Underground and Nico* album sleeve in 1967) provided a crucial context for the band's fascination with street culture and amorality which, in turn, was to influence Patti Smith's heroin track 'Land'.

Her other major influence at the time was her soul brother and part-time boyfriend Robert Mapplethorpe, whose photographs and images provide obsessive insights into the sexual imagery of the leather scene, S/M sex, homosexuality, flowers and contemporary icons such as Marianne Faithfull, William Burroughs, Andy Warhol, Iggy Pop and Debbie Harry. In essence, his work explores sexual ambiguities, for example his flowers 'with their drooping or thrusting penile leaves complement the concentrated postures of Mapplethorpe's men' (Hollinghurst 1983: 17) and his photographic images of Smith (with whom he lived for a while) have an ambiguity that challenges the onlooker, exacting a complex emotional reaction.

It is therefore apparent that the New York scene of the 1960s provided an environment that fostered individualism, and that this included a play on gendered identity – whether demonstrated through Mapplethorpe's array of images and discourses *about* sexuality, or in the camp strategies and performance art of The Factory's Exploding Plastic Inevitable. Patti Smith's adoption of the black and white insignia of Bohemian dress-codes, the black leathers and white T-shirt associated with Jim Morrison, thus incorporated a range of meanings, the most culturally prominent of which pivoted on gender. Her clothes, her stance, her attitude served as outward marks of difference that were both fluid and curiously asexual. What was at stake in this experience of the dualism of gender and sexuality was the possibility of distancing the feminine through an assumed persona that denaturalized sexual difference. Like Virginia Woolf's *Orlando*, the transformation offered an androgynous subversion of gender fixity.

While her adoption of leathers is the most obvious challenge to the notorious sexism of the 1960s[7] – change the clothes, change the sex – it is evident that the sexual dynamics of her performance owe much to her ability to morph into characterizations of rock heroes, so bringing both integrity and identity to the text. She becomes Johnny as he 'gets up, takes off his leather jacket', challenging the Angel whose taunt, 'Oh pretty boy, can't you show me nothing but surrender?' provokes her controlling gaze at the camera, where an emotional and physical closeness is combined with a suddenly ominous detachment – 'you got pen knives and jack knives and switchblades preferred'.

While the monotonal recitation of events owes more than a little to Bob Dylan, whose whining, nasal tone and abrasive intensity complement lyrics that focus on human and intellectual injustices, Patti Smith's feeling for the theatricality of (her) performance is evidenced more in her adoption of the masculine persona in the 'dance' sequence. Here image and vocal tone converge – with her hair over her face, she assumes a characteristic Morrison pose, her left shoulder pulsating to the lascivious tone of her voice as she moves into the dangerous territories of illicit desire ('I want your baby sister, give me your baby sister, dig your baby sister') and the voyeuristic ('Rise up on her knees, do the sweet pea, do the sweet pee-pee'). At the same time, she evokes memories of Morrison's own self-presentation, his self-conscious feminized preening that characterized his eroticized male image,[8] his hair long and curled over the collar of his white T-shirt, his skin pale, 'his face more than handsome ... it was pretty ... and the way he cocked his head slightly, exposing his alabaster white neck, displayed a vulnerability that most men would be afraid to reveal ... his eyes were penetrating, his cheeks hollow and slightly sunken like a fashion model's' (Riordan and Prochinichy 1991: 15–16).

In contrast, the emphasis on Smith's mouth, lips and teeth conjures up a comparison with Mick Jagger, not least when she orally caresses the microphone – 'do you like it like that'. But her characterization contains more than his goading, teasing, ritualized sexuality. Rather, her androgynous appearance and self-invention parallels that of Jagger himself in that it involves a complex gender-identity that is, at one and the same time, a macho performance style and a characterization that is ambiguous and sexually ambivalent.[9] Like Jagger, Patti Smith's performance is sexually sophisticated. The play between similarity and difference is blurred and replaced by a fantasy of eroticism that challenges the traditional sense of masculine/feminine dualism.

It is, however, the dark features of Keith Richards that she most evokes. As a young girl[10] her interest in the *sound and appearance* of rock music had been modelled on the lead guitarist of the Rolling Stones who, by the early 1970s, had become increasingly addicted to drugs. Most famously, Jagger and Richards were arrested at the latter's Sussex home 'Redlands' and charged with drug offences. Their trial in June 1967 became a cause célèbre, which culminated in heavy fines and a salutary prison sentence. A leader in *The Times*, written by its editor, William Rees-Mogg, and entitled 'Who Breaks a Butterfly on a Wheel?', offered an eloquent plea in their defence, and The Who rallied to their cause, releasing a single which coupled 'Under My Thumb' and 'The Last Time'. The sentences were duly quashed on appeal in July, but Richards's drug addiction continued. In January 1977, he was fined by an English court for possession of cocaine and only three months later, more seriously, he was arrested in Toronto on charges of dealing heroin. Clearly, his drug problems would not have emerged fully by the time that 'Horses' was released, but nevertheless his increasingly ravaged looks and headline rock persona provided a compelling model for Johnny and his realization, in performance, by Patti Smith. Thus, while her own guitar playing is little more than fiercely strummed three-chord rock, her powerful interaction with Lenny Kaye, as the tempo increases against the rising momentum of the piano and drums, morphs into the image of the archetypal guitar-hero, driving the 'do the watusi' instrumental break into a frenzied evocation of power-driven rock.

While I am not suggesting that Patti Smith consciously modelled her persona on Morrison, Jagger or Richards, her characterization of Johnny and the dramatizing of the heroin experience through performance relate both to her self-identification with rebels (both past and present) and to the keen sense of observation that distinguishes her frenetic poetry. As such, there is a merging of identities that informs her performance of 'Horses', which works to blur the rigid boundaries of gender and sexuality, and scramble the components of 'man' and 'woman' into a sexually-enticing androgyne. Given that Patti Smith's only female hero, Joan of Arc, was herself a de-sexed martyr, her self-styled sexual ambiguity is not too surprising. As a woman who is conventionally defined by her body, her performance masks her femininity, but rather than constituting a denial of her identity, it becomes, instead, an assertion of her autonomy – a strong, sexy woman challenging both the confines of gender and the fratriarchal structures of progressive rock, 'dancing around to the simple rock'n'roll song'.

Time and place

'Seize the possibilities ... the time is now'

Patti Smith's acute sense of sexual politics is given a particular context in her live performance of 'Horses'. Unlike the album track, which moves straight into the narrative of Johnny, she initially confronts the camera with a measured four-line recitation interspersed with a muttered 'Jah lives': 'Mr Death ... Oscar Wilde ... Mr Thorpe ... The time is now, the time is now'. The dedication provides a specific contextualization for the 'outsider', linking Johnny (the heroin addict) to others who have experienced both condemnation and alienation by a judgemental society, dedicated to upholding the status quo of so-called normality.

The tremors surrounding the 'outing' of Jeremy Thorpe, former leader of the Liberal Party, were already shaking the walls of the establishment in 1975. Accused of having a homosexual relationship with Norman Scott, who claimed to have been threatened by Thorpe after the end of their affair, he was subsequently one of four defendants in a court case, but was acquitted of attempted murder.[11] The ensuing scandal ruined his parliamentary career, and the animosity and hysteria directed at him by the media provoked comparison with Wilde, who had been found guilty of homosexual offences and sentenced to two years' imprisonment with hard labour in 1895. Both were at odds with society, both subverted the 'wholesome, manly, simple ideals of English life' (Dollimore 1993:

635), both relate to the 'outsider' – the misfits, repressed and oppressed because of their individuality and sexuality.

The extended investigation into 'the sea of possibilities' that closes the 'Horses' section of 'Land' is thus given a new focus in Patti Smith's live performance. While the underlying sentiments remain (the acoustic play on words, sea/seize possibilities), the words are given a sense of immediacy:

Go man go!
I'm calling to you
Oh God, I'm calling to you
Oh God, I hear you
Oh God, have no fear
There's a possibility
In taking more than one possibility
If you are male, choose other than female.

The inferred homosexual address that prefaced 'Horses' is thus given a sense of action: 'you must take responsibility for holding the key to freedom'. It is, then, no accident that the end of 'Horses' segues into the opening chords of 'Hey Joe' (her first single, in 1974)[12] with its sustained reference to urban terrorist Patty Hearst, so confirming, once again, Patti Smith's identification with the rebels and outsiders who shaped her powerful rock poetry, and her conflation of the cultural with the historical that marks this performance as topical, moving between the real and the unreal. The cry to God, to Jah, the direct address to 'Mr Thorpe' within a track that deals primarily with the outsider in its focus on heroin, is both demanding and challenging. Allied to her own androgynous appearance that contradicts the norms of femininity, the live performance of 'Horses' embodies a fierce sense of defiance, an example of punk at its most powerful in its identification with the marginalized and repressed.

Coda

Patti Smith's performance of 'Horses' provides a particular insight into her sense of individuality, in particular her confrontational style and image, which was to initiate a specific focus for both the feminization of rock and the arty garage rock of the 1990s and beyond. Not least, she was interested in both the *sound* and the *appearance* of rock, and her fusion of 'three chord rock with the power of the word', allied to her androgynous appearance, undoubtedly helped to define the New York punk scene of the 1970s.[13]

While I have focused on three particular aspects of the live performance of 'Horses', it is also apparent that her framing of the song (the 'Jah lives' of the introduction and the cry to God in the outro) owes much to her religious faith and her identification with the art and spirituality of William Blake. As a political and religious artist who was often in opposition with his artistic peers and with organized society, government and religion, his writings provided an inspiration for fusing her visionary insights with a politicized and often troubled interpretation of contemporary reality. This is subsequently reflected in her references to biblical figures, which set up the theme of religious revisionism consistent with Rimbaud's portrait of a redeemed Cain in *Mauvais Sang* and a materialized Christ at the conclusion of *Adieu*. As Jaures Noland has observed,

> the allusion to Cain turns out to be a particularly rich and useful one for Smith, for it serves to mythologize not only the poet but also his double in the poem, the originator of rock'n'roll, Little Richard ... just as Little Richard 'baptised' America and 'Arthur' baptises his siblings in the river, Smith resacralizes the world through music (1995: 594).

This questioning energy and often-violent mysticism, which attempts to communicate an idea of God with a living sense of spiritual and religious purpose, is evident both in her albums and in her radical rock journalism: for example, 'Jukebox Crucifix', an account of her trip to Jim Morrison's grave in Paris, provides a specific insight into the connections between mythic American rock, visionary religious language and her own sense of an artistic calling.

It is considered that any artist who continues to conflate cultural and historical influences with his/her own inner life will have lasting relevance regardless of age, but it is the sensual, androgynous figure of Patti Smith that gives 'Horses' its real impact and sexual appeal. She is/was nothing short of electrifying and, for me, this was sufficient reason to re-explore my attraction to a woman who embodied the perverse spirit of 1970s rock.

Notes

1. 'Land' is broken down into three continuous sections: 'Horses', 'Land of a Thousand Dances' and 'La Mer'.
2. See 'Daughters Of Chaos' in Whiteley (2000: 95–119).
3. Living with Robert Mapplethorpe in 'cold lofts and cheap hotels in New York, Smith's second great literary passion, for the French criminal, political activist and novelist Jean Genet, began to define her writing and describe her own experience in attempting to write in and about a state of near vagrancy. Genet's writing, like Smith's, was driven by a desire to live in opposition to social orthodoxy, and to confirm an outlaw status through a life of degradation. His criminality, as well as his prose, articulated a deeply moral view of society, in which his homosexuality and sexual fantasies became parables of personal, artistic and political freedom. As such, he was the perfect patron saint for Mapplethorpe and Smith's artistic union' (Bracewell 2003: 334).
4. Her determination to get to New York is reflected in her song 'Piss Factory' (1970).
5. I have written extensively on Jim Morrison, Jimi Hendrix and the relationship between death and rock; see 'Little Boys' in Whiteley (2003: 130–56).

6.   The Factory was the name given by Andy Warhol to his multi-media 'freak-show'. The Velvet Underground – Lou Reed (guitar, vocals), John Cale (bass, viola), Sterling Morrison (guitar), Maureen Tucker (drums) and Nico (vocals) – were part of his touring 'total environment' show, The Exploding Plastic Inevitable.

7.   While the 1960s appeared to offer personal freedom in its challenge to the traditional concepts of career, family, education and morality, it is apparent that this negated the experience of women, who were little less than 'the passive squaws of patriarchal hippy men' (Bracewell 2003: 18). See also 'Repressive Representations' and 'The Personal is Political' in Whiteley (2000: 32–43, 44–50).

8.   It is an image that arguably drew on the Marlon Brando/James Dean school of the 1950s.

9.   See 'Little Red Rooster v. the Honky Tonk Woman: Mick Jagger, Sexuality, Style and Image' in Whiteley (1998: 67–99).

10.   See her interview in *The Guardian*, July 9, 2003: *The Guide*, p. 26.

11.   The son of a Conservative MP, John Jeremy Thorpe (b. April 29, 1929) was educated at Eton and Trinity College Oxford, and was called to the bar in 1954. In 1959 he entered parliament as Liberal MP for North Devon, and in 1967 became party leader after the resignation of Jo Grimond. Thorpe's style, in contrast to Grimond's, was youthful and dynamic, and he was sometimes ridiculed as too gimmicky. Following the death of his first wife, he married Marion, a former concert pianist and ex-wife of the Earl of Harewood. In 1976 he was forced to resign the party leadership after being accused of a homosexual relationship with Norman Scott. He lost his parliamentary seat at the general election of 1979 and retired from public life. Not long after the end of the trial he was diagnosed with Parkinson's Disease.

12.   Funded by her 'soul twin', Robert Mapplethorpe.

13.   As Patti Smith has observed, 'When I was a small girl, "punk" was a very negative term. If you called someone a punk, it meant they were stupid or a jerk. Then, in America at least, in the seventies, punk translated into something very intelligent and philosophical. I'm not talking about the trappings and the clothing, but the actual meaning of the word. Whoever invented the punk movement – which certainly wasn't myself – shifted the meaning' (Bracewell 2003: 340).

Chapter 9

Print the truth, not the legend
The Sex Pistols: Lesser Free
Trade Hall, Manchester,
June 4, 1976

Sean Albiez

The Sex Pistols' first performance at Manchester's Lesser Free Trade Hall on June 4, 1976 has become widely accredited as 'year zero' in the history of Mancunian rock music. It is claimed that those attending the gig experienced a personal epiphany, going on to change the fortunes of the local music scene and eventually to shape the future development of Anglo-American rock. Perhaps more than any other performance in this collection, the gig is understood to have had an immediate and profound *local* impact. This chapter will propose that it may indeed have contributed something to the development of broad based alliances between twenty-something Mancunian musical activists, disaffected musicians and young music fans in a small but vibrant scene. But it will also suggest that it was only one of several Sex Pistols-related events in Manchester that acted to kick-start that scene.

Fundamental problems with previous representations of the gig and its dubious status as 'history' need to be recognized. To exemplify why this is a necessary concern, I will briefly examine the most recent, widely known and problematic reconstruction of the Lesser Free Trade Hall performance, in Michael Winterbottom's film *24 Hour Party People* (2002).

The movie tells the story of Factory Records and surrounding events in the Manchester music scene from 1976 to 1992. Its narrative is hinged upon the premise that the Sex Pistols gig of June 4, 1976 is a central moment in Manchester's musical and cultural history. It suggests that many who attended formed bands and labels, became cultural commentators and activists, and contributed to future developments in popular music. The film self-consciously and explicitly denies its basis in truth[1] yet simultaneously and implicitly promises historical veracity through the often handheld, DV, docudrama qualities of its photography and production (Gilbey 2002). Its re-staging of the Lesser Free Trade Hall performance additionally incorporates inter-cut 8 mm footage of the original event, which underpins its claims to authenticity. For those in the cinema audience without any previous knowledge of the gig, *24 Hour Party People* plausibly stands in for history, but this substitution is more than a little problematic; this is not to condemn the film for failing to be something it does not claim to be, but simply to point out its shortcomings as a historical record.

In fact, many of the details of the performance as represented in the film are wildly inaccurate. In gauging its significance for the Manchester music scene, the awkward problem of ascertaining who actually attended the gig is central. For example, the attendees with reasonable corroboration include Pete Shelley, Howard Devoto and Steve Diggle of the proto-Buzzcocks; Bernard Sumner and Peter Hook (later of Joy Division/New Order); Paul Morley (later an author and music journalist); Morrissey (later of the Smiths); the Sex Pistols and their entourage, including Malcolm McLaren and Jordan (original Sex boutique assistant, style guru and one-time manager of Adam and the Ants); and the support band, Solstice. Others who certainly attended (somewhere between 30 and 100) included Eddie Garrity (later of Ed Banger and the Nosebleeds), Ian Moss (later of the Frantic Elevators, with Mick Hucknall – who was not there) and John the Postman, a committed and omnipresent figure on the punk and post-punk scene in Manchester.

David Nolan's Granada TV documentary *I Swear I Was There* (2001), and its accompanying book, go to heroic lengths to set the record straight, and yet there is still confusion over the gig. As Nolan suggests, the reasons for this uncertainty may be the deliberate or accidental conflation of the band's performance on June 4, 1976 and its later one at the same venue on July 20, 1976, and the flawed nature of memory and oral history as historical evidence. Considerable doubts have therefore been created about who actually attended the first gig, and who did not but 'swore they were there'.

For example, based on Nolan's research for the television documentary (and inconsistencies found across many of the published accounts of the gigs), it appears that there are disagreements over Mark E. Smith (and the early Fall's) attendance at the first gig (although they certainly attended at least one of them)[2] as well as uncertainties over the presence of Tony Wilson (Granada TV and Factory Records). Shelley and Devoto (who organized both events) and John the Postman have no recollection of Wilson being there, despite knowing him from his local television appearances. Rogan suggests that Wilson was sent a Sex Pistols demo tape, and an invitation to the July 20 gig, by Devoto *after* the first gig (1993: 82); if true, this casts doubt on any claims to authenticity of *24 Hour Party People*, in which Wilson is portrayed as the filmic narrator of the first gig.

The significance of this fact-sifting is that although we can suggest that the direct consequences of the June 4 performance were perhaps important for some, we are reminded that no single performance makes a music scene. It may be, as Nolan and Haslam (2000) suggest, that it was a combination of the two Sex Pistols visits that kick-started the Manchester scene. I would go further by arguing that it was a combination of many *local and national* factors. These would include national music press coverage in *Sounds*, *New Musical Express* and *Melody Maker* throughout 1976; the Lesser Free Trade Hall gigs; the group's TV appearance on Granada's *So It Goes* on September 1; a 'mystery' gig at Didsbury College, Manchester[3] on October 1; the group's infamous interview with Bill Grundy on Thames Television's *Today* programme on December 1, which received huge national press attention and was heavily covered in the *Manchester Evening News* because of Grundy's north-west connections (Haslam 2000: 112); and the post-Grundy 'Anarchy Tour' gigs at the Electric Circus in Collyhurst, Manchester on December 9 and December 19. The critical punk mass that developed in Manchester finally culminated in the Buzzcocks' DIY release of their 'Spiral Scratch' EP in February 1977. Together, these events all contributed to the development and establishment of a Manchester punk scene.

My main focus, however, will remain on the contexts and events of June 4 (and, briefly, July 20) in assessing how the Sex Pistols' longitudinal influence over the development of the Manchester scene in 1976–77 was, for some key players, traceable to those performances. I will also examine the responses of those who attended the gig as evidenced through their recent testimony. As these accounts will have been coloured by subsequent punk memories, shifting personal perspectives and self-conscious or inadvertent omission and embellishment, we should be wary of their claims to historical accuracy. However, we should also acknowledge the capacity that such narratives possess to provide an insight into the personal impact of the June 4 performance on those few who did attend.

1970s Manchester and music pre-Pistols

Manchester's vibrant music and club culture of the 1960s (Lee 2002: 17–86) had become increasingly impoverished by the early 1970s. Rock acts such as David Bowie, Lou Reed and Led Zeppelin appeared at major venues in the area, but only acted to re-affirm the gulf between the aspirations of local musicians and the opportunities to hand. The confidence and musical achievements of the previous decade (the Hollies, Herman's Hermits, Freddie and the Dreamers, Wayne Fontana), bolstered by the triumphs of the neighbouring Liverpudlian Mersey sound, had diminished. Successful local groups such as Barclay James Harvest (from nearby Oldham) or 10cc were far removed from the everyday experience of musicians and fans alike. Middles encapsulates the situation in the Manchester of the mid-1970s:

> For so long, there had been no real reason to actually physically start playing in a band as the gap between local halls and dizzy success just wasn't expected to happen. Rock stars, it had long since been concluded, were hallowed beings who hailed from somewhere else – America or the south of England – and owned fish farms in Hertfordshire (1996: 13).

Equally significant and damaging were national attitudes to the north-west. Urry describes the region as being broadly viewed as a cultural 'no man's land' by a general, southern consensus which believed that the north-west of England possessed little of interest, either historically or culturally:

> It was a 'place on the margin' of British life ... the culture of the area was not thought of as worth knowing about. It was 'up there', well away from the supposed centres of British public and artistic life which have for some centuries been based in the south east of the country (1995: 158).

While this reads as a caricature of southern attitudes of the time, it is, within Urry's terms of reference – the 'pre-history' of cultural tourism and the heritage industry – a valid perspective. It can also be suggested that the attitudes of London-based record companies, apart from RCA and CBS who had small promotional offices in Manchester in the 1970s (Middles 1996: 75–9), were not dissimilar to those he describes ... apart from sending successful British and international artists to perform at the Manchester Apollo, why would A&R or any other record company staff wish to travel there?

It has been argued that this inequality extended to more than just a perceived impossibility of opportunity. Alongside the geographical prejudices in British cultural life, there were very real impediments to the success and exposure that bands needed in order to prosper in post-1960s Manchester. Even though universities and colleges in the city potentially provided local musicians with opportunities to perform, there was, in effect, a closed shop operated by London-based booking agencies:

> The major problem was one of celebrity status ... the groups that the social secretaries were booking into their college venues were the ones promoted by the big London agencies, Chrysalis, Virgin, etc, and these bands tended to be ones who had record contracts with the majors. There was simply no space in the scheme of things for a local band (Lee 2002: 90–91).

However, it would be unfair to suggest that music fans in the north-west responded to this southern hegemony with resignation and cultural compliance. The Northern Soul phenomenon, which originated in Manchester's Twisted Wheel club in the 1960s, was an example of the fierce northern self-sufficiency which would later be central to the punk and post-punk Manchester scene. Joanne Hollows and Katie Milestone have claimed that Northern Soul rejected

> the authority of 'the south' of England [in favour of] the American North, in particular, Detroit ... Northern Soul is [an] ... example of the ways in which British working class culture has produced an 'imaginary' identification with America as an 'escape' from native cultural traditions (quoted in Connell and Gibson 2003: 107).

Northern Soul fans can therefore be viewed as (hyper)active consumers, who created a semi-autonomous regional scene with its own distinct consumption practices (not least in obsessively seeking out obscure Detroit soul releases), styles of dance and dress, and a network of venues. Their DIY ethic was a precursor of the Manchester punk and post-punk scene. Furthermore, key figures in Manchester's post-punk club and dance music culture such as Rob Gretton (Joy Division/New Order's manager and the person who conceived the idea of the Hacienda) and Mike Pickering (Quando Quango, T-Coy, M People and Hacienda DJ) were involved in, and inspired by, the Northern Soul scene (Haslam 2000: 116).

In Manchester itself, Music Force, a socialist-based musicians' co-operative, was – perhaps more than any other pre-punk phenomenon – pivotal to the future trajectory of music-making in the city (Lee 2002: 92), bridging 1960s pop/rock and 1970s punk. Its central aims were to support local musicians by developing a network of low-key venues, and to promote local bands on a regional and national basis. As a result of its success Music Force not only prepared the way for punk by establishing access to venues in a collective framework, but also by proselytizing about the meagreness of rock music in this period, using remarkably punk-like rhetoric. In 1975, its in-house magazine polemically stated:

> ROCK MUSIC has lost a lot of the cultural dynamism that steamhammered the 60s and early 70s. Now, far too often, the music squeaks in falsetto for a decaying aristocracy of greasy management and gilded superstars, or mumbles incoherently to cloistered coteries of musicians (Lee 2002: 111).

It seems Manchester was not only primed for change, but had created the very conditions for the renewal that would be set in motion by punk. Ironically, it was to be a London-based catalyst that provided the final push, resulting in a renewed and reinvigorated Manchester music scene.

Sex Pistols: Lesser Free Trade Hall, June 4, 1976

Numerous commentators have written about the Sex Pistols' first appearance in Manchester (Savage 1991; Middles 1996; Haslam 2000; Nolan 2001; Lee 2002). Two bootlegs of the gig exist, which reveal that far from being musically inept, the Sex Pistols were a powerful and accomplished rock band. There is also film and photographic evidence that can be used to support eye-witness testimony. Based on the recollections of those attending the performance, the immediate response was a mixture of utter shock, bemusement, admiration, perceptible disdain and disinterest. We therefore need to establish why and how an event that seems on tape to be a competent and powerful rock show was perceived by some of those attending as a major paradigm shift, and in particular how the physical performance and presence of the band contributed to such an effect.

The Sex Pistols came to Manchester in June 1976 through the efforts of Salford-based Bolton students Peter McNeish (Shelley) and Howard Trafford (Devoto). Like others in the Manchester audience, they had been struck by Neil Spencer's review in the *New Musical Express* of February 18, 1976, of an early Sex Pistols gig at the Marquee in London. It described them as 'a musical experience with the emphasis on Experience', noted that they played an 'Iggy and the Stooges item', reported that a band member countered a heckler who shouted 'You can't play!' with the response 'So what?' and recorded that there were 'two scantily clad (plastic thigh boots and bodices) pieces dancing up front'. Spencer also wrote that one of the band confided in him 'Actually, we're not into music … we're into chaos.' The review promised that the Sex Pistols 'experience' was about sex, violence, insolence and anarchy (1976).

Devoto later said of the review, 'Well it clicked with me and it just so happened that I could borrow a car that weekend … it was the weekend that changed our lives' (Nolan 2001: 23). Devoto and Shelley journeyed to London to see the Sex Pistols, attending their gigs at High Wycombe College Of Higher Education on February 20 and Welwyn Garden City on February 21. After the events they spoke to the band's manager, Malcolm McLaren, and offered to organize a gig in Manchester. Whether it was these two February gigs or the *New Musical Express* review that marked the point of their musical awakening, Devoto and Shelley clearly felt the Pistols 'experience' was something they wished to share, and booked the Lesser Free Trade Hall at a cost of £32 for the evening of June 4, 1976.

The Free Trade Hall was the main venue in Manchester for classical music (the Hallé Orchestra) and one of the central venues for major rock bands. On June 4, in the upstairs 'lesser' venue, the Buzzcocks were unprepared and unable to support the Sex Pistols as they had hoped. Instead, they arranged for local band Solstice to fill in. Peter Hook remembered them as 'complete dyed-in-the-wool, Deep Purple/Led Zeppelin-types' (Nolan 2001: 51), who conformed to mid-1970s expectations of dress and hair-length for bands on the rock circuit, as indeed did the audience. As such, they provided an illuminating backdrop for the drama to follow, through their validation of contemporary expectations of rock performances, including their interpretation of Mountain's 'Nantucket Sleighride' which confirmed the obligation for aspiring rock musicians to play exceptionally well. For many in the audience, it was probably easier to imagine joining the string section of the Hallé Orchestra, than to envisage themselves as competent enough to join even the low-key college rock circuit.

In contrast, the Sex Pistols' performance was fundamentally shocking, leaving many of the audience open-mouthed, if generally appreciative. However, some recall the audience response to be relatively restrained. Paul Morley remembers that 'everyone was just sort of very polite' (Nolan 2001: 52) and Peter Hook states that 'people didn't get up and dance – it was very sedate' (*From The Factory Floor*, *24 Hour Party People*, DVD2).

The 8 mm film footage of the Sex Pistols used in *24 Hour Party People* and *I Swear I Was There* clearly shows Rotten wearing roughly assembled and customized second-hand clothing (including a sleeveless cream jacket/cardigan) rather than McLaren and Vivien Westwood's Sex shop chic. Morrissey, who was intrigued but largely unimpressed by the Sex Pistols at this and a subsequent Electric Circus performance on December 9, assessed the band's appearance by insisting in the *New Musical Express* that 'I'd love to see the Pistols make it ... maybe then they'll be able to afford some clothes which don't look as though they've been slept in' and telling *Sounds* that 'I consider it something of a joke that the [New York] Dolls should be compared to such notoriously no-talents as the Ramones and the Sex Pistols' (Rogan 1993: 82–4). His misgivings about the band were shared at the time by Bernard Sumner and Peter Hook, although after hearing a bootleg tape of the June 4 performance, Hook later revised his opinion, suggesting that the immediate audience reaction was astonishment, and only half-jokingly adding that 'it was just shock really [because] they sounded so awful, it was just so shit ... [but] it wasn't the band, it was the sound, it was terrible ... and it was the sound guy, I think, that inspired all those people' (*From The Factory Floor*, *24 Hour Party People*, DVD2).

The tape confirms that the Sex Pistols played a set which included some of their own songs ('Pretty Vacant', 'Problems', 'Seventeen', 'Did You No Wrong') and some covers of late 1960s rock and pop tracks by the Monkees ('Stepping Stone'), the Stooges ('No Fun'), The Who ('Substitute') and the Small Faces ('Whatcha Gonna Do 'Bout It'). For a band pointing the way to the future, the Sex Pistols relied heavily on material from a more innocent time before the romanticist decadence of the early 1970s had beset rock music. Nevertheless, their performance of these tracks was far from reverential, revisiting and subverting the spirit of American proto-punk and bubblegum, and the energy of British 1960s beat music.

With Rotten up front, it was clear that nostalgia had no part to play in these references to the past. His confrontational stage persona overrode rather than hid behind the music. It was as if the Pistols had opened a door to another way of being a rock band, and the audience had no clear or existing criteria through which to make sense of the spectacle before them. Rotten was at the centre of this general bemusement. Audience member Iain Grey remembered that 'Johnny Rotten ambled on ... and that was just like a shock. He was one of the most frightening people I'd ever seen at that time, this lad with a thousand yard stare, just stood there. And then he started playing ... and it was just as though he was staring at me' (Nolan 2001: 54). Another attendee, Ian Moss, recalled how the audience's expectations, largely due to the *New Musical Express* review, were aroused. Anticipating what they assumed would be an inevitably outrageous event, they nevertheless underestimated the astonishing, not to say disturbing, nature of Rotten's physical and vocal performance:

I think the audience were sat there waiting to be impressed … or disappointed. So the attitude was coming from the stage and almost exclusively from Johnny Rotten … just the way he moved, the way he sounded, the little asides between songs. It was just not the same preening rock star, it was a completely different performance to any I'd ever seen and I'd seen hundreds of bands. Completely different. (Nolan 2001: 55).

The customary relationship between band and audience seemed shattered. The sense that rock performance had to self-consciously 'put on a show' – partly derived from the post-1960s celebration of formidable musical virtuosity ('Clapton is God') and the self-conscious theatricality of the performances of David Bowie – seemed immediately irrelevant. The expectation that the audience should look on from afar, with a clear demarcation between the space of stage and space of reception (the only exchange either appreciative or derogatory depending on the 'quality' of the performer and the performance) was unmistakably challenged. Rotten made the members of the audience aware that he was alert to their presence, demanded a reaction, challenged them, communicated directly to each and every one of them. It was an affront, an assault and it dared the audience to take a stand. The message had little to do with show business. It was a call to arms and was suffused with realism and tangible authenticity.

Yet meanwhile, guitarist Steve Jones was unreservedly aping the stage moves and look (boiler suit) of The Who's Pete Townshend (Nolan 2001: 57). In this sense, the performance contained elements of both the familiar and the strange, creating a kind of cultural noise or interference. The Sex Pistols presented a clear message about the 'here and now', breaching a path through an intransigent musical terrain, showing the way for others wanting to express their disaffection with rock music and society at large. They were accessible and rooted in the Britain of 1976, not in an inaccessible, mid-Atlantic, rock Never-Never (ever) land disconnected from provincial imaginations. Morley asserts that 'the kind of rock music that you'd loved over the years, like Led Zeppelin and The Who, seemed a little before your time. The Pistols brought everything bang up to date; it was absolutely for you. It was about the times' (Nolan 2001: 59).

Therefore, the assaultive noise of the performance, due to a badly mixed live sound rather than the Sex Pistols' assumed incompetence, was itself an eloquent message, above and beyond the fleetingly heard lyrical slogans – a state of the nation address (and what a state!). It was about anger and a kind of hatred of the rock music of the present, through its deconstruction of rock conventions. It seemed a socially located music 'dramatizing' the changes and discontent felt in British society (Hebdige 1979). When considering the Sex Pistols' performance we need to emphasize the manner in which it too was embedded in these changes and this discontent.

Music should be seen as inextricably a social production, the product of human desires as expressed in a particular space and time. The value of music does not lie therefore in its ability to escape its social character, but in its ability to reflect, discuss, contest, reshape or re-imagine what it means to be a human at a particular time and place (Kahn-Harris 2003).

The significance of the 'embeddedness', authenticity and perceived realism of the Sex Pistols' performance was, in Morley's view, crucial: 'He meant it man ... and you felt that more than anything else you had come across before' (Nolan 2001: 54). It was particularly noted in Rotten's authenticity (or novel performance of it) after years of apparent rock complacency and performative atrophy. However, we should be wary of suggesting that their performance was about 'truth' per se – about 'dole queue rock' speaking for a disenfranchised working class. The drama of the performance was, in part, considered and conceptual, prompted perhaps by McLaren and Westwood's cultural-political interests. Frith has pointed out that 'the pioneering punk rockers themselves were a *self-conscious* artful lot with a good understanding of both rock tradition and populist cliché; the music no more reflected directly back onto conditions in the dole queue than it emerged spontaneously from them' (1980: 167, my emphasis).

While claims of 'working class' realism and authenticity may seem partly misplaced with the Sex Pistols, their *performance* of these qualities (including the performance at the Lesser Free Trade Hall) has to be read in conjunction with the historical context within which they were made. Indeed, Lee contends that 'the majority of punk musicians were middle class, adopting a working class pose for the duration of their involvement in the movement' and agrees with Home (1995) that their self-conscious 'adoption of a class stance ... [was] a rejection of a middle class world incarnate' (2002: 133–4). I would further add that this adoption was a performance of an idealized working classness that used clothes and accent as tools of both alienation (from middle-class values) and solidarity (creating a hierarchical 'flatness' within the punk scene).[4] As such, the Sex Pistols appealed to 'youth-like' impatience with the perceived impotence of provincial life, across classes and age groups. Within this impatience with defeat, a strong emotional investment in cultural phenomena that expressed the malaise of post-industrial northern life was, paradoxically, a release from it.

While the 'extreme' performance of the Sex Pistols on June 4 was important for those who witnessed it, it would become increasingly important when repeated in four further gigs in Manchester in 1976. Perhaps the performance expressed something the audience had half-consciously recognized – that bitterness and resignation need strong medicine to incite action. Whatever the previous social or cultural experiences of those who attended, there was a shared moment of revelation, repeated in subsequent performances, that would go on to change Manchester's music and to impact upon the future of rock. But who were the audience that night? Moreover, why is this event still viewed as so significant for the Manchester punk and post-punk music scene?

The aftermath

As previously stated, the audience on June 4 1976 included the impressed proto-Buzzcocks, the shocked Hook and Sumner, the astonished Paul Morley and the underwhelmed Morrissey. Martin Hannett (of Music Force and later an influential record producer), Rob Gretton (associate of Slaughter and the Dogs, and later Joy Division's manager), Mick Hucknall (later of Simply Red) and Alan Erasmus (Factory Records co-founder) certainly were not at the performance, despite *24 Hour Party People*'s portrayal of the events. Mark E. Smith and the fledgling Fall attended either the first, second or both gigs, but the evidence is contradictory.

However, it is important to note that there were at least 30 other people there, who seemingly got on with their lives regardless. It should also be noted that at the better-attended return gig on July 20, many in the audience were from Wythenshawe (in south Manchester) and were there to see Slaughter and the Dogs, rather than the Sex Pistols or the Buzzcocks. Many of them had little interest, or any future involvement, in punk. In valorizing the 'stars' to be, we should not forget that there was a normality of experience at the core of these gigs, as well as the experiences of the 'exceptional'. Vanessa Corley, a Slaughter and the Dogs fan, says of the second gig, 'it was rubbish ... at the time I probably thought it was a waste of money, I'd rather be somewhere else' and Lorraine Joyce states 'I'd never heard of punk, nobody knew what punk was ... I mean, I actually don't like punk rock' (Nolan 2001: 97, 86).

Notwithstanding the confusion engendered by *24 Hour Party People*, the future roles of Hannett, Gretton and Erasmus were to be crucial. Alongside Wilson at Granada TV, a middle generation too young to have fully participated in the countercultural events of the 1960s and an older disaffected generation disillusioned after the defeated promise of 1960s rock were crucial to developments in Manchester in the post-punk period. They would also all be inspired by the Sex Pistols' later forays into Manchester in 1976, whether these were first or second-hand experiences. They started labels (Factory and Rabid Records) and set up or commandeered venues such as the Electric Circus, The Squat and the Factory Club that were important in creating a live infrastructure for new bands.

Furthermore, Dick Witts and Trevor Wishart's Manchester Musician's Collective (MMC) at the Band on the Wall was important in providing a creative space for a diverse range of musicians to develop publicly, including Joy Division, A Certain Ratio and, most notably, The Fall (Smith and Middles 2003: 77–80). The collective was a ramshackle, cross-class alliance of local musicians working in jazz, blues, rock, funk and punk, and Witts and Wishart were fascinated by the range of music developing outside closed contemporary music circles. At the very least, the collective provided space for the new Mancunian bands to perform and experiment in a relatively supportive context. At the most, it provided non-traditional musicians such as Hook, Sumner, Ian Curtis and Mark E. Smith with a sense of the wider experimental possibilities of avant-garde music-making, and conceivably encouraged them to stray from the confines of mainstream punk.

In one way or another, the four key Manchester bands to develop in the wake of the Sex Pistols performances – the Buzzcocks, Magazine, Joy Division, The Fall – matured into individualistic bands who more immediately 'got' Rotten's message than many punks. The irony of Rotten's novel appeal was that his performance persona was soon systematized by both himself and many punk bands that followed. Rotten felt that central to his message was an absolute belief in individual expression, honesty and integrity that was widely missed by those who sought to adopt a 'punk uniform' and copy the Sex Pistols' power-chord musical template (Albiez 2003). However, it can be argued that more than any other centre of post-Pistols activity, the city of Manchester listened long and hard to Rotten and created, in several cases, idiosyncratic new music.

In producing these sounds the bands perhaps looked to the Sex Pistols for philosophical rather than musical inspiration – often invoking the Velvet Underground and Lou Reed, the Stooges and Iggy Pop, Can, Kraftwerk, Roxy Music, David Bowie and Brian Eno as their sources. Rather than leading to faithful reproductions of the Sex Pistols, this resulted in innovative new ways of constructing and arranging rock music. On the early demos of the Buzzcocks and Warsaw/Joy Division, there is a speed and urgency in their music which is clearly an initial response to the Sex Pistols, but both bands eventually matured with distinctive sounds. The members of The Fall, on the other hand, although inspired by the Sex Pistols, immediately perceived they had very little connection with early British punk, and little that they produced from 1976 onwards has any parallels with it.

The Manchester punk and post-punk scene included several other bands such as The Worst, the Distractions, Ed Banger and the Nosebleeds, Slaughter and the Dogs, and the Drones, all of whom were, at the time, more popular locally than The Fall or Warsaw/Joy Division. However, they often created a very Pistols-like punk sound that quickly dated. While the local Manchester punk scene had musical similarities to London, it contained more underlying musical diversity, and it may well be that the Manchester bands who lacked longevity were those that allied themselves too closely to the language and modes of the national punk scene, and those that thrived emphasized a certain local idiosyncrasy in their music.

The Buzzcocks and Magazine

> Howard Devoto: My life changed the moment I saw the Sex Pistols. I immediately got caught up in trying to make things happen (Savage 1991: 174).

> Steve Diggle: There was Rotten with bright yellow teeth. Straightaway, he's spitting, and fuck this and fuck that … forget all those stories about the Pistols not being able to play. I hadn't seen or heard anything like this in my life … England was indeed fucking dreaming at that time and this was its wake-up call (Rawlings 2003: 42).

The Buzzcocks were at the zenith of the Manchester punk hierarchy as they were responsible for bringing the Sex Pistols to Manchester, and were the only non-London band at the Sex Pistols/Clash gigs at Islington's Screen on the Green on August 29, 1976. The band's 'Spiral Scratch' EP, released on their own New Hormones label, arguably instigated the DIY discourse of independent punk labels in Britain. Devoto left the band soon after its release, and Pete Shelley took over on vocals. The remaining Buzzcocks developed a sound that was fast, insolent and told tales of everyday life through melodic and tightly structured songs. Magazine, Devoto's post-Buzzcocks project, more clearly drew from British and German art rock influences and relied on a broader range of musical textures than punk, deploying synthesizers and more complex arrangements. Magazine are less celebrated today than are the Buzzcocks, but their 'progressive post-punk' legacy may be found in the more cerebral areas of contemporary post-rock bands such as Radiohead, thus demonstrating that the Sex Pistols instigated much more than a revival of three-chord garage rock.

The Fall

> Mark E. Smith: Yeah, it was crap the Lesser Free Trade Hall, and anyone who says different is lying. But what it did do was to break things down ... we came away certain we could do a lot better than that. I mean, I loved the Pistols, really. I loved Johnny Rotten's vocals [but] the Pistols were a pretty bad heavy metal band (Smith and Middles 2003: 70).

> Martin Bramah: We'd heard about ... [the Sex Pistols] already through the music press. There was a photo of a guy with short hair [Lydon] and I was wondering what these 'skinheads' were doing covering Stooges' songs ... I went along thinking I could heckle or something but I was really bowled over (Ford 2003: 16)

The members of The Fall (Smith, Bramah, Una Baines, Tony Friel) had already musically experimented as a 'hobby' at home in Prestwich, north Manchester, but had assumed that what they were doing would have little possibility of being publicly performed. After seeing the Sex Pistols, they realized that such assumptions were redundant. Through many subsequent changes of personnel, Smith remained the only constant and he has unfailingly held a strong identification with aspects of working-class culture and everyday life. In Rotten, Smith recognized a kindred spirit and appreciated that he was grappling with class as a mode of performance and identification, and as a valid position from which to critique society. Rotten also recognized this quality in Smith's work, admitting 'he always seemed to voice the things that I was thinking. There was some kind of link. We were both working class and ... more intelligent than people gave us credit for' (Smith and Middles 2003: 63).

Joy Division

> Bernard Sumner: They were terrible. I thought they were great. I wanted to get up and be terrible too (Rimmer 2003: 29).

> Ian [Curtis] was ecstatic. Seeing the Sex Pistols ... re-affirmed Ian's belief that anyone could become a rock star. After the [July 20] performance everyone seemed to move quickly to the door. It seemed as if we had all been issued with instructions and now we were set to embark on a mission (Curtis 1995: 37).

The day after Sumner and Hook attended the Lesser Free Trade Hall gig, Hook bought a bass guitar and together they set about putting together a band that eventually became Joy Division. Perhaps more than any other band in the post-punk period, Joy Division's legacy has been picked over, mythologized and misunderstood. Yet, however we try to approach their music, we must return to the Lesser Free Trade Hall in the summer of 1976 and the Electric Circus performance on December 9, at which Curtis first met Hook and Sumner. Curtis, obsessed with Bowie, Lou Reed and Iggy Pop, felt the Sex Pistols represented the common becoming the uncommon, and that he had every right, given the opportunity, to stand alongside his personal heroes. Without these gigs, Sumner, Hook, Curtis and Steve Morris would not have formed Joy Division, we would have had no New Order or Hacienda, and a very different Mancunian and Anglo-American musical terrain. Joy Division at the turn of the 1980s became a template for U2, a touchstone for indie music-makers worldwide and an embodiment of the Lesser Free Trade Hall message that 'anybody can do it'. At its base was an implicit challenge to the hegemony of received standards of musicality in popular music, derived either from high culture (progressive rock) or from the closed shop mentality of professionalized musicians. Ironically, it was Hook and Sumner's mistaken assumption of the Sex Pistols' musical ineptitude that started them and others on this road.

Conclusions

The Sex Pistols' incursions into Manchester in 1976 were an important catalyst for some of the musicians who would go on to have international success in the 1980s and beyond, and therefore had perceptible repercussions on the development of Anglo-American 'alternative' rock. However, it is equally apparent that the mediations of the band, whether in the music press, regional and national newspapers or television coverage, contributed much more to the broader awareness of the Sex Pistols in Manchester and across Britain. Their early Manchester performances were attended by members of Joy Division, The Fall, the Buzzcocks and the Smiths, but their reactions were diverse, and the inspirations taken from the Sex Pistols were differently constituted. Because of the historiographical problems of reconstructing the events of June 4, 1976, it is doubtful that we can ever gauge the full importance of this particular performance, but we can undoubtedly suggest that it contributed to the musical awakening of some of the future participants in the rebirth of Manchester music. With the support of other crucial agents who were primed for musical and cultural change, a Manchester post-Pistols scene developed that had far reaching musical and cultural implications. Notwithstanding the varied personal assessments of those who witnessed the initial Lesser Free Trade Hall performances, they had an affective and immediate impact that helped shape the future trajectory of Manchester music, and their aftershocks are still felt into the present.

Acknowledgements

Many thanks to David Nolan of Granada TV whose research for the book and documentary *I Swear I Was There* and advice in e-mail and telephone conversations have made this chapter possible.

Thanks to Pete Walsh of Milo Books for permission to draw from the testimony of audience members in the book *I Swear I Was There: Sex Pistols and the Shape of Rock* (© Granada Media Group Limited 2001).

And thanks to Peter Jones for keeping me on track.

Notes

1. Tony Wilson's foreword to his 'novelization' of *24 Hour Party People* explicitly asserts that 'a lot of what follows is pure bloody fiction and never actually happened' (2002: 5) and goes on to state 'although there's a whole bunch of lies in this book – between the truth and the legend, print the legend' (2002: 13). While this leads to a complex, inter-textual and comedic postmodern narrative, the assumption of many of my students and friends who saw the film was that the Lesser Free Trade Hall reconstruction was historically accurate.

2. Smith is certain he attended the June 4, 1976 performance, but in Haslam's account, he is quoted as saying 'I saw the Buzzcocks and I thought I'd better form a group, I can do better than that! I actually remember coming out of the gig at the Lesser Free Trade Hall and thinking that' (2000: 110). He is probably referring here to the July 20, 1976 gig when the Buzzcocks did support the Sex Pistols.

3. The Didsbury College date on October 1, 1976 is an enigma – not one writer on the Manchester punk scene has acknowledged this gig, the first post-Lesser Free Trade Hall Manchester performance. Perhaps low-key and poorly attended, it therefore may not fit comfortably with the notion that the Lesser Free Trade Hall gigs launched punk on the Manchester scene. Further research is necessary, but it is possible that there was a lull in punk activity in Manchester, and that it was the Sex Pistols' television interview with Bill Grundy, and further music press coverage, that ignited a wider participation in the punk scene in late 1976.

4. How far this solidarity was felt among ruthlessly ambitious punk musicians in the Manchester scene is very debatable. The scene as a whole did not pull together in 'punkish camaraderie' and was often riven with jealous inter-band feuds (Smith and Middles 2003: 67).

Chapter 10

'I need contact' – rock'n'roll and ritual
Peter Gabriel: *Security* tour, 1982–83

Jeffrey Callen

From the back of the concert hall, the five-person ensemble, four dressed in simple black clothing and one in simple white, proceeds through the crowd, playing drums. As they reach the stage, the synthesizer takes up the same rhythm and the band members pick up their instruments and don headsets. The singer, dressed in white, re-appears from the back of the stage, his face, now clear in the stage lights, in stark black and blue make-up that recalls, to some, a shaman from some non-specified culture and, to others, the image from his latest video.

Peter Gabriel's *Security* tour in 1982–83 (also known as 'Playtime 1988')[1] crystallized a moment in rock performance. The visual and auditory images that created the particular aesthetic of Gabriel's performances drew heavily upon his experience in the British progressive rock group Genesis, and also incorporated the minimalism of performance art, the immediacy of punk rock and a frequently disorienting use of auditory and visual elements from African, Asian and Native American sources. As the leader of Genesis in the early 1970s, Peter Gabriel had helped move rock performance to new levels of theatricality; after leaving the group in 1975, his work was increasingly characterized by socially conscious lyrics and atmospheric, rhythm-driven music. Gabriel explored this new territory through an increasing employment of computer technology and non-western musical sources. The intertwining of these elements reached its peak in 1982, with the album *Security*, whose sound was highly 'technological' while remaining viscerally human, and eclectic in its musical sources without crossing the line into exoticism or stereotype. In his early post-Genesis performances, Gabriel had moved away from the extravagant showmanship of his later years with the group in favour of a minimalist stage presentation. Now, with the *Security* tour, Gabriel sought to move back towards a theatrical presentation built around the minimalist aesthetic that had characterized his previous solo performances. The album, and the tour of Europe and the United States that supported it, thus marked a turning point in Gabriel's career and sealed his impact on rock performance.

At the end of the scene offered as the prelude to this chapter, the insistent rhythm of the drums becomes the song 'The Rhythm of the Heat', the high-intensity opening of an album that is itself structured as a progression of songs of higher and lower musical intensity. The persistently slow rhythm of the album tracks (even the faster songs seem to be 'dragging', as if in self-parody) and frequent use of rhythmic displacement creates a visceral response that simultaneously involves and disorients the listener. In the same way, the *Security* concerts (which included some additional material from Gabriel's earlier solo albums) are also structured around moments of higher and lower musical energy. However, in concert, the immediacy of the performance, which adds a visual element to the aural elements of the songs, acts to bring a sense of completion, as an experience of *re*-orientation is added to the initial *dis*-orientation of the listener.

The fusion of visual and aural images had been a focus of Gabriel's performances since his later years with Genesis. In fact, as one of the most commercially successful of the British 'progressive/art rock' groups of the early and mid-1970s, Genesis had increasingly emphasized the 'spectacle' of their music, both on albums and in concert. The epic storytelling that began with their second album *Trespass* (1970) culminated in the 'rock opera' *The Lamb Lies Down on Broadway* (1974). Their albums were conceived and constructed as 'concept albums' in which the individual songs were linked together thematically to create a unified work. The 'concept album' tradition in rock'n'roll had been initiated in the mid-1960s with the release of three seminal works: the Beach Boys' *Pet Sounds* (1966), Frank Zappa and the Mothers of Invention's *Freak Out* (1966) and the Beatles' *Sgt Pepper's Lonely Hearts Club Band* (1967). The format had subsequently been extended into more narrative-driven trajectories by albums such as The Who's *Tommy* (1969) and Pink Floyd's *The Wall* (1979) both of which related a single story through a progression of songs within a mythic presentation. This tradition, which can loosely be labelled 'rock opera', brought a frankly theatrical element to the concept album which inevitably changed the concert performances of the works. These live rock operas melded elements from a variety of traditions, including rock'n'roll, opera, British music hall and Broadway theatre, to create a unique and innovative genre of musical performance.

From *Trespass* onwards, the stories and characters of Genesis's songs increasingly took on mythic proportions; and Gabriel's performance in his role of lead singer became increasingly dramatic. He had begun to emphasize the use of costumes, masks, make-up and props to create on-stage characters that were 'part comic-strip horror cartoon, part Peter Pan, part faerie' (Kamin and Goddard 1984: 50). *The Lamb Lies Down on Broadway* told the story of a young New York City street hustler, Rael, and his journey of self-discovery and confrontation with mortality, presented in romantic proportions via the narrative structure of a quest. After the tour to promote that album, Gabriel announced his intention to leave

Genesis in order to redefine the direction of his career. In particular, he wished to reject the role of rock star he felt was being thrust upon him, and to escape from the constrictions imposed by the group's style of music.

His first solo album was released in 1977; entitled *Peter Gabriel*, it is also, informally, known as *Rainy Windshield*.[2] He has explained that his intention at the time was to jettison most of his previous stylistic associations, arguing that although the strong visual sensibility of 'art rock' was an asset, the genre had a tendency to take itself too seriously (Hutchinson 1986: 71). Expressing nervousness about facing audiences in his home country, he chose to begin his solo touring career in the United States. Unlike the extravagant performances for which he had become known with Genesis, he favoured a restrained, unostentatious style, often dressing in a plain boiler suit. While some of his early concerts received glowing reviews in British music magazines such as *Sounds* and *New Musical Express*, his appearance on the BBC-TV show *Top of the Pops* (singing 'No Self Control') showed him looking and sounding very much like a member of any other contemporary synthesizer-based new wave band.

Established as a solo artist, Gabriel did begin to rebuild the lyrical subjects he addressed and the musical styles he utilized. His first two albums – *Rainy Windshield* and *Fingernails* (1978) – both included songs that dealt with substantially darker issues than he had addressed before, which explored themes of isolation and estrangement. Although *Rainy Windshield* contained some Genesis-like tracks, the cabaret-styled 'Excuse Me' and the lounge jazz 'Waiting for the Big One' displayed his growing idiosyncrasies, and 'Moribund The Burgermeister' and 'Humdrum' were early clues to the darker atmosphere that would pervade much of his later work. These songs were the first to exhibit the 'hard simplicity' (Kamin and Goddard 1984: 75) for which he was searching. Among the contributing musicians were bassist Tony Levin (also a member of the influential progressive rock band King Crimson) and keyboardist Larry Fast, both of whom would become key members of Gabriel's band during the 1980s.

Fingernails (produced by King Crimson guitarist Robert Fripp) featured a sound that was more experimental, but stylistically disjointed, and which lacked the cohesion his later albums would show. 'On the Air' and 'D.I.Y.' clearly demonstrated the transformations in his musical ambitions. The layers of synthesizers, driving rhythms and highly processed guitar sounds sat comfortably within the sound of late 1970s new wave rock, but were also prototypes of the evocative and rhythmic music he would perfect with *Security*.

His third solo album *Melting Face* (1980) displayed a stylistic unity that the previous two had lacked. The aural picture it created skilfully matched the lyrical subjects with a sound that was more ominous and driven than anything Gabriel had produced before, and which clearly distanced his work from his progressive rock roots and new wave preoccupations. It effectively established a distinct identity for Gabriel and, in fact, many of the album's songs were a central part of his live repertoire for the next decade (in contrast, he would only regularly perform three songs from the first two albums). *Melting Face* also introduced some new components that would become increasingly significant in his later work: the reference to political subjects, a consistent use of electronic tones, the incorporation of non-western musical elements (particularly rhythms) and a fresh approach to songwriting. In general, the political subjects Gabriel addressed were rarely explicitly stated, but 'Biko' was the definitive exception. A passionate homage to the South African anti-apartheid activist Steve Biko, who was murdered by the country's security forces in 1977, the song signalled the beginning of Gabriel's exploration of non-western musical sources. The track opened and closed with field recordings of South African funeral music, whose rhythms provided the foundation from which Gabriel created the song.[3] Although 'Biko' was the only overtly political song on the album, other songs dealt with similar subjects more elliptically ('Not One of Us', 'Games Without Frontiers') or on a personal/psychological level ('Intruder', 'Family Snapshot').

On *Melting Face*, Gabriel began to make extensive use of studio technology, including sound processing and synthesizers. It was the first album on which he employed the Fairlight CMI,[4] which allowed him to achieve the sound that would come to dominate his solo work by colouring synthesized sounds with the 'human element' through extensive filtering. A vision of a 'primitive electric music' began to develop in which the application of technology would not only individualize sounds, but also break down barriers between performer and audience – objectives which reached their public climax with the *Security* tour. In the live performances following *Melting Face*, Gabriel began the practice of entering the concert hall from the back of the audience that he would use to dramatic effect during the *Security* tour, in order to challenge the typical concert experience that 'you can get close but you can never touch':

> I always find that walking through the audience, you see people and their surprise ... and I find that the eye-contact on a one-to-one level as you pass people is much better for perspective, than if you walk from the dank pit of the dressing room into that huge bath of floodlights (*Bristol Recorder* 1981).[5]

Believing that too many concerts were 'safe, predictable rituals in which the audience sits passively to be spoon-fed this supposed nectar from the stage' (*Bristol Recorder* 1981), Gabriel wanted to transform the concert experience into an event in which the audience was actively involved – an objective that was to become an increasingly important element in his work and which would serve as the implicit framing device for the *Security* tour two years later.

At the same time, Gabriel also made a decision to change his approach to the process of songwriting that led to significant shifts in both his recorded work and his live performances. Speaking of his prior songwriting, Gabriel explained:

> Usually I approached the music from the aspect of melodies and harmonies and filled out the rest later. But Larry Fast suggested I work from a particular rhythm, that it

was the backbone of the music that could be fleshed out later (Kamin and Goddard 1984: 75).

He decided to build on a rhythm, to experiment, and to invite the other musicians to experiment with him. On 'Biko', he began with an African rhythm; on 'Lead a Normal Life', a Bo Diddley beat. To leave space in the high range for the electronic sounds he used, and in order to match the 'primitive feel' of the rhythmically based sound he wanted, Gabriel asked his drummers not to use cymbals. He was increasingly placing his work on what he regarded as 'the fringe of rock' (alongside such musicians as John Lydon, who had left the Sex Pistols to form Public Image Limited). His need to experiment led Gabriel to incorporate influences from a variety of sources outside mainstream popular music; this included the work of avant-garde composers such as Steve Reich whose approach incorporated musical 'grooves', borrowings from non-western musics and an application of *musique concrète* techniques.[6] Gabriel also admitted that an increasing concern with 'the world out there' (Kamin and Goddard 1984: 78) had persuaded him to address a broader range of subjects (personal and political) in his lyrics and to introduce new elements in his music. He suspected that 'conventional rock rhythms would lead to conventional rock writing' (Hutchinson 1986: 72) and wished to move into less familiar territory.

From this point, his songs started to move away from traditional rock'n'roll structures towards longer formats well suited to the slow build-up that would become an integral part of the songs on *Security* and of the performances during the subsequent tour. Characterized by themes of social isolation, often from the perspective of the 'outsider', they allowed him to continue his exploration of role-playing. Frequently, he made use of masks to create an experience through which audiences could explore alternative sides of their personalities, something he felt had an important social value: 'if people have something in their culture, or entertainment, that allows them to experience harmlessly this part of their personality ... they're humans' (*Bristol Recorder* 1981).

The device of the mask is used effectively on *Melting Face* in a number of songs that address different situations but which all revolve around forms of estrangement: the protagonist of 'Family Snapshot' is an adult preparing to assassinate a prominent person or, alternatively, a neglected child watching his parents move toward a divorce; 'I Don't Remember' reveals the singer as a victim of amnesia or as someone who simply no longer cares. The use of the mask in performance would be a central part of Gabriel's performances during the *Security* tour in which he would use one visual image to portray many approaches to the theme of isolation and the need for contact and social integration.

When Gabriel began work on his fourth album (entitled *Security* for the US market as a concession to his new record company), he thus had a clear idea of the sound he intended to create – one constructed around rhythm, percussion (but not a regular drum kit-trap set) and synthesizers. The new compositions continued the device of building tracks up from initial rhythms: African rhythms provided the basis for 'I Have the Touch' and 'The Rhythm of the Heat'; 'Shock the Monkey' (the album's hit single) was inspired by dance club rhythms. While the songs' foundations remained percussion and synthesizers, other instruments (guitar, bass, trap set and keyboards) were used to emphasize transitions or other highlighted sections.

However, the album's inclusion of rhythmic and melodic elements from Africa, Asia and the Americas were referenced less to their geographic origin (as 'Biko' had been) than to their sonic elements. Gabriel explained that he was not trying to create pastiches of African musics, but rather to use their influences to go 'somewhere else within his own music' (Hutchinson 1986: 72). Non-western musical elements, electronic tones and environmental sounds (such as the sound of dragging concrete in the opening section of 'Lay Your Hands on Me') were integrated into the songs via the Fairlight CMI to achieve a heavily textured sonic construction, and their rhythmic intensity was additionally heightened by an often slow tempo that accentuated the layering of the synthesized tracks. Lyrically, the predominant focus continued his investigations of the psychological impact of isolation and the need to dismantle barriers, both personal and political, without the patina of appropriation and exploitation that marked the 'world music' efforts of other western musicians, such as Paul Simon, Brian Eno, David Byrne and Sting.

The recording of *Security* began in early 1981 in the studio at Gabriel's Bath home; subsequently, Gabriel, recording engineer David Lord and Larry Fast edited more than seven hours of recorded material.[7] When the album was finally released in 1982, around 18 months of work had gone into its creation and it was distinguished by a coherence missing from his previous solo albums. The atmospheric sound, powerful rhythms and longer 'conceptual' songs gave it an immediate and noticeable intensity that reflected the length of time that went into its production (Bright 1999: 201–3).

The release of *Security* coincided with the popular music industry's early recognition of the significance of music video and the appearance of MTV. The video of 'Shock the Monkey' (directed by Brian Grant) was a watershed moment in Gabriel's career, not only promoting interest in *Security*, but also firmly establishing a distinctive and innovative image for the performer. Presenting him in stark facial make-up, it mixed the iconography of the businessman with that of a shaman – a 'modern primitive' image which perfectly complemented the darkly atmospheric tone of the song, and provided the visual and ideological motifs that were to be essential components of the tour that followed.[8]

Gabriel's performances during the *Security* tour synthesized the theatricality of his work with Genesis (minus its props and elaborate staging) and the minimalism of his prior tours as a solo artist. He no longer had any interest in re-visiting the 'mythology' that had characterized his work with Genesis, and chose to emphasize instead the use of 'ritual' as an element of his work (Hutchinson 1986: 71). Indeed, the tour was not just marked but, in many ways, *defined* by his emphasis on ritual elements – repetitive rhythms, growing intensity, physical enactment and emotional/dramatic climax (or catharsis). He continued to open concerts by entering with his band from the back of the concert hall. The band members moved onstage to continue the rhythm they had begun at the rear of the hall, which would then resolve into the beginning of the first song, usually 'Across the River' or 'The Rhythm of the Heat'. As the first song began, Gabriel would re-appear, in view of the entire audience, to the insistent drumming that commences both songs. The hymn-like 'Across the River' introduced 'I Have the Touch', whose metronomic 4/4 pattern on the traps set became part of a polyrhythmic accompaniment as additional layers of rhythm were added and increasingly complex textures were introduced by the melodic instruments. Gabriel would walk the stage, acting out the lyrics and emphasizing the attempts made by the protagonist, who lives in a world of rush hours, to break his sense of isolation:

> Pull my chin, stroke my hair, scratch my nose, hug my knees,
> Try drink, food, cigarette, tension will not ease,
> I tap my fingers, fold my arms, breathe in deep, cross my legs,
> Shrug my shoulders, stretch my back but nothing seems to please.

He returns repeatedly to the phrase 'shake those hands'. He approaches the guitarist and attempts to shake hands, but is rebuffed and stretches his hand out to the audience. When he later (successfully) shakes hands with the bassist, they leap up and down together. At the climax of the song, he attempts to recreate the experience (at a distance) with the audience, by alternately offering his right and left hands, while repeatedly singing the closing line: 'I need contact.'

Songs performed during the tour came from all of his four solo albums, although those from the first three – narratives such as 'Intruder' and 'I Don't Remember' or evocative pieces such as 'Solsbury Hill' and 'Humdrum' – were generally more subdued than those from *Security*, which created the effective rationale for the performances, and which also relied on a strong visual component. Some, especially 'The Family and the Fishing Net', seemed incomplete without the mix of the visual and aural that occurred in live performance. Progressions to moments of high dramatic intensity culminated in Gabriel's performances of 'I Have the Touch', 'The Rhythm of the Heat' and 'Lay Your Hands on Me'.

'The Rhythm of the Heat' (originally titled 'Jung in Africa') relates the story of an incident reported by psychologist Karl Jung in which he became overwhelmed by the power of the ritual drumming and dancing at an event he attended during a visit to the Sudan in 1925. At the height of the ritual, Jung, fearing that his 'shadow' was beginning to appear and that he would lose control, ran around the ritual circle to all the drummers in an attempt to prevent their playing. The song's dramatic trajectory is matched by Gabriel's increased physical involvement in telling the story as the 'rhythm takes control'. The performance builds until

Gabriel falls to the ground, singing the words 'I submit to trust', only to rise again to dance to – or fight against – the powerful drumming that closes the song.

The climax of each concert on the tour was 'Lay Your Hands on Me'. The song reveals the internal conflict faced by the singer as he contrasts the emptiness of his daily life with the 'warmth' that nevertheless flows through him. At its peak, he calls out to some unidentified other (or others):

> I am willing – lay your hands on me.
> I am ready – lay your hands on me.
> I believe – lay your hands on me, over me.

After beginning the song by pacing the stage in a subdued manner, Gabriel's performance parallels the musical accompaniment to a striking level of interaction with the audience. At the start of the tour, he would leave the stage to walk through the audience, touching and being touched by them. In later concerts, he would stand at the edge of the stage and fall backward into the outstretched arms of the audience, who would carry him around the concert arena while he continued to sing. Criticized by some in the music press for indulging in messianic delusions, Gabriel responded that he was simply attempting to dramatically serve the moment in the performance of the song.

Musical moments (songs, performances, styles) occur, like any 'act of meaning production', in a discourse with other moments (both past and present) within a 'stylistic intertextuality' (Middleton 2000: 11–13). Musical performances cannot be experienced or interpreted outside the context in which they take place – they are a part of the tenor of their times. The times of Peter Gabriel's *Security* tour were an unsettled period in the history of rock'n'roll. Punk, new wave/modern rock, corporate/stadium rock and disco had faded or were nearing the end of their commercial success and influence. Musical tastes and directions were in a state of flux, without a set of ready clichés in place to (re)define genres and commercial slots. In this state of flux, the adoption and/or adaptation of musics from the margins of popular culture received an unexpected attention.

Peter Gabriel was not an isolated figure in the stylistic decisions he undertook in order to create and perform music during the early years of the 1980s. His use of ritual and the starkness of his performing style echoed the minimalism of those performance artists (most notably Laurie Anderson) who were enjoying a relatively wide exposure and influencing others' performance styles, not just in rock'n'roll, but also in theatre and film. Gabriel and David Byrne (of Talking Heads) may have been among the most prominent musicians to bring elements from performance art into their concert appearances, but numerous, less celebrated musicians, such as Indoor Life and Gang of Four, also explored those options. Others, including Jon Hassell, Kate Bush, Hulgar Czukay and Brian Eno, borrowed compositional techniques from avant-garde classical composers, such as Karl Stockhausen, Terry Riley and Steve Reich.

In particular, Brian Eno was a key figure in bringing new approaches and perspectives into the popular music of the early 1980s. Through his work as a producer and a musician – David Bowie's *Lodger* (1979), Talking Heads' *Remain in Light* (1981) – Eno helped to introduce new sensibilities about what could be included within the canon of popular music. They included ambient music, as demonstrated on *Ambient 1: Music For Airports* (1978) and *musique concrète* collages (built from combining synthesized music with tape samples) such as *My Life in the Bush of Ghosts* (1981). The release of *Security* came before the 'world music' phenomenon reached its greatest public exposure via the participation of mainstream pop stars like Paul Simon and Sting, but at a time when a wide variety of popular musicians were beginning to look outside Western Europe and North America for musical influences and resources. Indeed, Talking Heads' *Remain in Light* was probably the first commercial recording to combine African polyrhythms and rock'n'roll.

The lyrical themes of isolation and separation that Peter Gabriel visited repeatedly during the late 1970s and early 1980s were also frequently explored by other contemporary musicians, including Laurie Anderson, David Byrne and David Bowie. In this respect, Gabriel's success was to straddle the line between performance and pop, between mainstream and fringe categories. However, by the late 1980s, themes and styles had shifted. Gabriel's album *So* (1985) included only a few songs, such as 'Red Rain', that recalled the sound of *Security*. Its two most memorable tracks were the tongue-in-cheek dance song 'Sledgehammer' and the epic political ballad 'Don't Give Up'. In an interview in 1986, Gabriel confessed that with the completion of the soundtrack for Alan Parker's movie *Birdy* (1985) and *So*, he had driven the desire to create music based on rhythm and texture out of his system, and wanted to get back to writing 'songs' (Hutchinson 1986). In live performance, while he continued to seek interaction with the crowd, he now did so as a 'pop star', without the ambiguity of his *Security* performances. The spectacle and showmanship of the concerts increased, re-integrating some of the theatricality of his work with Genesis, but the emphasis on the ritual of performance faded. Peter Gabriel had moved on. It was also a signal that a window for experimentation in mainstream popular music that had opened in the early 1980s had closed.

Notes

1. The 'Playtime 1988' tour comprised 23 performances in 1982. Following the release of *Peter Gabriel Plays Live* (1983), Gabriel initiated a second, more extensive tour of 56 performances which maintained the same repertoire and performance elements. The itinerary of the two tours is listed below:

'Playtime 1988'

16 & 18/7/82	Shepton Mallet, UK (WOMAD Festival))
28/10/82	Boston, MA, USA (Orpheum Theatre)
1/11/82	Poughkeepsie, NY, USA (Civic Center)
2/11/82	Utica, NY, USA (Performing Arts Center)
5/11/82	Montreal, Canada (Forum)
6/11/82	Ottawa, Canada (Civic Center)
8/11/82	Toronto, Canada (Maple Leaf Gardens)
9/11/82	Buffalo, NY, USA (Shea's Theatre)
13/11/82	Passaic, NY, USA (Capitol Theatre)
14/11/82	Washington, DC, USA (Warner Theatre)
16/11/82	Philadelphia, PA, USA (Spectrum)
20/11/82	Ann Arbor, MI, USA (Hill Auditorium)
26 & 27/11/82	New York, NY, USA (Palladium)
1/12/82	Milwaukee, WI, USA (Performing Arts Center)
2/12/82	Chicago, IL, USA (Pavillion)
6/12/82	Kansas City, MO, USA (Kemper Arena)
7/12/82	Carbondale, IL, USA (S.I.V. Arena)
12/12/82	Houston, TX, USA (Music Hall)
14/12/82	San Diego, CA, USA (Civic Auditorium)
18/12/82	San Francisco, CA, USA (Civic Auditorium)
19/12/82	San Jose, CA, USA (Civic Center)

'Plays Live Tour'

30/6/83	Rouen, France (Parc des Expositions)
1/7/83	Paris, France (Palais des Sport, two shows)
2/7/83	Torhout, France (Rockwood Festival)
3/7/82	Werchter, Holland (Rockwood Festival)
5/7/83	Ferrara, Italy (Stadio Comunale)
6/7/83	Prate, Italy (Stadio Comunale)
9/7/83	London, UK (Selhurst Park)
18/7/83	Toronto, Canada (Maple Leaf Gardens)
20/7/83	Montreal, Canada (Place des Nations)
23/7/83	Philadelphia, PA, USA (Mann Music Center)
24/7/83	Saratoga Springs, NY, USA (Performing Arts Center)
27/7/83	Worcester, MA, USA (E.M. Loew's Theatre)
29/7/83	New York, NY, USA (Forest Hills)
2/8/83	Chicago, IL, USA (Poplar Creek)
8/8/83	Vancouver, Canada (PNE)
10/8/83	Seattle, WA, USA (Paramount Theatre)
12 & 13/8/83	Berkeley, CA, USA (Greek Theatre)
15/8/83	San Diego, CA, USA (Open Air Theatre)
16/8/83	Los Angeles, CA, USA (Greek Theatre)
5/9/83	Southampton, UK (Gaumont Theatre)
7, 8 & 9/9/83	London, UK (Hammersmith Odeon)
10/9/83	Birmingham, UK (NEC)
12/9/83	Glasgow, UK (Apollo)
14/9/83	Edinburgh, UK (Playhouse)
15/9/83	Newcastle, UK (City Hall)
17/9//83	Manchester, UK (Apollo)

18/9/83	Liverpool, UK (Empire Theatre)
26/9/83	Brussels, Belgium (Forest National)
27/9/83	Den Haag, Holland (Congressgobow, two shows)
29/9/83	Oslo, Norway (Ekebergshalle)
30/9/83	Stockholm, Sweden (Isstadion)
1/10/83	Copenhagen, Denmark (Falkoner Theatre)
2/10/83	Hamburg, Germany (CCH)
4/10/83	Düsseldorf, Germany (Philipshalle)
5/10/83	Frankfurt, Germany (Alte Oper)
6/10/83	Munich, Germany (Cirsus Crone)
8/10/83	Wien, Germany (Stadthalle)
10/10/83	Hanover, Germany (Niedersachselnhalle)
11/10/83	Berlin, Germany (Eissporthalle)
12/10/83	Boblingen, Germany (Sporthalle)
15/10/83	Clermont Ferrand, France (Maison des Sports)
19/10/83	Avignon, France (Parc des Expositions)
20/10/83	Grenoble, France (Palais des Sports)
21/10/83	Dijon, France (Le Chapiteau)
22/10/83	Strasbourg, France (Le Chapiteau)
24/10/83	Lille, France (Parc des Expositions)
25/10/83	Paris, France (Espace Ballard)
27/10/83	Nantes, France (Parc de la Beaujoire)
28/10/83	Brest, France (Salle de Penfeld)

2. Gabriel's first three solo albums are all entitled *Peter Gabriel* but are probably better known by short descriptions of their cover art as *Rainy Windshield* (1977), *Fingernails* (1978) and *Melting Face* (1980).
3. The song was later to be featured in Richard Attenborough's *Cry Freedom* (1988) with rhythmic accompaniment provided by the Ekome Dance Company, an African drumming ensemble based in the UK. The song became an anthem for the South African anti-apartheid movement. Gabriel's work with African artists on this project was also an inspiration for his founding of WOMAD (World of Music, Arts and Dance) in 1980.
4. The Fairlight CMI was also central to the work of singer-songwriter Kate Bush.
5. The *Bristol Recorder* (also known as the *Bristol Recorder Talking Book*) was a combination magazine/record album that published three issues in 1979–81, from Bristol. In its written work, it addressed issues of community, politics and culture, and the accompanying recordings presented work from local bands. It also included a few works by more established artists, such as the Thompson Twins and Robert Fripp. For the January 1981 issue, Gabriel donated concert performances of three songs: 'Not One of Us' (1980), 'Humdrum' (1980) and 'Ain't That Peculiar' (1977).
6. *Musique concrète* is a compositional technique, developed in the 1940s by classical composers such as Karlheinz Stockhausen, in which musical tones (sometimes electronically generated) or environmental sounds are transformed electronically, recorded on tape, then re-combined to create an aural collage. This technique was subsequently applied to popular music, most notably by Beatles producer George Martin. Martin's use of *musique concrète* on *Sgt Pepper's Lonely Hearts Club Band* in 1967 influenced many other popular musicians to make use of the technique.
7. The first performance of material from *Security* was at the first WOMAD (World of Music, Arts and Dance) festival in 1981. It was also the first occasion on which Gabriel performed publicly with non-western artists, supplementing his five-person

band with the African percussion ensemble Ekome and South Indian violinist Shankar. When the *Security* tour began in 1982, Gabriel appeared with that five-person band: Gabriel, Tony Levin (bass), Jerry Marotta (guitar), Larry Fast (keyboards) and Tony Banks (drums).

8. Before filming the 'Shock the Monkey' video in September 1982, Gabriel had investigated recent developments in video technology during his tour of the US. He had also viewed video works of performance artist Laurie Anderson, avant-garde rockers the Residents and experimental video artists at New York's Museum of Modern Art (Bright 1999: 251–2).

Chapter 11

Michael Jackson: *Motown 25*, Pasadena Civic Auditorium March 25, 1983

Jaap Kooijman

[Michael] Jackson's passage from music superstar to a world historical and cultural figure was ritually enacted on May 16, 1983, with his mythic dance performance of the 'moonwalk' on the *Motown 25* television special, which was beamed to almost 50 million viewers around the globe. Jackson's uncanny dexterity, disciplined grace, and explosive imagination coalesced in a series of immortal movements, which, in their turn, freeze-framed the recrudescent genius of street dance, summarized the important history of Fred Astaire-like purposeful grace in executing dance steps, and extended the brilliant tradition of African-American performers like Bojangles, Sammy Davis, and Katherine Dunham surging against the odds to create vital art (Dyson 1993: 42).

Referring to Michael Jackson's performance of 'Billie Jean' at the *Motown 25* television special, Steve Ivory, editor of *Black Beat*, remembered: 'I don't think I've seen anything like that before. I was stunned. Michael truly became a legend that night. Watching the performance on videotape pales in comparison to the exhilaration I, and everyone else who was there, felt at seeing Michael's act in person' (Taraborrelli 1991: 291–2). Ivory was not the only one who was blown away by the event, as the performance has been widely considered as a groundbreaking moment in the history of pop music, which would, according to *Rolling Stone*, 'energize the music scene once again and set in motion all the forces that would go on to shape the popular culture of the 1980s' (Shuker 2001: 182). It was a pivotal transition in that it marked the shift of emphasis from musical performance to visual presentation. In stark contrast to the other, live, performances of *Motown 25*, Jackson performed to a pre-recorded soundtrack, lip-synching to his multi-layered pre-recorded voice, thus indicating that the visual re-enactment of music video imagery had become an integral, and perhaps dominant, part of live performance.

In retrospect, it is difficult to gauge how spectacular Michael Jackson's performance really was at that time. Since *Motown 25*, his performances – live on stage and in his often-controversial music videos – have become ever more outrageous (King 1999). Also, his reputation as 'Wacko Jacko' has added another layer of controversy, as rumours about him sleeping in a hyperbaric chamber, the alleged whitening of his skin and cosmetic alterations to his nose and body, his marriage to Lisa Marie Presley, the mysterious births of his three children and, most seriously, the accusations of child molestation, have made him an easy target for tabloid journalism and sensationalist 'unauthorized' biographies (Taraborrelli 1991; Andersen 1994). Compared to Jackson's current star image, and more than two decades on, the *Motown 25* performance seems innocent and relatively 'simple'. Yet, on May 16, 1983, when *Motown 25* was broadcast on US national television by NBC (reaching an audience of around 50 million Americans and even more viewers worldwide) Jackson's performance was singled out as the most exciting moment of the show (O'Connor 1983; Pond 1983; Shales 1983). Moreover, it proved to be a major commercial promotion of his album *Thriller*, originally released in December 1982. Although the album had been selling well before the television special (and 'Billie Jean' was already a Number One single), sales skyrocketed after the broadcast, making it – with more than 45 million copies sold worldwide – the best-selling album of all time, and simultaneously catapulting Michael Jackson into global mega-stardom.

The significance of the *Motown 25* performance is twofold. First, the performance is an important contribution to the star-text that constitutes Jackson's star image. As both Dyer (1979, 2004) and Goodwin (1992) have shown, the star-text consists not only of the star's actual performances, but also of other texts such as interviews, promotional material, critical reviews and gossip. *Motown 25* proves to be a key moment in the construction of Michael Jackson as a crossover star. Second, the performance should be positioned within the emergence of music video as the prevalent medium through which to present pop music. With its emphasis on the visual rather than the musical, Jackson's 'Billie Jean' at *Motown 25* is a key moment in the history of the performance of pop music, in which spectacle has increasingly become its most celebrated component.

Motown 25: Yesterday, Today, Forever

Taped on March 25, 1983, at the Los Angeles Pasadena Civic Auditorium, the television special *Motown 25* was broadcast by NBC on May 16, 1983. It proved to be both a commercial and a critical success, reaching a wide audience and winning an Emmy award in the category of 'Outstanding Variety, Music, or Comedy Program'. Subtitled *Yesterday, Today, Forever*, *Motown 25* was a celebration of the 25th anniversary of the legendary Detroit record label and a tribute to its founder and president Berry Gordy. By the 1980s, many of the big Motown stars, including Marvin Gaye, Diana Ross and Michael Jackson, had left the label, but that night, as Ross pointed out to Gordy in her speech, they all came back. Marvin Gaye gave a moving performance of 'What's Going On', Stevie Wonder sang a couple of his greatest hits and the Temptations and the Four Tops performed together in an electrifying medley. To attract a more versatile and younger audience, white British pop star Adam Ant had been invited to sing the Supremes' hit single 'Where Did Our Love Go' – although it was their former lead singer Diana Ross who received most of the cheers when she joined Ant on stage to do a bump-and-grind. The current Motown sound was represented by the groups DeBarge and High Inergy, but their performances paled in comparison to those by the artists who had made Motown a legendary label in the 1960s, thereby emphasizing that by the 1980s Motown had become 'just another record company'. Ironically, the show 'contrasted Motown's robust musical past with its mediocre present' (George 1986: 193).

The grand finale of *Motown 25* reinforced this notion that the 'real' sound of Motown belonged to 'Yesterday' rather than 'Today'. The highly anticipated reunion of Diana Ross and the Supremes was supposed to be the evening's climactic moment, but instead the performance turned into controversy as Supreme Mary Wilson claimed that Ross tried to push her (again) into the background. Accounts about what exactly happened differ, but the performance was cut short and the controversial 'shove' was edited out of the television broadcast. As a result, two *Motown 25* moments stood out in the media: on the one hand, the disappointing reunion of Diana Ross and the Supremes and, on the other, the electrifying performance by Michael Jackson, which only seemed to confirm that it was not Motown but Michael Jackson who was the sound of 'Today'.

The show's producers knew that they needed Michael Jackson – by then, the hottest star the label had ever produced – in order to make the television special a success. As both Jackson and Berry Gordy confirm in their autobiographies, Jackson had initially refused to appear, partly because he was reluctant to work with his brothers again, and partly because he wanted to avoid over-exposure on television. It was Gordy himself who went to see Jackson to persuade him to participate. He eventually agreed, with one condition: he wanted to sing his current Number One hit 'Billie Jean' (Jackson 1988: 208; Gordy 1994: 378). Jackson's demand was significant as 'Billie Jean' would be the only non-Motown song to be performed that night. Gordy and his fellow producers realized that they had no choice: the only way to secure Jackson's presence was to let him perform the song even though the single had been released by another label (Epic). In return, Jackson agreed to take part in a Jackson 5 'greatest hits' medley with his brothers.

The Jackson 5 reunion segment began with film clips from the Motown archives, including their original audition in 1968, in which a 9-year-old Michael Jackson danced around like James Brown. Following the clips, Michael Jackson joined his five brothers (including Jermaine, who had stayed with Motown after the Jackson 5 left the label, and Randy, who had replaced Jermaine at that time) on stage. Dressed in fashionable 1980s costumes, the reunited Jackson 5 performed a medley of 'I Want You Back', 'The Love You Save' and 'I'll Be There'. On the last song, Michael and Jermaine shared the lead vocal, emphasizing that their performance was indeed a reunion. Once the medley was over, the audience enthusiastically cheered them on. Before leaving the stage, the Jackson brothers hugged Michael and each other. Then Michael Jackson was left alone on stage. He addressed the audience: 'I have to say those were the good old days. I love those songs. Those were magic moments with all my brothers, including Jermaine.' Then Jackson paused, looking at the audience as if about to reveal something extraordinary: 'But, uh, you know, those were the good songs. I like those songs a lot. But especially, I like … the new songs.' At that moment, on the opening beats of 'Billie Jean', Jackson grabbed his black hat, spun around, and struck a pose. The contrast was clear. With both his speech and his moves, Michael Jackson made the definitive statement that the Jackson 5 were history, and that his solo performance of 'Billie Jean' was the future. Even Berry Gordy had to admit that Jackson's performance – the only non-Motown song, lip-synched, by a former Motown star – outshone the magic of Motown itself: 'It was the most incredible performance I'd ever seen. He had touches of many of the greats in that one performance – Sammy Davis Jr, Fred Astaire, Jackie Wilson, Marcel Marceau and James Brown. But it was his own moonwalk that blew everybody away' (1994: 378).

Both audience and critics seemed to share Gordy's amazement. Dressed in black pants with silver-glittery socks, a silver-glittery shirt, and a black sequinned jacket, Michael Jackson enacted a long tradition of African-American dance movements in one performance. Nelson George called the performance 'epochal', claiming that Jackson combined 'Jack Wilson's athleticism, James Brown's camel walk, the intensity of the Apollo amateur night, and the glitter of Diana Ross' (1988: 194–5). Undoubtedly, the performance is best remembered as the moment that Michael Jackson showed the world how to do the moonwalk. One could hear the audience gasping as he moved backward, while seemingly walking forward, as if he was floating on air. Nobody seemed to care that the moonwalk was really called the backslide, or that he was not the first one to perform it on television. The dancers of the television show *Soul Train* had performed the moonwalk before, and it had been one of those dancers, Geron 'Casper' Candidate, who had taught the step to Jackson (Andersen 1994: 119). However, after *Motown 25*, the moonwalk became synonymous with Michael Jackson, who would later capitalize on his new trademark by naming his 1988 autobiography *Moonwalk* and his 1988 self-written, feature-length, promotional video *Moonwalker*. But although the moonwalk stood out, it was only one of several visual elements that constituted his trademark performance. The single white sequinned glove grasping his crotch, the staccato movement of his pelvis and his angry gaze into the camera have all become classic elements of the Michael Jackson star persona, reappearing in his other 'live' performances and music videos. It was the accumulation of these visual elements, rather than the song he lip-synched, that made the performance legendary. The *Washington Post* noted that 'Jackson's voice hasn't really changed much over the years. But the *moves* have. Oh, how they have changed! Michael Jackson is more dazzling than a Fourth of July fireworks display. He redefines showmanship right in front of your amazed little eyes' (Shales 1983).

As Michael Jackson revealed in his autobiography, it was not until later that he realized how pivotal that performance was to be for the future of his career. Although he later admitted that 'there were many changes in my life in the aftermath of *Motown 25*', he was initially unable to grasp the magnitude of his appearance.

> I turned around and grabbed the hat and went into 'Billie Jean', into that heavy rhythm; I could tell that people in the audience were really enjoying my performance. My brothers told me they were crowding the wings watching me with their mouths open, and my parents and sisters were out there in the audience. But I just remember opening my eyes at the end of the thing and seeing this sea of people standing up, applauding. And I felt so many conflicting emotions. I knew I had done my best and felt good, so good. But at the same time I felt disappointed in myself. I had planned to do one really long spin and to stop on my toes, suspended for a moment, but I didn't stay on my toes as long as I wanted. I did the spin and I landed on one toe. I wanted to just stay there, just *freeze* there, but it didn't work quite as I'd planned (Jackson 1988: 211–12).

Michael Jackson's recollection may be perceived as modesty, befitting his star image, but at the same time it reveals the magical amazement shared by all who saw him that night. In this way, his account contributes to the near-mythical status of *Motown 25* as a key moment in the construction of his own star image and in the history of pop music.

Yesterday: Motown's crossover dream

Founded by Berry Gordy in 1958, the Detroit-based Motown – 'The Sound Of Young America' – became the largest independent record label and the largest black-owned business in America of the 1960s. Known for its assembly-line production, Motown was a true hit factory, releasing hit after hit by Diana Ross and the Supremes, the Temptations, the Four Tops, Martha and the Vandellas, Marvin Gaye, Gladys Knight and the Pips, Little Stevie Wonder et al. Rivalled only by the British Invasion (especially the Beatles), the Motown sound became the soundtrack of 1960s America, crossing the borders between black and white, old and young (George 1986: Early 1995; Smith 1999). The Jackson 5 joined Motown in 1969 and would be the last group shaped according to its assembly-line production policy. With the young Michael on lead, their first four singles – the first three written and produced by a collective of songwriters fittingly named 'The Corporation' – all became US Number One hits: 'I Want You Back', 'ABC', 'The Love You Save' and 'I'll Be There'. In addition, the group regularly appeared on national television (including *The Ed Sullivan Show*), in its own TV specials and (as animated characters) in the Saturday morning cartoon series *The Jackson 5 Show*.

As part of Motown's marketing strategy, Diana Ross was announced as the one who had discovered the Jackson 5. Subsequently, it was she who introduced them to American television audiences on *The Hollywood Palace* on October 18, 1969, followed by the release of their first album entitled *Diana Ross Presents The Jackson 5*. Like Michael Jackson, the popularity of Diana Ross (then lead singer of the Supremes) was not only based on her music, but also on the visual presentation of her on national television (Kooijman 2002). That Jackson was both singer and dancer was evident during the *The Hollywood Palace* broadcast. After the Jackson 5 performed their first single 'I Want You Back', Ross singled out the young Michael and asked him to show the audience how incredibly he could dance. Jackson immediately stole the show with a short, seemingly improvised, James Brown-styled routine. By explicitly connecting Michael Jackson to Diana Ross, Motown succeeded in making both stars more spectacular. Ross had been Motown's greatest crossover star, leading the way to wider and more diffuse (black, white, teenage, adult, Las Vegas, television) audiences. From the start, Motown groomed Michael Jackson in the same way (Harper 1996: 88–9).

The 'special' connection between Diana Ross and Michael Jackson continued to develop, as they were joined in the public's mind through the myth that Jackson 'really' wanted to become Diana Ross. As was generally suggested by the tabloid press, Jackson did not only imitate Ross in his stage and TV performances, but also altered his body through cosmetic surgery to make himself look more like her (Hadleigh 1991: 59–63). Whether true or not, the public perception of Jackson as an imitator of Diana Ross who was quite prepared to physically transform his appearance has contributed to his star image. The press reports about him lightening his skin and straightening his nose – supported by photographs – have become part of the Jackson mythology in which what is 'true' or 'false' has become largely irrelevant. In fact, the difficulty in distinguishing between actuality and gossip emphasizes the (racial and sexual) ambiguity contained within the Jackson persona, as described by Mercer:

> neither child nor adult, nor clearly either black or white, and with an androgynous image that is neither masculine nor feminine, Jackson's star image is a 'social hieroglyph' as Marx said of the commodity form, which demands, yet defies, decoding … he may sing as sweet as Al Green, dance as hard as James Brown, but he looks more like Diana Ross than any black male soul artist (1994: 34–5).

By the early 1980s, the association between Ross and Jackson was at its height. They performed together in the film *The Wiz* (Sidney Lumet, 1978) and television specials such as CBS's *Diana* (1981), and often appeared together in public. Described by Jackson as 'my mother, my lover, and my sister all combined in one amazing person' (1988: 69), Diana Ross embodied the same crossover dream as Jackson. 'Diana and Michael: the undisputed king and queen of entertainment' announced *Ebony* in November 1983, featuring a front-cover portrait of the two stars (Sanders 1983: 29).

It has been argued that Motown's crossover strategy into mainstream American popular culture was, while successfully employed by Diana Ross, taken to the extreme by Michael Jackson (Tate 1987; Harper 1996: 88–9). In his provocatively titled essay 'I'm White! What's Wrong With Michael Jackson?' Tate asserts that 'Michael Jackson has crossed so way far over the line that there ain't no coming back ... the difference between Gordy's crossover dream world and Jackson's is that Gordy's didn't preclude the notion that black is beautiful' (1987: 96). Others have argued that what Jackson presents is less a black image transforming into a white image than a black image challenging the stereotypical black image. Jackson does not offer 'a fixed identity ... [but] something closer to drag' (Fuchs 1995: 22); or, through his androgynous image, 'Jackson not only questions dominant stereotypes of black masculinity, but also gracefully steps outside the existing range of "types" of black men' (Mercer 1994: 50). Thus, instead of simply 'selling out' to mainstream culture, the Jackson star image invites new definitions of identity that cross the borders of race and gender. In her analysis of his 'Bad' (1987) video, Wallace goes further in suggesting that Jackson might even constitute a third racial category, a fantasy identity, beyond the limitations of race (1990: 87). What these arguments share, regardless of whether they perceive the Michael Jackson star image in negative or positive terms, is the emphasis on visual (re)presentation. It is his visual image, his body, and the movements that he makes with his body, rather than his music which take priority in the construction of his star image.

Today: MTV and the dominance of visual (re)presentation

The dominance of visual (re)presentation in Michael Jackson's *Motown 25* performance needs to be located within the broader development of the emergence of music television during the early 1980s. With the introduction of the American cable channel MTV (Music Television) in 1981, music video became the preferred medium through which to promote pop music. That MTV chose 'Video Killed the Radio Star' by the relatively obscure band the Buggles as its first broadcast video was no coincidence. In the world of pop music, vision/television had become more important than sound/radio (Goodwin 1992; Shuker 2001: 188–91). This is not to say that visual (re)presentation had been unimportant before. The famous 1956 performance of Elvis Presley, shot from the waist up, on *The Ed Sullivan Show* is a clear and early example of the impact of visual performance in pop music. And of course, the music video as a separate genre existed before the introduction of MTV, with Queen's 'Bohemian Rhapsody' (1975) as its most familiar example. However, MTV's 24-hour rotation of music videos, seven days a week, dramatically increased their impact on the promotion of pop music and pop stars. Their increased significance also raised the question of whether the music video was best seen as a commercial for the pop song and its star, or if the pop song had been reduced to the soundtrack of the video.

Jackson has claimed that the videos for 'Billie Jean', 'Beat It' and 'Thriller' were part of the original concept of the *Thriller* album: 'I was determined to present this music as visually as possible. I wanted something that would glue you to the set, something you'd want to watch over and over' (1988: 200) – a perception of his music and its visual representation as intertwined, as intrinsically belonging to each other. Although predominantly shot in freeze-frames, *Thriller*'s first music video 'Billie Jean', released in March 1983, focused on Jackson's dance moves, showing him walking and dancing on a street (which clearly was a studio set), with the tiles of the pavement lighting up whenever he stepped on them. Although the moonwalk was absent, he did execute the other dance moves that would reappear in the *Motown 25* performance, including the spin ending with a still shot of Jackson on his toes. To a certain extent therefore, the *Motown 25* performance could be perceived as a re-enactment of the 'Billie Jean' video.

Even though Michael Jackson was already a successful pop star before the release of *Thriller* and 'Billie Jean', it proved to be difficult to break the racial barrier of MTV. During its first few years, MTV was considered to be a 'rock'n'roll' channel, meaning that it predominantly featured white, male artists. The success of the *Motown 25* performance helped Jackson's record company, CBS, to increase pressure on MTV to include 'Billie Jean' and 'Beat It' in its rotation. Jackson, together with Prince, can be considered as a crossover artist who helped to break the barriers between dance and rock, and black and white, that initially defined MTV as a white channel (Goodwin 1992: 133; Shuker 2001: 119). Over the years, his videos would become major media events, beginning with MTV's legendary 'exclusive premiere' of 'Thriller' in December 1983; 15 minutes long and directed by John Landis, 'Thriller' could be justifiably considered as a short film, rather than a 'mere' music video.

In his assessment of the 'Thriller' video, Mercer expands Laing's (1985b) argument that music videos are no longer promotional commercials for pop songs, in which the visuals are subordinated to the soundtrack. Another convention has become more important:

> that of an alternation between naturalistic or 'realist' modes of representation (in which the song is performed 'live' or in a studio, and mimed to by the singer or group) and 'constructed' of fantastic modes of representation (in which the singer/group acts out imaginary roles implied by the lyrics or by the atmosphere of the music) (1994: 37).

This distinction may also be applied to Michael Jackson's *Motown 25* performance in which, similarly, visual (re)presentations – dance movements, bodily poses – were not subordinate to the soundtrack. This is not to say that sound was no longer important, but that the *live* performance of sound had become seemingly irrelevant. That Jackson lip-synched 'Billie Jean' is, in itself, not extraordinary, but the fact that it did not change the impact of the performance is extraordinary; whether the performance was live or lip-synched made no difference to the audience. Jackson was not singing live, but was acting out the visually constructed and imaginary role of 'the star', Michael Jackson.

His *Motown 25* performance can thus be seen as a pivotal moment that marks a shift from live performance to the re-enactment of the imagery of the music video. In the years since, numerous pop stars have chosen to successfully build their live performances around the conventions of their music videos – Madonna, Janet Jackson, Britney Spears, Justin Timberlake. The knowledge that many (if not all) of the vocals have been pre-recorded is largely uncontested, suggesting that contemporary audiences prefer to see their superstars present a visual spectacle that re-enacts the music video, rather than hear them sing a live rendition of their hit songs.

Forever: *Motown 25* re-enacted

At the 1995 MTV Awards, Michael Jackson presented a 'medley' of some of his best-known songs, although 'bricolage' may be a better word to describe his performance. The soundtrack consisted of pre-recorded short segments of his greatest hits – 'Don't Stop 'Til You Get Enough', 'The Way You Make Me Feel', 'Scream', 'Thriller', 'Beat It', 'Black or White' – the last of these with an instrumental solo from Guns'n'Roses guitarist Slash. Jackson did not sing live, but lip-synched extracts from the songs. During Slash's extended solo, Jackson left the stage to re-appear in costume very similar to that worn in the *Motown 25* performance of 12 years earlier. The bricolage continued with 'Billie Jean', during which Jackson literally repeated his *Motown 25* performance; this time, however, the lyrics were kept to a minimum, as he performed the moonwalk to the song's backbeat.

With this performance, Michael Jackson had come full circle. He no longer performed a song, but instead gave a visual representation of his earlier – now 'epochal' – *Motown 25* performance, providing a visual image that referred back to the 'imaginary' image of the pop star Michael Jackson in the early 1980s. The 1995 MTV Awards performance turned out to be the *Motown 25* performance in the extreme – a distilled version, reduced to its basic, visual elements: the sequinned black jacket, the black hat and, most importantly, the moonwalk. Only the single white sequinned glove was missing. As the performance made clear, Michael Jackson had become a postmodernist sign, a visual representation, far removed from 'live' musical performance, that reiterated and reinforced the shift towards the dominance of the visual presaged by his *Motown 25* performance of 1983.

Chapter 12

Live on tape
Madonna: *MTV Video Music Awards*, Radio City Music Hall, New York, September 14, 1984[1]

Gary Burns

Madonna and MTV have been a match made in heaven since they almost simultaneously burst upon the American musical and televisual scenes in the early 1980s. At that time they were both part of the Warner conglomerate, so that their 'marriage' made perfect, proto-synergistic sense: Madonna recorded for the Sire label, distributed by Warner Bros Records; MTV was owned by Warner Amex Satellite Entertainment Corporation. Oddly enough, after the sale of MTV to Viacom in 1985, Madonna became even more firmly 'wedded' to the cable network. Viacom, which does not own a record company, seems content to let its influence be felt in the recording industry through its (now) numerous cable TV networks, which, in the United States at least, serve a domineering gatekeeper function for all the large record companies.

Although the original, US MTV channel has veered away from its initial 24-hour music video programming formula, the MTV brand, which now covers numerous international channels, subsidiaries (BET, CMT, VH1) and US spinoffs (MTV2), remains substantially devoted to 'format' programming. MTV's networks, as a group, mostly play programmes that have some sort of musical focus. The original name 'Music Television' is not heard much today but remains present by implication in the MTV acronym. 'Music' programming, in turn, is operationally defined as music video on most MTV channels most of the time. As MTV continues to invent new channels, a pattern becomes evident. When the channel is launched, it plays music videos almost all day almost every day, with few if any commercials. As the channel becomes older, it starts playing commercials and primitive programmes (which initially may be nothing more than named time blocks of videos grouped by musical genre). This was the trajectory of the original MTV channel, which ultimately went much further and became the teenage-lifestyle channel that it is today, with music videos truncated, talked over, obliterated by other images and (especially) relegated to fringe time slots.

Before all that, when there was only one MTV and when most of MTV's schedule consisted of music videos, the channel was highly dependent on photogenic rock singers and striking videos, which Madonna produced in abundance. Madonna, for her part, has long been a multimedia star, but more than almost any other musician she owes her stardom to music video. Even as Madonna's live performances have been celebrated as theatrical events, their renown stems primarily from their circulation as home videos, cable telecasts and re-runs.

Madonna's performance of 'Like a Virgin' at the 1984 *MTV Video Music Awards* (often abbreviated *VMA*) is a paradigmatic case in point. The performance is somewhat canonical as Madonna's 'coming out party' for a national, prime-time TV audience. It is less often noted that the broadcast served a similar 'coming out' function for MTV, which was in its 'second launch' phase – the second stage in its history (Goodwin 1992: 135) – when it became available on the cable systems in Manhattan and Los Angeles, the two largest media markets in the US and the places where the people who run the media businesses live and work.

A prime-time awards show served as punctuation in the MTV schedule, which in 1984 was still a 'format' of round-the-clock videos. At that time, videos were so unfamiliar, the 'formatting' idea was so new in television programming and competition for 'eyeballs' was so weak that MTV as a whole constituted something of a 'destination' for viewers – especially those interested in music.

Such viewers had previously been underserved by US television stations and networks. But before MTV provided its solution, it was not entirely clear what kind of programming might succeed on a 24-hour musical TV channel. For example, alternatives to MTV-style video rotation might have included 24-hour live studio performances by musicians, or the re-running of old TV variety series, or the playing of sound recordings under abstract video images or even a black screen (as on satellite TV music channels now).

But MTV did not do any of those things. Instead, it played videotapes produced and provided free by the record companies. The videotapes were mostly films of bands lip-synching to hit records. This became the familiar model of music video and of 'music television'; E. Ann Kaplan's (1987) cultural analysis of the channel (the book's subtitle includes the expression 'music television' but not 'MTV') is about both music video and MTV, but generally conflates the two subjects. The model was borrowed from Top 40 radio and it meant that the 'music' on MTV would be mostly recorded and not live.

In the light of MTV's extraordinary success, the decision to play videos in an almost nonstop rotation seems in retrospect to be a stroke of genius. In more mundane terms, MTV was merely carrying to an extreme the programming principle known as 'parsimony' (Head 1976: 146–7) which states that TV (or radio) programmes should be produced as cheaply as possible, networked geographically and re-run until some hypothetical point of diminishing return.

If we examine the music video format under this rubric, we see that MTV has minimized production costs by not producing many programmes. Especially in its early days, MTV mainly produced the ultracheap VJ segments between the videos. The videos themselves were originally obtained free from record companies, then later for payments in exchange for exclusive use of the videos by MTV, in order to drive competing music channels out of business (Banks 1996: 63–79).

But even when MTV has had to pay to obtain videos, the cost has been amortized by re-running the videos incessantly. Record companies, which are usually the owners and financers of the videos, have an interest in gaining every possible exposure for the videos, since each airing promotes the recording artist's career and, especially, the individual sound recording. Thus, the record companies have been compliant partners in the ascendancy of the MTV business model with its reliance on the rerunning of free, cheap or amortized videos.

Other re-runs, in addition to videos, showed up later in MTV's history, but these were also forms of cheap programming – *The Monkees*, *The Young Ones*, *Speed Racer* and other off-network recyclings. Eventually MTV started producing its own programmes, partly for the banal but highly practical reason that this was necessary in order to ensure listings for the network in *TV Guide* and similar publications (Boehlert 1996). Even so, some of the so-called programmes were little more than a slice of the network's usual format to which a fresh name was attached (such as *Postmodern MTV*) demonstrating a new form of parsimony, which today is called 'contexting' (Boehlert 1998). As previously suggested, this pattern of evolutionary development – from format and re-runs to primitive pseudo-programmes (and later to more elaborate original series) – became a recurring strategy for MTV Networks as the company launched additional channels. When MTV finally became seriously involved in TV series production in the late 1980s, it was usually in supercheap genres such as the game show (*Remote Control*, *Singled Out*) and the reality series (which MTV more or less invented with *The Real World*).[2]

Interestingly, MTV does not produce music videos. The closest it comes is in occasionally staging concerts and variety shows. Some of these have been actual series, such as *Unplugged*, but equally important are those that are framed as special events, such as the yearly New Year's Eve specials and the annual awards celebrations. The first *Video Music Awards* show occurred on September 14, 1984 at New York's Radio City Music Hall. The programme has been an annual production since then and has become a ritual pseudo-event that interrupts the otherwise rather uneventful flow of recorded programming on MTV.

Indeed, at first glance the *Video Music Awards* would appear to be an anomaly in the MTV programme schedule – an expensive production whose value is immediately used up. However, several mitigating factors offset its high cost. First, as the trade journal *Broadcasting & Cable* noted:

> the show is a windfall in ratings and revenue for MTV. MTV reaps seven to ten times what it costs to produce the show (about $3 million) in revenue from advertisers, according to network sources … [It] is MTV's highest-rated show, earning ten times

MTV's average total-day rating, and the network reaps some of the largest cable audiences year after year for the program, according to Nielsen data (Petrozzello 1998: 26–7).

Second, MTV may recover some of its cost by charging admission to the live event. Tickets for the 1984 show were $100 and approximately 5800 people attended (Small 1984; Goldstein 1985). Third, musical performers may accept low fees for appearing on the *Video Music Awards* because their appearance brings them good publicity. As Warner Bros Records executive John Beug noted in 1998, it is 'a high priority for record labels to get their acts on that show' (Petrozzello 1998: 27). Fourth, the programme, or portions of it, may be sold on home video or to broadcasters for syndication. For example, the 1984 show was syndicated as a two-hour special in more than 80 US television markets (Seideman 1984; Small 1984). In addition, the audio portion of the programme was simulcast live on radio (Terry 1984: 115). As of March 16, 2004, the WorldCat database (www.firstsearch.oclc.org) listed four home video releases drawn from *Video Music Awards* telecasts (along with a few other items of *VMA*-branded merchandise in other media).[3] Fifth, MTV typically re-runs the entire programme several times. And sixth, it re-runs parts of the show separately and calls them music videos. In *that* sense, MTV does produce music videos, and the value of an expensively staged concert is not immediately exhausted after all. MTV mixes these 'videos' in its rotation so that they mingle with the more expensive-looking, single-camera, filmed, stand-alone videos provided by the record companies.

Madonna's performance at the 1984 *Video Music Awards* show was one of the first of these 'so-called' videos – a live rendition of a song for an MTV event, repackaged as a music video. It allowed MTV to perform several rhetorical sleights of hand. By re-running the live-but-recorded performance as a music video, MTV seemed to say: 'Here is a significant live performance that occurred on our air, and it is also a video. We set the agenda and claim the buzz. We define music video as an artistic category worthy of receiving awards. We bestow the awards. We give the awards mostly to musicians, for their videos. Thus, music video is a form of music. But the performances we recycle as videos are often those that are exciting primarily as television, not as music. And although this performance did not itself win an award, it is praiseworthy as a stand-out representative and memoir of the awards programme.'

Madonna has become something of a regular at the MTV awards, having contributed at least three performances that were exciting enough as television to be recycled as videos.[4] By this I mean that even though these were not especially interesting *musical* performances they were striking *televisual* events. The performances in question are 'Like a Virgin' (1984), 'Express Yourself' (1989) and 'Vogue' (1990). In addition, the 2003 *Video Music Awards* saw Madonna – with Britney Spears, Christina Aguilera and Missy Elliott – performing 'Like a Virgin' (in a medley) as a sort of reprise, updating and celebrating her 1984 appearance. This further buttressed the canonical status of Madonna, her 1984 performance and the *Video Music Awards*. The impact of the 1984 'Like a Virgin' is felt throughout Madonna's subsequent *VMA* appearances, and should also be considered in the context of her overall image and self-presentation, especially as reflected in her other music videos.

Within this framework, Madonna is a paradigmatic case of the 'sluttification' of women in music video, rock music and popular culture. This trend had a long pre-history but did not reach its full fruition until MTV. Later instances included the Dixie Chicks 'tak[ing] on their critics' by posing nude on the May 2, 2003 cover of *Entertainment Weekly* and the formerly squeaky-clean Janet Jackson exposing her breast in a Super Bowl halftime performance on CBS TV on February 1, 2004 (in a programme segment produced by MTV).

'Like a Virgin' is a one-woman performance on a stage decorated with an oversized 'wedding cake'. Madonna, dressed as a bride, stands at the top of the cake next to a mannequin 'groom'. As the performance unfolds, she descends the layers of the cake and performs a mini-striptease with various pieces of her wedding attire, all the while singing the song. By the latter part of the number she is writhing on the floor and humping it, which may be the MTV equivalent of a 'money shot'. Significantly, throughout the song she performs for the mobile, handheld TV cameras more than for the Radio City audience, so that the recorded product has some of the trappings of music video – in particular, a large quotient of direct address to the camera. At the end of the piece she is lying on the floor, apparently having had an orgasm.

In this (and many of her other performances) Madonna simultaneously spoofed sluttification and was the apotheosis of it: 'even jaded members of the cut-throat music industry sat dumbstruck. The performance, which went on to rank as one of her most-watched videos, set a standard for calculated tastelessness that Madonna would spend years attempting to transcend' (Andersen 1991: 126). Well, not *that* many years.

Undoubtedly, the most shocking thing about such a display in 1984 was the humping of the floor. Journalist Billy Altman proposed a mock award for Madonna for 'Best Impression of a Heifer in Heat' (1985: 48). Certainly, Madonna appeared to be a slut, but the spoofing part of the video, which makes it funny, is the wedding-cake motif and the hyperbolic idealization of marriage. This angle is emphasized in the *VMA* performance but is quite in keeping with the iconography of Madonna's 'Virgin Tour', from the same period, in which Madonna again performed 'Like a Virgin' in a wedding dress. In fact, the *VMA* performance may be seen as a stripped-down, tarted-up version of the 'Virgin Tour' routine – stripped-down, in that there were no musicians or backup singers present on stage at the *VMA* show. (The tour version of the song is available on the 1985 video-cassette *Madonna Live: The Virgin Tour*.)

The same kind of humorous excess occurs in her 'Express Yourself' (1989) and 'Vogue' (1990) performances – semi-pornographic dancing and stage business combined with spoofing in the form of exaggeration and context. In 'Express Yourself', Madonna and two female backup singers, dressed in male attire, furiously bump and grind their way through a straightforward vocal rendition of the song. The dancing and blocking of the number include humping, simulated masturbation and momentary storage of the performers' wireless microphones inside their bras. Again, Madonna is a trollop (this time, along with her accompanists), but again it is (also) a joke, by virtue of the drag costumes and the comical hiding of the microphones.

In 'Vogue', we find a farcical masquerade of 'Snow White/Madonna and the Seven Fops', presented in what Madonna triviaphile Matthew Rettenmund describes as 'eighteenth-century French gear *à la* Marie Antoinette' (1995: 120). Madonna, two female backup singers and seven male dancers (all from the 'Blonde Ambition Tour') perform the song in a complicated and highly stylized pantomime and dance routine. Madonna is ostensibly a 'proper lady', but also one who occasionally lifts up her comically voluminous dress or allows herself to be fondled by the effeminate, gnatlike dancers. She is a playfully sadistic queen or boss, obsequiously attended by the masochistic dancers and imitated by her ladies-in-waiting/backup singers. The improbable context of camp and period decadence and the sheer excessiveness of the pantomime humorously undercut the pornographic nature of the performers' antics.

Since I am arguing that the significance of Madonna's *VMA* performances is primarily televisual rather than musical, an analysis and comparison of the staging and shooting of these three 'videos' is in order. The three performances were all production numbers which became more elaborate, difficult and impressive over the course of six years, demonstrating that Madonna was probably the hardest-working woman in show business. But to underline the idea that music occupies a somewhat subsidiary position in these productions, we may note that in each case we see no instrumentalists – only Madonna, plus two backup singers in 'Express Yourself', and two backup singers and seven dancers in 'Vogue'.

In all three videos, the main visual point of interest is dancing, which is skilfully choreographed and directed for the camera. In all three, there appears to be live miking but also a backing instrumental track and probably a backup vocal track. One can surmise the live singing from the synchronization of lip movements, and because Madonna's voice is occasionally flat on 'Like a Virgin' and 'Express Yourself'; one can deduce the presence of backing vocal tracks because the singing sounds as good as it does and, on 'Express Yourself', because Madonna's voice sometimes sounds doubled when there appears to be only one person singing.[5]

We can note some commonality in the dramatic structure of these three videos. Madonna has a star entrance in all three, more clearly marked in the latter two, by which time she was being called the most famous woman in the world. Her entrance in 'Like a Virgin' and 'Express Yourself' places her at the top of stairs ... the music has already started. In 'Express Yourself' and 'Vogue', an air of expectancy is created by showing the other performers waiting for her entrance. In 'Express Yourself', we see Madonna dancing behind a screen in silhouette before she steps forward to appear in glorious flesh. As producer Joel Gallen recalled:

> MTV told me to strive for one surprise every half hour, which is sort of impossible – it's like five or six surprises. The opening of the show was Madonna singing 'Express Yourself'. There was no introduction, no laundry list of who is going to be on the show. We just faded up from black, the curtain opened, and there was Madonna behind a screen in silhouette. Cold open. The place just went nuts and it set the tone for a show with surprises (Hoye 2001: 122).

In all three videos, there are still figures that come to life. In 'Like a Virgin' it is the 'bride' Madonna atop the wedding cake. In 'Express Yourself', it is again Madonna, frozen in silhouette behind a screen at the top of stairs, before she starts to dance and emerges from behind the screen. In 'Vogue', all-powerful Madonna magically freezes and unfreezes her fellow performers by pointing at them.

We can also note considerable progress in the ambition and technique of the productions from 1984 to 1990. 'Like a Virgin' is a solo performance by Madonna; 'Express Yourself' features three people; 'Vogue' features ten. The blocking of the performances became correspondingly more complex and ranged over a wider area of the stage, somewhat mirroring the increasing elaborateness of Madonna's tours as she became a bigger and bigger star.

On the video recording of 'Like a Virgin', we are scarcely aware of the live audience, and they do indeed seem 'dumbstruck' at the end, although journalist and in-person eyewitness Toby Goldstein suggested that 'acts who acknowledged the in-house audience got more applause than those who knew that cameras were on them and acted like we didn't exist, such as Madonna' (1985: 38). This criticism of the live performance reveals the tension being played out between an aesthetic of authenticity, live musicianship and rock vs. the new MTV model of synthesizers, lip-synching and recorded television. Madonna's later *VMA* appearances more successfully resolved this tension. On 'Express Yourself', the live audience is highly visible and audible and clearly enjoys the spectacle. On 'Vogue', the seven fops are an internal-internal audience who applaud the women, and the concert audience (the internal audience) is loudly appreciative and appears to be very close to the stage. The effect of the concert audience and the fops is to cue the television audience to admire the performance.

The endings of the three videos illustrate a growing sensitivity to narrative structure from 1984 to 1990. The ending of 'Like a Virgin' is weak. Madonna has descended from the wedding cake, swirled around and around in the manner of Stevie Nicks, done a striptease and humped the floor. She ends by writhing on the floor – which was a familiar component of many of her early videos. Madonna goes from high to low, top to bottom, and this ending is like a fade instead of a cold close. The entrance is strong, the exit is weak. The ending of 'Express Yourself' is more emphatic, and is similar to a bookend in that Madonna returns to the top of the stairs. The music and dancing end with a cold close. After this, Madonna says 'yeah', while exiting to loud applause, in a sort of coda that underscores the comical effect of the performance and of Madonna's status as the boss. 'Vogue' also has a coda – a highly effective stage exit and a sharp and funny little piece of character business. Madonna is seated on a divan, breathing heavily from the strenuous song and dance she has just given, and the fops pick up the couch and carry her off stage. Their cue to do this is Madonna hitting one of them with her fan. As she is carried off, she looks at the audience through her period binoculars.

Televisual technique is an important ingredient in all three of these performances, and again we see progress from 1984 to 1990. In interview, Madonna has said that MTV tricked her on 'Like a Virgin', employing two cameras at the rehearsal, but six at the actual shoot, and that is why there were shots of her underpants (Bego 1992: 97–8). In effect, she said she was angry at MTV for violating her privacy, a charge she repeated several years later, when claiming 'I didn't know what I was doing [apparently because it was the first *VMA* show] … I had no idea my dress was up' (Hoye 2001: 261).

But there are several inconsistencies here. First, it is hard to figure out what shots she is referring to; we may get an indirect glimpse of Madonna's underwear, but it is hardly the case that the cameras go looking for it. Second, it is disingenuous to claim modesty when one has just given a performance like the one Madonna gave. Third, it strains credulity that a programme of this type would be planned for only two cameras or that it would be rehearsed with one camera configuration and then shot, for live transmission, no less, with a drastically different configuration. Fourth – beyond the speculative nature of the preceding point – Madonna mugs for the camera several times, in a manner that suggests she knows exactly where the cameras are going to be, in contradiction to her assertion that she was fooled. Fifth, there are no shots showing any other camera in the picture, which would be a likely result of using so many cameras, unrehearsed, in that kind of a shoot.

Be that as it may, and although I am hard-pressed to count six cameras, it remains possible that there were that many. But in that case the video should be better than it is. The shots are rather wide and the cutting rather slow for a six-camera shoot. And, although it is not directly related to the number of cameras used, it should be noted that Madonna leaves the frame once, and that is probably a mistake. This could be taken as support for her being tricked, but it is more likely evidence of the relatively frugal and unspectacular staging of the 1984 programme as compared with later years.

The six-camera approach (if that is what it is) seems to have become standard and perfected by 1989 for 'Express Yourself'. This camera deployment represents a doubling of the standard three-camera style for a studio-TV shoot. It allows for cutting to be twice as fast, but is thereby twice as demanding on the director. In 'Express Yourself', there are at least five cameras – two from each angle, except possibly only one from screen left.

In 'Vogue', there appear to be at least six cameras – two cover shots, three low angles from the apron area and one high angle from screen left. The faster cutting, combined with the concept, makes 'Vogue' almost look like a filmed video, and indeed it is included on Madonna's second compilation of videos. Even at that, the theatrical metaphor effectively acknowledges the live audience, as when the fops 'tour the apron' at the beginning.

The perfection of the performances in 'Express Yourself' and 'Vogue' is notable, and the camera choreography and direction also come close to perfection. One possible mistake occurs in the latter, when a fop grabs Madonna's breasts from behind at screen right. We do not get a very good view of it, and the timing of the cutting seems off. The large number of cameras used on 'Express Yourself' and 'Vogue' (and possibly on 'Like a Virgin') also suggests that some editing may have occurred in the versions that have been re-run (and in the version of 'Vogue' that appears in the 1990 video compilation *Madonna: The Immaculate Collection*). The most likely purpose of any such editing would be the correction of mistakes, although, as I have pointed out, at least one apparent mistake in cutting remains in 'Vogue', and in 'Like a Virgin' there exists a mistake in camera choreography when Madonna leaves the frame for an instant. It is exactly because of the painstaking choreography and rehearsal that had to go into these productions that it is unlikely that they were corrected much, or at all, in post-production. The cameras are so efficiently used that any redundancy seems unlikely and possibly even counterproductive.

The historical importance of Madonna's performances at the *MTV Video Music Awards* derives primarily from their televisual venue. As good as Madonna's songs are (which is not often enough acknowledged) her own singing is at best unexceptional, and her backup singers (in 'Express Yourself' and 'Vogue') are excellent but not the focus of attention. The performances are striking primarily as high-energy, provocatively choreographed, dance production numbers. They stress the 'TV' part of MTV and herald the arrival of the network as a cultural arbiter.

In Hoye's 'official history' of MTV, significant space is devoted to the annual *Video Music Awards* programmes; and this indication of the shows' importance to MTV has been readily confirmed in numerous statements by MTV personnel:

Les Garland: 'This is our Super Bowl' (Schneider 1986).

Bob Pittman: 'The hope was that it would become ... *the* thing ... the hot party, the show that the artists really cared about and viewers would look forward to ... and it's lived up to its promise' (Hoye 2001: 26).

John Sykes: 'The *VMA*'s idea came from Bob Pittman wanting to do a signature channel event. We got Don Ohlmeyer, an accomplished sports producer, to do the show for us instead of the traditional Oscars group ... it redefined music events on television by trying to relay our sarcastic tone to the big TV event' (Hoye 2001: 26).

Kurt Loder: 'MTV is just great at staging shows like this. There's a whole department of people at MTV who just specialize in parties and fun' (Hoye 2001: 26).

Tom Freston (chairman, MTV Networks): 'We wanted to build an annual franchise to make music videos a more credible art form. The *VMA* brought legitimacy to the music video genre' (Petrozzello 1998: 30).

The mystique of the live event establishes that the musicians can actually 'deliver' and are willing to do so for MTV. Forever after, the performances are fondly remembered as MTV moments, as much corporate milestones as musical keepsakes, even when the musical virtuosity involved is greater than that of Madonna. And these performances are short. They are live for the purpose of being recorded, re-run and re-packaged. This is deliberate and primary, not accidental or incidental. Although Madonna and MTV have an ongoing symbiosis, the primary benefit Madonna has gained from this relationship is the interminable re-running of her music videos, of which those derived from her *Video Music Awards* performances are only a small percentage. The more important legacy of 'Like a Virgin' is the (albeit ambiguous) legitimacy it lent to MTV at a time when MTV was trying – by the roundabout means of award ceremonies and live music – to convince the world (and perhaps itself) of the worthiness of music video.

Notes

1. An earlier version of this chapter was presented at the conference of the Popular Culture Association, Dublin, August 6, 2003.
2. *Remote Control* producer Joe Davola confirms the presence of a second stage in MTV's approach to programming: 'MTV was moving into the second phase – doing stripped programming. Half-hour shows other than videos' (Hoye 2001: 84).
3. See also Denisoff (1988: 332).
4. It is quite possible, and even likely, that some or all of Madonna's other *Video Music Awards* performances have been replayed as music videos (although I have not seen them in that format). Her *VMA* performances, in addition to those mentioned in the text, include 'Causing a Commotion' (1987), 'Bye Bye Baby' (1993) and 'Shanti'/'Ray of Light' (1998). In addition, she has appeared as a presenter at the event on several occasions.
5. I do not think and do not wish to suggest that Madonna, or her backup singers, lip-synched any of these performances. However, the *New York Times* review of the 1985 *VMA* show offhandedly noted that 'too many performers clearly were lip-synching' (Schneider 1986).

Chapter 13

Popular music performance and cultural memory Queen: Live Aid, Wembley Stadium, London, July 13, 1985

Susan Fast

> What we remember is highly selective and how we retrieve it says as much about desire and denial as it does about remembrance ... All memories are 'created' in tandem with forgetting; to remember everything would amount to being overwhelmed by memory. Forgetting is a necessary component in the construction of memory. Yet the forgetting of the past in a culture is often highly organized and strategic (Sturken 1997: 7).

Was Queen's performance at Live Aid the high point of the 16-hour concert? What was a certainty to me about the event when I began to write this chapter has become an intellectual tangle that revolves around the issues of cultural memory and the study of performance. When I came to read accounts of the 'mega event' written shortly after the concert, Queen's performance was nowhere particularly singled out; it is mentioned as having been *good* – indeed, *very* good – but so too are those of other performers on the day (especially U2). Yet I was certain that this performance was widely hailed as 'the best', a view confirmed in discussions with other contributors to this book, and so I knew on some level that I had not simply made this up myself. Where did this idea originate? Whose memory is it? On what is the memory based? What politics of remembering might be operative?[1]

How can we begin to answer these questions? For Live Aid, the enterprise of analysis is complicated by several factors. We must first ask, 'what *was* Live Aid, and for whom?' A much-too-simple answer is that it was a benefit concert for African famine relief, organized by Boomtown Rats singer Bob Geldof, that occurred in two live venues, Wembley Stadium in London and John F. Kennedy Stadium in Philadelphia. It featured about 60 different artists, and was aired on television in 160 countries. The concert began in London at 12.00 noon local time. Some of this early portion of the concert was shown on television in North America, although which performances one saw depended upon which channel one watched. Performances began in JFK Stadium at 9.00 a.m. local time. At 12.00 noon local Philadelphia time, the two concerts were linked via satellite, and live acts alternated with acts shown on video screens at the two stadiums. So, for example, Bryan Adams played in Philadelphia at noon, and this was transmitted live to Wembley, where it was seen on video screens; U2 played next at Wembley and this was shown, live, on video screens at JFK Stadium; both performances were shown on television. This description of the 'concert', however, does not take into account that in addition to the 'main' live shows in London and Philadelphia, there was also Oz For Africa, which occurred on the night of July 12 in Sydney, as well as benefits held simultaneously on July 13 in numerous other countries, with names other than Live Aid, but which were all inspired by it and staged for the same cause of African famine relief. The familiar description, therefore, of Live Aid as a concert that took place in London and Philadelphia, marginalizes these other shows in a way that replicates the global hegemony of Britain and the US, as does, in fact, singling out a British band as having given the best performance (rather than, for example, the widely praised performance of INXS as part of Oz For Africa). In addition, the show was broadcast on radio as well as television, and money was raised for the cause through locally organized telethons held via all these media. Although there was a single satellite feed for the London/ Philadelphia show, it was reported in *Rolling Stone* that for the Philadelphia portion of the event alone

> at least twenty-five video cameras covered the action in JFK stadium. These signals were fed to what were called the stadium trucks, where various producers decided which camera shots to use and when to use them. Another truck handled the signals from London, Australia, Japan, the Soviet Union, Holland, Austria, Yugoslavia and West Germany. All those signals were then routed to the various networks, each of which put its own spin on what would eventually be seen or heard (Goldberg 1985: 32).

As Neal Ullestad has noted, 'Live Aid was first and foremost a media event of the highest order. The aid, the music, and the musicians were quite secondary to the event itself' (1992: 45). While this might be slightly overstated, the fact is that the magnitude of this event – the spectacle of it – was, indeed, overwhelming, and its organization and very existence tend to overshadow, in many accounts, its specific moments. Indeed, when I watched the complete MTV broadcast in order to write this chapter, my initial response was how absurd it seems that anyone *could* single out a particular performance in the wake of 16 hours of television that included not only a heart-wrenching social cause, but also a parade of popular music celebrities, the appearance of any one of which makes heads turn. The range of performances, from reunions (The Who, Led Zeppelin), through acoustic performances of hits (Phil Collins, Sting), to spectacular collaborations (Mick Jagger and Tina Turner), across vast stylistic differences (Queen v. Sade v. Patti Labelle v. the Beach Boys), makes the whole enterprise of picking a 'best' seem suspect, to say the least. My response is congruous with that of reviews written directly after the concert, in which most performances are given equal weight and none is particularly singled out. But, of course, choosing a 'best' performance is one avenue through which the event can be remembered in some coherent way; as Hayden White has observed, 'the value attached to narrativity in the representation of real events arises out of a desire to have real events display the coherence, integrity, fullness and closure of an image of life that is and can only be imaginary' (Sturken 1997: 8).[2] The desire for narrative closure pushes us to remember some things and forget others, which, in this case, allows us to make sense of a complex event. The question is, of course, who articulates the narrative, and why?

A further difficulty in writing about Live Aid is that there was never a commercial video or soundtrack album released (unimaginable now) and the acquisition of a video or audio recording has, until recently, been quite difficult. This may account for the relative lack of academic literature around Live Aid: those music performance events that have been captured on video and that are easily available have, perhaps, become more memorable and more profoundly embedded in our consciousnesses because we can view them repeatedly: 'camera images are central to the interpretation of the past' (Sturken 1997: 11). Are we then to rely on memory for the analysis of the event? If so, on the memories of those who attended the concert at Wembley or JFK, or of those in attendance at one of the events in another country, or of those who watched the BBC broadcast, the MTV broadcast, the prime time three-hour live special that aired on the ABC network, or of those who heard a radio broadcast? Do we rely on the television broadcast shown in, for example, France, which aired from 10.08 p.m. local time on July 13 until 5.00 a.m. the next morning (with a break for late night news at 11.40 p.m.) and which interspersed taped segments from performances that had taken place earlier in the day with live feed from the Philadelphia portion of the show? Is it ethically acceptable for the researcher in a situation such as this to rely on bootleg video?[3] Might we look to BBC-TV's ten-year retrospective, broadcast in the summer of 1995? Even if we were to rip Queen's performance out of the context of any one of these Live Aids, which is problematic, we would be dealing with different performances – complete, edited, differently introduced, interrupted by commercials and VJ banter, potentially not shown at all and so on.[4]

Hence there are numerous ways in which Queen's performance on that day might be remembered, might be privileged or not privileged. One way of thinking about the different means through which performances may be represented/ remembered is as 'technologies of memory – objects, images, and representations [through which cultural memory is produced]' (Sturken 1997: 9). I wish to present and discuss here six such technologies of memory with respect to Queen's performance at Live Aid.

1

If I had to rely on my own memory in writing this account, it would be a vague one, nearly 20 years after the fact, with no particular reason to remember Live Aid as an important or momentous occasion in my life. I watched parts of the concert in my apartment living room in Iowa City (I was in my third year of graduate school), my then-husband flipping back and forth between some sports event (probably football) and Live Aid. I was studying at our kitchen table and I recall wandering in and out of the living room as I heard familiar voices singing. By that point, I had lost the strong connection to popular music I had enjoyed while growing up, in favour of trying to be a 'serious' musicologist, and the entire event seemed strangely distant, yet familiar, to me. The most vivid memory I have is of watching the reunited Led Zeppelin performing 'Stairway To Heaven' and saying aloud what a pity it was that Robert Plant couldn't sing anymore. Having not followed his solo career, and not allowing that this performance might be an anomaly, this seemed to me an unfathomable loss. Queen's performance? I don't know whether I even saw it.

2

'I'm just not sure', I say to my friend and music afficionado Matt, 'how Queen's performance came to be hailed as the best one at Live Aid.' 'Have you seen it?' he asks. 'It was absolutely amazing.' 'Which version of it have you seen?' 'The one on the ten-year anniversary show.'

This exchange triggers my memory regarding where and how Queen's performance at Live Aid might have become privileged for me ... and perhaps for a lot of others as well. The version of the BBC retrospective that I watched and have on tape (so thankfully the patient reader does not have to endure my vague memories) was the one shown on MuchMusic in Canada in the summer of 1995. It is an eight-hour documentary that includes highlights from the concert, introduced and sometimes interrupted by interviews and commentary from the musicians themselves, by other performers who were part of the event, by concert organizers, and – importantly – by some fans who were at the Wembley concert. There is a kind of spectacle created in this documentary that is different from the spectacle created in the live broadcasts on the day of the concert; this is created in part by the way the performances are remembered for the viewer by those who made them, or by those who watched them. The documentary also includes long segments of film that show Geldof back in Ethiopia, where a substantial amount of the money from Live Aid (an estimated $90 million was raised) went to help people rebuild their lives, juxtaposed with horrific scenes of people starving in the same places ten years earlier. It is a moving testimony to the power of popular music, providing that one might hope against hope that the narrative represents reality. In fact, it is impossible to determine whether this documentary is more about remembering Live Aid or more about contemplating what Live Aid accomplished. In a very important way, it is also about the spectacle of contemporary technology which, the viewer is constantly reminded, was the means through which this event took its particular shape. In some ways, the performances and the cause were overshadowed by the 'triumph of technology' and, in fact, how well the technology worked is partly responsible for making some performances more memorable than others.

Certainly not all of the performances that took place at Live Aid were shown in this retrospective, so already the producers were remembering for us: who's in, who's out and why (or, as Sturken might ask, 'what do we forget in order to remember?'). Perhaps because the documentary was made by the BBC, none of the performances that took place in Philadelphia before noon were included, and although some of the American acts who performed later in Philadelphia were shown, the documentary has a distinctly British bias (only British musicians are interviewed). There is a construction of national identity here that mirrors that found in press reviews of the concerts; namely that when the concert is remembered from the point of view of British musicians, producers and reporters, it is the British portion of the concert that tends to be singled out. Likewise, of course, if the concert is remembered from the American point of view, American performances are privileged. In addition, all of the documentary's featured performers (except Sade in London and Tina Turner – with Mick Jagger – in Philadelphia) were white. One of the searing criticisms of Live Aid was that there were so few black artists on the bill (Goldberg 1985: 31; Garofalo 2002: 314). Geldof has insisted that he did contact a number of black artists, including Michael Jackson and Prince, but was unable to persuade them to participate (1986: 272, 280). However, it seems especially inappropriate that in the face of this criticism, a ten-year retrospective would edit out most of the performances by black artists that *did* take place on that day; for whatever reasons, they were clearly not considered worth remembering. That Queen's performance should be singled out as 'the best' is also interesting from the perspectives of national identity and of racial politics: why a white, British band?

Queen's performance comes a few hours into this documentary. They were introduced at Wembley by two British comedians, Mel Smith and Griff Rhys-Jones, dressed as policemen. They quip to the audience, 'We've had a bit of a complaint about the noise ... from a woman in Belgium!' Great cheers from the crowd. 'We'd like to introduce the next act which is ... Queen' and Rhys-Jones fumbles to remove his helmet in a gesture of mock respect, before saying 'Her Majesty!' Not all acts on this day are introduced (or, at least, not all of the introductions are shown on television) and those that are become singled out, privileged, in particular ways – as I will discuss below.

The camera captures a shot of the Wembley audience from the stage, including a woman holding a sign that says 'Queen works'. Other than signs and flags emblazoned with 'U2', Queen is the only other band that has prompted audience members to display such signs of allegiance; the camera seizing on this sign signals to the viewing audience that the band is especially important to members of the crowd and so, again, privileges this particular performance. The television screen is split in two and on the left side a preening Freddie Mercury appears before the crowd. He struts back and forth across the stage with exaggerated steps, chest out, arms in motion, working hard to transmit his physical energy to the huge crowd before him (72 000 at Wembley) as well as to those watching on the video screens at JFK and on television. On the right side of the screen appears an interview with Pete Smith, identified as the 'world wide event co-ordinator' for Live Aid, who sets up the performance in the following way:

> What we really wanted to achieve from a fund raising point of view was to get the artists to do what they're best known for, so in talking to everybody it would be a question of could you do your hits for us please and then we'll raise the most money. Looking back now I still find the segue that Queen did of all of their Number Ones not only exactly what they should have done but exactly what we needed.

Thus, before seeing Queen's performance, it is remembered for the viewer as the performance that best achieved the primary goal of the event, according to one of its senior organizers. How, therefore, can we not view what follows in those terms?

Watching Queen's performance, four elements emerge which worked to make it particularly powerful, and which may account for it being cited as the best of the day by so many; these are in addition to the obvious facts that it was musically tight (the group was on tour and so playing together regularly, and they spent three days rehearsing for Live Aid) and that there were no technical difficulties (such as the satellite feed) which plagued some of the other performances. Queen's performance was clearly part of the 'triumph of technology' of the day, in terms of both their musicianship and the equipment used to transmit it. But beyond this, there are (a) the way in which the performance was situated vis-à-vis the cause, (b) the manner in which it unfolded musically, (c) the nature and extent of audience participation, and (d) the way in which we view Mercury after his death from AIDS in 1991 that make this performance particularly special.

Before exploring these issues, I will describe some of the salient features of the performance as shown in the BBC documentary. It included, in part or whole, four songs, plus what I am calling an 'audience participation' segment:

1. 'Bohemian Rhapsody' (first two verses with chorus and guitar solo)
2. 'Radio Ga-Ga' (first two verses with chorus)
3. Audience participation segment with Mercury
4. 'We Will Rock You' (first verse only with extended chorus and guitar solo)
5. 'We Are the Champions' (complete).

After his initial walkabout at the front of the stage, Mercury sits down at the piano and begins to play the piano introduction of 'Bohemian Rhapsody', probably the band's best-known song. We can hear the massive audience singing along from the very beginning of the vocals, something that did not occur, to the same extent, in any other performance of the day. The camera is focused on Mercury and remains so throughout almost the entire performance, the most notable exceptions being shots of the crowd. The first of these comes as Mercury begins to sing, when the camera pulls away from him to an angle from behind the first 50 or so rows of the audience, and captures some audience members swaying their arms over their heads. The camera returns to the singer, still at the piano, and then pulls back out to a long shot of the stage for Brian May's guitar solo. A grand cadential chord is held while Mercury gets up from the piano and is handed a microphone; he begins marching around the stage again in time to the music, flirting shamelessly with the audience as the next song, 'Radio Ga-Ga', begins. At the chorus, he yells to the crowd 'Everybody!' and there is a shot of the audience (the same shot from about 50 rows back) pointing towards the stage, showing everyone in the camera's view with arms raised straight in the air while they sing 'All we hear is (clap, clap) Radio Ga-Ga (clap, clap)' followed by two short claps before the next line of the chorus, when they again punch their fists straight up in the air. The second time the chorus is sung, the camera captures the audience from the back of the stage, and we see a veritable sea of arms in the air, holding still and then clapping in tandem.

After 'Radio Ga-Ga' comes the first break in the music, and Mercury goes to the front of the stage to engage the audience in a round of call and response, using (as he often did in Queen concerts) musical gestures derived from classical music. They begin quite simply ('Eh-oh', dropping a perfect fourth, then rising a major second, which the crowd repeats) but become increasingly more complex, turning into vocalizations of considerable length and musical sophistication; he sounds like an opera singer warming up. But no matter what the complexity or dynamic level (from *ff* to *pp*) the crowd manages to follow him.

The band then launches into 'We Will Rock You', the anthemic song that has been used to rouse audiences at sporting events since it was released. Only a single verse of the song is sung by Mercury, before it goes into an extended chorus sung by the audience, into which Mercury interjects with comments such as 'I like it!' Of course, part of the impetus of this song comes from the simple but powerfully strong drum groove, which the audience again claps as it sings, and to which Mercury stomps forcefully across the stage. As the song's guitar solo begins, the television screen is split in two again, and we see Tony Hadley (of Spandau Ballet) saying of Mercury, 'he's just such a natural showman, and he just loved the day; and I've always been a fan of Queen anyway, great songs, great performance!' This is followed by members of Status Quo praising the performance, and by this endorsement from fellow musician Howard Jones:

> The power of their performance was just transcendent. Whether you like their music
> or not, you couldn't deny that it was just one of the best performances ever that
> anyone had done anywhere, ever.

The decision to cut away from May's guitar solo and insert interviews that frame
Queen's performance as spectacular by – importantly – fellow musicians, fellow
British musicians, keeps the focus on Mercury, instead of the band as a whole. The
television screen returns to a full shot of him back at the piano for 'We Are the
Champions' and this song features another stunning shot of the audience taken
from behind Mercury, a large segment of the crowd swaying back and forth, some
of the rows moving left to right, others moving right to left, to create an undulating
sea of humanity. The performance ends with another long-held cadential chord,
while the camera now pans out to show the entire stadium from above, and then
moves back to a final slow-motion shot of Mercury running across the stage.

Jennifer DeBoer has tracked Queen's reception in the rock media and noted the
often-negative way in which their music was covered. Considering press reviews
by writers such as Dave Marsh, Ken Barnes and Paul Du Noyer, she concludes that
'the reviews are filled with criticisms that betray a general dislike for Queen and
their music' (which she attributes to a widespread notion that the band was too
commercially successful to have any musical value), that they were regarded as
'arrogant', and that their music was characterized by 'histrionic vocals, abrupt and
pointless compositional complexity, a dearth of melody [and] emotional emptiness
dressed up as spectacle' (1999: 18–20). And in reviews of the band's Live Aid
appearance, the power of the performance is generally qualified in some way:
'Let's just say that if they could do it like this every time then even the MM team
would be queuing up for tickets. A guitar solo-free zone. Freddie, what about it?'
(*Melody Maker* July 20, 1985: 30). Even Howard Jones's hyperbolic praise of the
performance, quoted above, is qualified by the words 'whether you like their music
or not'. DeBoer argues that Mercury's flamboyant image and the band's particular
brand of musical excess challenged notions of rock authenticity, especially in
terms of how these relate to normative ideas of gender performativity in rock
music. She theorizes Mercury's image, using the term 'camp sensibility' (1999:
67–81) and emphasizing the notions of ironic self presentation, excessiveness and
superficiality. However, she does not carry over the idea of camp to Queen's music
(even though she does explore it as 'feminized' in comparison to other kinds of
hard rock). I would suggest that it was not only Mercury's stage persona that
enacted a camp aesthetic, but that this aesthetic was also operative in Queen's
music, for it is here that they so often 'prise[d] the form ... away from the content
... revelling in the style while dismissing the content as trivial' (Dyer 1999: 113).
Perhaps the best example of this is the mock opera 'Bohemian Rhapsody', a
song which 'parodies various elements of opera in its use of bombastic choruses,

sarcastic recitative and distorted Italian operatic phraseology ... not to lend musical cachet but rather to mock the musical conventions of [opera]' (McLeod 2001: 192). Rather than think about these features purely in terms of parody, however, we might think of them in terms of camp. Some of the defining elements of opera are present, but they work as surface, as de-contextualized artifice, illustrating Esther Newton's observation that what is important has shifted 'from what a thing is to how it looks, from what is done to how it is done [which] results in an overwhelming presence of excess and exaggeration' (DeBoer 1999: 69). There is in 'Bohemian Rhapsody' the 'invisible wink', the humour of camp performativity (DeBoer 1999: 70), which the rock critics who dismissed it undoubtedly missed. In fact, this camp sensibility is present in much of Queen's music – certainly in similar grandiose pieces such as 'We Are the Champions', but also in a song such as 'Crazy Little Thing Called Love', in its borrowings from rockabilly style.

How is this important to the band's performance at Live Aid? Garofalo has commented that 'the character of Live Aid and certainly most of the reportage about the event were decidedly apolitical' (1992: 28). What, exactly, is meant by the term 'political' in this context is an important question to ask – must it be the explicit mention of African famine relief, or song lyrics that are 'political', or words from the performers spelling out the terms of the African famine crisis and its relationship to western governments? I also wonder whether it is not so much what the concert *was*, or what the media coverage *was*, as it is our memories that want to make it apolitical. In watching the ten-year retrospective, and the complete MTV broadcast, and in re-reading coverage of the event, both before and after it occurred, I was struck by how much the issue of African famine relief was foregrounded. A particularly wrenching moment of the concert came at the end of David Bowie's performance, when instead of playing the fifth song he had planned, he introduced a CBC documentary that began by depicting a tiny, starving, African child trying to stand up, to the strains of the Cars' ballad 'Drive'. There are shots of audience members at Wembley in tears as they watch this on the video screens. Interestingly, although Bowie gave a remarkably good musical performance, his is nowhere singled out as 'the best'. My conclusion from this is that Queen's camp performance, including the campy introduction by the British comedians, made people feel good, made them laugh, and lightened the terribly heavy load of the day. And the call and response segment allowed the audience to participate in the creation of camp, instead of merely watching it being created. What is both humorous and terribly cheeky about that segment is that the vocalizations that Mercury expects audience members to copy should, theoretically, be much too difficult for them; he pulls gestures out of a musical repertory that belongs to elite culture, which only a privileged few should be 'talented' enough to (re)produce, and yet manages to get a massive rock audience to succeed at the task. As Dyer has recognized, camp can 'demystify the images and world-view of art. We are encouraged by schooling to be very solemn in the presence of art. Camp can make us see that what art … give[s] us are not the Truth or Reality but fabrications. It stops us thinking that those who create the landscape of culture know more about life than we do ourselves' (1999: 115). The exaggeratedly grand style of the music, Mercury's extravagant, tongue-in-cheek flirtations with the audience and with the camera (including sticking his wiggling tongue out at it to punctuate one of those long, cadential chords), pulled viewers away from the horrors of the African famine, or maybe made it bearable. Why *not* remember what makes us feel good? But the real power of camp in this performance comes from the way in which that sensibility can allow a serious undertone in; for some gay men, for example, camp is 'a form of self-defence … the fact that gay men could so sharply and brightly make fun of themselves meant that the real awfulness of their situation could be kept at bay' (Dyer 1999: 110). Although I am sensitive to the personal politics of claiming camp specifically as a site of empowerment for gay men, I would like to suggest that it may be possible to extrapolate on the idea that it was a mode of self-defence during Live Aid as well. Thus, Queen's performance is fun, but the 'invisible wink' makes us understand that the fun lies only on the surface, and provides only a slight gloss over a terrible situation. This, it seems to me, makes their performance quite profoundly political.

The audience participation in Queen's performance is also worthy of further comment. Geldof insisted that artists play their biggest hits at Live Aid because he was certain that this would raise the most money. He conceived of the event as a 'global jukebox', which meant that popular musicians with enormous influence (generally meaning those most commercially successful) would each play their greatest hits for 15 minutes (Geldof 1986: 264). Queen not only adhered to his suggestion, but replicated the recorded versions of their songs almost exactly, and in a particular way. Instead of performing the entire song, in most cases they played abbreviated versions, turning the performance into a medley of their hits, thus allowing themselves to reference more of their hits than if they had played entire songs. This strategy also allowed them to deliver the most familiar parts of these songs, typically the choruses. The result was not only that Queen performed more of their hits, but that these were paced in a particular way – movement from one hit to another was swift, creating over and over again that rush of adrenaline that we feel upon hearing an 'old friend' of a song performed live. Furthermore, the constant arrival at a chorus allowed audience members to participate more often, and more fully (although they did also sing the verses of 'Bohemian Rhapsody', as mentioned above). Mercury also orchestrated the audience's physical engagement with the music, modelling strong gestures that indicated how and when they should clap, or put their fists in the air. The camera shots showing the audience's (apparent) unanimous participation are incredibly powerful, and are perhaps also an indicator that this performance was 'the best': in no other performance was there this level and intensity of audience participation. Physical engagement with a performance, whether through singing, clapping or bodily movement, makes one feel invested because there is participation in the creation of the performance.

Finally, what makes this performance memorable is Mercury's body, which is athletic, strong, lithe, healthy; it exudes excess energy that can hardly be contained, that makes him appear playful and almost giddy (campy, to be sure) in combination with decisive, angular gestures that project strength and control. His attire is simple – jeans, sneakers and a white sleeveless vest that reveals a tanned, muscular, upper body. There is something about the way in which Mercury constructs his body here that conforms to notions of idealized masculinity often exhibited through the bodies of, for example, manual labourers and athletes: strength, hardness, control, endurance (Connell 1995). Perhaps my attention is drawn to this aspect of the performance because Mercury has since died of AIDS, and the photographs and video of his thin, fragile body just before death offer such a stark contrast to the image of him at Live Aid. Could it be that, in retrospect, it is this that makes Queen's performance on that day so special, so singular? The television documentary, made four years after his death, does seem to present Queen's performance at Live Aid as a kind of memorial to Mercury: the nearly complete focus on the singer (as opposed to Brian May during his guitar solos) and the slow motion shot of Mercury at the end of the performance (the only time this editing technique is used) which suggests 'that the action [is] tak[ing] place in a dream or fantasy ... [or as] a way of dwelling on a moment of spectacle or high drama' (Bordwell & Thompson 1993: 80). The slow motion pulls his image out of ordinary time, making him appear either other-worldly or emblematic of the past (and creating a nostalgia for him).

Or is it the stark difference between this healthy, strong body and the wasted bodies of starving Africans with which it was juxtaposed on the day of Live Aid that makes us want to remember Queen's performance as 'the best'?

3

On a website called *Live Aid: The Greatest Show On Earth*, there is a page devoted to 'Memories of Live Aid', which the owner of the site solicited around the time of the tenth anniversary of the concert (www.herald.co.uk/local_info/la_memories.html). There are 31 different accounts of the concert posted; of these, ten mention Queen's performance – the comments range from 'they stole the show' to inclusions of the band in a list of the day's great performances. Five of these ten people attended the Wembley show, and one watched on British television (the others watched on Dutch and Australian television; one person did not specify location). Only one person who mentioned Queen as a highlight of the day watched on American television, and no one who was at the JFK show saw the band as a highlight.

Similarly, press reviews of the concert tended to privilege those performances that took place in the presence of the reviewer. *Melody Maker*'s review of the live portion of the concert at Wembley largely ignored the American acts that appeared on the video screens and the review ended by commenting on Elton John's performance (there was, however, an additional review of the television broadcast). Richard Williams paid very little attention to the American side of the concert in *The Times* (1985) whereas the coverage in the *New York Times* began by reporting that Joan Baez opened the show in Philadelphia, went on to include short interviews with audience members in attendance there, but hardly mentioned individual musical performances at all (Fein 1985:). In *Billboard*, Paul Grein, who attended the Philadelphia show, described the appearance of Teddy Pendergrass as 'the first peak' of the show, as it was the first time the singer had appeared in public since his near-fatal car crash; he cited the performance of Mick Jagger and Tina Turner as the 'high point' of the show (1985: 3), and he overlooked the performances shown on video screens. None of the reviews referred to Queen's performance at all.

Both the website memories and the reviews of Live Aid indicate the centrality of 'liveness' in making a determination of 'the best' performances. Fellow contributor Philip Auslander has asserted that

> the use of giant video screens at sporting events, music and dance concerts ... is a direct illustration of [Walter] Benjamin's concept [of a mass desire for proximity]: the kind of proximity and intimacy we can experience with television, which has become our model for close-up perception ... can be reproduced only by means of their 'videation' ... The ubiquity of reproduction of performances of all kinds in our culture has led to the depreciation of live performance (1999: 35–6).

Although this is undoubtedly true, I wonder whether the Live Aid event – where there were both live and video performances – might offer evidence that the embodied presence of performers, as opposed to, or at least in addition to, their video representations, is not only preferred, but, in fact, offers a more powerful, and hence more memorable, experience.

4

The introduction of Queen on the MTV broadcast begins with American comedians Chevy Chase and Joe Piscapo in Philadelphia. The television screen is split in half and they appear on the right side; on the left side of the screen is the stage at Wembley, which is being prepared for Queen's performance. Chase and Piscapo introduce the band as follows:

> Chevy: We have a special treat for you; I believe Joe wants to tell us about it, from London. Joe, what's it all about?
> Joe: Well, very excited, ah we're going to go to London, which you'll be able to see on your Diamond Vision screens. Queen has done a little something for us.
> Chevy: We're going to see the Queen?
> Joe: No, no the rock group Queen is actually what I was talking about.

Chevy: It is not the queen?
Joe: No it's not.
Chevy: Are they queens?
Joe: No, no, no, no, no, I don't want to get anybody in trouble here. This is Queen,
this is straight, this is not royalty *per se*, this is just Queen, rock and roll.
Chevy: Oh, there are no queens here and this is not Prince!

At least for the Philadelphia crowd, Queen's performance was thus positioned as 'gay' through this overtly homophobic introduction (even though Piscapo tries to deny that there's anything un-straight about to happen). How might this have affected the reception of Queen's performance for the Philadelphia and MTV audiences? Can a 'gay' band be considered 'best'? (Is it, in fact, homophobic fear that makes those who do praise Queen's performance at Live Aid feel the need to qualify it in the ways they do?) Throughout the band's performance we are offered several shots of MTV VJs Nina Blackwood and Alan Jackson watching Queen's performance on video monitors, in some cases with their backs turned to the camera, bobbing their heads or playing a little air guitar along with Brian May. They are certainly engaged with the performance, but not in the way they are with other performances of the day; they model for the viewer an interest, but not an emotional investment. Of course there are none of the framing interviews that tell the viewer how good the performance is.

This version of Queen's performance includes the song 'The Hammer Will Fall' which they performed after Freddie Mercury's operatic interaction with the audience. The band played the entire song, and I wonder whether this was edited out of the ten-year retrospective not only because of its length, but because it is a relatively unfamiliar song, whose complete performance (as opposed to an excerpt) detracts somewhat from the tightness of the edited version. The one interesting performance element of the song missing from the television retrospective is Mercury's decision to address the television camera directly, in addition to the live audience. He peers directly into the lens, touching it, dancing with it, much as Bono did years later in U2's 'Zoo TV' tour, where the video camera became a kind of cyborg partner for the singer. This tends to weaken, somewhat, the strong connection between the live audience and Mercury. There is also a greater coverage of Brian May's guitar solos; this draws attention away from Mercury and his interaction with the crowd, diluting to some degree the potency of the performance, and certainly the memorializing tendencies of the retrospective.

MTV decided to cut away to commercials at this point – seven of them, to be exact. They sold Camay oily skin formula soap; Chevy Cavalier ('live today's Chevy, with an interior that comforts your very soul'); Sun Country wine cooler; Foot Locker ('when you've got your body going, we've got the shoes'); Chevy Camero: Pepsi (pitched by Lionel Ritchie); a General Electric cassette player ('the power of music: no one lets you experience it like General Electric'); and English Leather men's cologne ('with its clean masculine scent'). There is something obscene about selling luxury products such as these, with their self-absorbed hook lines, in the midst of a benefit concert for famine relief. The BBC broadcast did not include commercials (easier for it to do, since it is a public broadcaster). More recently, the spate of benefit concerts shown on television following the terrorist attacks of September 11 did not include commercials, even though they were broadcast on the main US commercial networks.[5] Interrupting the everyday televisual flow, especially the commercial part of that flow, for a benefit concert enhances the specialness of the event and signals the willingness – momentarily – to set aside capitalist self-interest for a particular cause. That MTV chose to show commercials during Live Aid (along with the focus on the VJs and their generally vacuous commentary) places the station as, at least, out of touch with the seriousness of the issue (Goldberg, Hendrickson and McNamara 1985; Garofalo 2002).

The show returns to the VJs after the commercials; we can faintly hear Queen's performance of 'We Will Rock You' behind the VJ's introduction of Marilyn McCoo, one of the hosts of the syndicated television broadcast of Live Aid. The camera cuts away to a pre-taped interview with McCoo, in which she is asked how she became involved with Live Aid (this is the standard question asked of celebrities that day). The camera returns to a live shot of the VJs, and Queen's performance of 'We Are the Champions' can be heard in the background. The two VJs proceed to talk about the heat, how everyone has donated their time and about some of the upcoming performers. Their conversation is interrupted when VJ Alan Jackson announces that they are going to 'do some more Queen'. They rejoin Queen for the last chorus of 'We Are the Champions', capturing the sea of swaying bodies at Wembley and the final, powerful cadence of the song.

Although the opening three songs of the performance are shown in their entirety, and a good deal of the energy and momentum of Queen's performance is offered during that time, the power of the performance is compromised by the homophobic introduction, by the commercial break and by the decision to use the audio of some of the performance as background to interviews and VJ banter. In the light of this, it is difficult to imagine how someone might single out this version of the performance as being the best of the day.

5

The *Live Aid World-Wide Concert Book* (Hillmore 1985), published immediately after the event, is largely a picture book, but also includes a prose narrative through which the event is remembered. The first image in the book is a shot of the finale at Wembley that covers a full two pages; the last image shows the finale at JFK, also covering two full pages. These finales were musically ragged affairs, but they did bring the majority of artists who had participated in the live concerts together on stage to sing, respectively, the two songs with which the drive to raise money for African famine relief had begun in 1984 – the British 'Do They Know

It's Christmas' and the American 'We Are the World'. Framing the event with photographic images that, in effect, 'sum up' the day's performances is a neat, compact way of remembering, of bringing coherence to – or bringing together in one image – the vast array of individual events that occurred on that day. It also privileges moments that were particularly spectacular in terms of 'star power'. Contained between them is a chronological presentation of photographs and a narrative account of the performances. While Queen is privileged with four pages of pictures (not the only performers to be afforded this much space), most of them of Mercury, there is only a single, short paragraph of prose that does not mark the band's performance out in any particular way.

6

A bootleg video of the performance as it was broadcast on the BBC appears in my mailbox and another two pieces of the cultural memory puzzle fall into place. This is the 'complete' performance, unedited and uninterrupted, which includes a performance of 'Crazy Little Thing Called Love' not shown in the other two versions I've seen. This song follows 'The Hammer Will Fall'. It occurs to me that the reason this song might have been excluded from the ten-year retrospective is that it is so stylistically different from the other songs included there. 'Bohemian Rhapsody', 'Radio Ga-Ga', 'We Will Rock You' and 'We Are the Champions' are anthemic, epic, theatrical, incredibly grand pieces of music; heard back to back, with the operatic audience participation segment included, they create a stylistically cohesive unit which acts as an aural equivalent to spectacle, and which also keeps the camp aesthetic in the forefront of the performance. 'Crazy Little Thing Called Love' is stylized rockabilly – it is fun, light, corny, camp, yes, but different to the other songs. On the other hand, the song was one of the band's biggest hits, and the crowd responded enthusiastically when Mercury began to sing it; its familiarity provided another peak in the performance – another moment when a familiar song was begun. Its stylistic contrast to the other songs in the set may also have provided a crucial break from their uniformity. Just before the song begins, Mercury speaks to the crowd (the only time he does so during the performance) to thank them for coming and making it such a special occasion. While it is always enthralling when a performer speaks to an audience, the fact that this was edited out of the ten-year retrospective keeps Mercury at more of a distance from the viewer, and locates the power of his performance entirely within the framework of the music. It is during 'Crazy Little Thing Called Love' that the only technical glitch of Queen's performance occurs – an annoying recurrence of feedback. Given some of the other technical problems that occurred on that day – the power at Wembley went out during The Who's performance and the satellite feed was temporarily severed, and Paul McCartney's microphone failed during 'Let It Be' – this was relatively minor, and to hear it now is a reminder of just how technically impressive Queen's overall performance was.

In addition, the performance is framed by interviews with members of the band before and after Live Aid. A few days before the concert, they are shown rehearsing – something that is important within the discourse of their performance having been 'the best', since one of the things 'best' means is that they were musically accurate; not all performers were so accurate on the day, and in those cases the performances became more about the audience seeing them than hearing them. In a BBC interview with Brian May given the day after the concert, the reporter (the white, male, British reporter) begins by saying, 'by all accounts you were the total hit of the concert'. Although the performance was not singled out by the press in the immediate aftermath of Live Aid, it may be that it was singled out by television (and, perhaps, British television broadcasts in particular) with the result that British audiences who watched these interviews probably had it embedded in their memories that Queen's performance was singled out, without necessarily remembering that it was the television interview, unrepeated, fleeting, that gave them this idea.

A final technology of memory that occurs many years after the concert comes from Bob Geldof. In a biography of Freddie Mercury written after his death, he reflects on Queen's performance at Live Aid (and, again, notice the way in which he qualifies his praise):

> Queen were absolutely the best band of the day. Whatever your personal taste was irrelevant. When the day came, they played the best, they had the best sound, they used their time to the full. They understood the idea *exactly* – that it was a global jukebox, as I'd described it. They just went and smashed out one hit after another. It was just unbelievable (Jones 1997: 348).

Notes

1. I wish to thank Karen Pegley for initially problematizing the received idea that Queen's performance was the highlight of Live Aid, and for suggesting that there may be a politics of remembering surrounding this notion. I also wish to thank Liss Platt, Claudia Manley, Christina Baade and my research assistant Matt Caldwell for their invaluable assistance.
2. The list of performers and the order in which they appeared is far too long to include here; a reliable source for this information is the website entitled *Live Aid* (www.live-aid.chez.tiscali.fr).
3. I would not normally raise the issue of ethics with respect to using bootleg video, but in this case bootleggers are making a profit from the illegal sale of a charity event. As Bob Geldof has pointed out, this is money that could be – should be – going to help feed hungry people, and he himself has been instrumental in exposing a bootlegger and putting him out of business. Further, Geldof promised to release a commercial

DVD of the concert by the end of 2004, the proceeds of which would go to charity. In writing this article I have relied on a bootleg copy of the MTV version of the concert and also on a compilation video of live Queen performances. Although I do not pretend that this solves the problem, I have made a contribution to charity, equal in value to what I spent on the bootleg tapes.

4.   Karen Pegley's (2002) work on MTV and MuchMusic is my model for analysis of this kind of television event. She examines not only individual videos, but also the context in which they appear, which is important in terms of how we understand them.

5.   For analysis of some of these events, see Susan Fast and Karen Pegley 'America, a Tribute to Heroes: Music, Mourning, Body, Nation After 9/11' (forthcoming) and Susan Fast and Karen Pegley 'Nation Building in a Time of Crisis: Canadian and American Responses to 9/11 via the Benefit Concert' (forthcoming).

Chapter 14

Nirvana:
University of Washington,
Seattle, January 6, 1990

Tim Hughes

The ascendance of Nirvana's *Nevermind* (1991) to the top of the *Billboard* album charts is widely regarded as a crucial event in the history of popular music. Often referred to as the first punk record to reach Number One, thereby representing the acceptance of punk by the mass market, it has also been described as a triumph of independent music over corporate pop, the end of metal, the beginning of the 1990s, and in numerous other vague, but deeply reverential, ways:

> Nirvana announced the end of one rock & roll era and the start of another. In essence, Nirvana transformed the 80s into the 90s. They didn't do it alone, of course – cultural change is never that simple. But in 1991, 'Smells Like Teen Spirit' proved a defining moment in rock history. A political song that never mentions politics, an anthem whose lyrics can't be understood, a hugely popular hit that denounces commercialism, a collective shout of alienation, it was '(I Can't Get No) Satisfaction' for a new time and a new tribe of disaffected youth. It was a giant fuck-you, an immensely satisfying statement about the inability to be satisfied (DeCurtis 1994).

But perhaps the most enduring aspect of Nirvana's legacy is the way they changed the 'sound' of popular music, increasing the intensity level of mass-market music in the United States and around the world. In making this claim, I am not trying to be poetic, to 'fruitlessly describe the greatness of music that needs no apologist' (Hughes 2000: 168); rather, I am referring to a specific, tangible quality of their music and lyrics that was the result of a fusion of diverse musical traditions into something that was entirely new in 1991.

The transformation wrought by Nirvana was largely the result of a studio recording, yet the key to *Nevermind*'s success lay in the ability of producer Butch Vig and engineer Andy Wallace to capture the raw power of a live punk band on CD. Just as with many other revolutionary acts such as Billie Holiday, Charlie Parker, Jimi Hendrix and the Ramones, the source of Nirvana's remarkable success as a studio act is found in their live performances. In this regard, it is instructive to examine Nirvana's live sound in as unadorned a fashion as possible.

In this chapter I will focus on the music of the Nirvana concert that took place on January 6, 1990, in the ballroom of the Husky Union Building (HUB) of the University of Washington in Seattle. Unlike the other performances analysed in this volume, the concert itself is not in itself unique, nor historically important, nor particularly remarkable. It is, however, *representative*, of a particular time, a particular place and a particular stage in the evolution of a band. It was not their first performance at the HUB, although it was their last (numerous Nirvana websites state that they were banned from campus after this show, although I have seen no documented evidence of this). As a (relatively) local band, Nirvana played in Seattle frequently, so the audience was already familiar with them.[1] In addition, the concert took place well before Nirvana's rise to stardom in late 1991 – roughly halfway between the release of their first album, *Bleach* (1989) and *Nevermind*. This is important because it was not until after the release of the latter album that anyone – including the band members – had any idea that they would become stars. As a result, the concert provides a candid and revealing document of their live performance and sound, at a time when the foundations of their forthcoming and huge global presence were being fashioned in venue after venue.

From beginning to end, Nirvana was led by Kurt Cobain, who played guitar, sang and wrote all their original songs, and Krist Novoselic, who played bass. In January 1990, they employed their more familiar, three-person line-up, with Chad Channing playing drums. This was one of Channing's last shows with Nirvana; he was replaced by Dave Grohl later that year. The band had just returned from an often difficult European tour alongside Tad, and so a performance in Seattle was something of a homecoming. They had just recorded 'Sappy', but would not record again until the sessions which produced 'Sliver' in July.

The recording I used as a source is a bootleg, transferred directly to CD from a soundboard cassette.[2] My choice to use a bootleg recording requires some discussion. Scholarly analyses of popular music have generally been based on studio recordings. The few exceptions, such as Brackett (1995) and Boone (1997), have generally been based on commercially released live recordings. However, for a number of reasons, commercial recordings rarely document live performances accurately. Because legal permissions and contracts are involved, musicians know when they are being recorded for a live album or broadcast and, as a result, may consciously or subconsciously alter their style. In addition, live albums are frequently assembled from highlights of multiple shows, sometimes over substantial spans of time – Nirvana's own *From the Muddy Banks of the Wishkah* (1996) features songs recorded over a span of more than four years. Furthermore, in most cases live recordings are remixed in the studio, edited or selectively altered – following Jimi Hendrix's performance at Woodstock, three of the six musicians (percussionists Juma Sultan, Jerry Velez and guitarist Larry Lee) were entirely omitted from the commercially released recordings. Some musicians even overdub new parts in the studio – Frank Zappa often added new instruments and vocals to his 'live' records. And 'In Memory of Elizabeth Reed', from the celebrated *The Allman Brothers at Fillmore East* (1971), is actually a composite of two entirely different performances, spliced together. In contrast, bootleg recordings are much less likely to have been significantly altered, simply because editing and remixing is an expensive process and bootlegs are generally made as cheaply as possible. As a result, if care is taken in selecting the bootleg version, it can provide a document of a band's live sound of lower 'quality', but greater accuracy.

The set

The bootleg recording of Nirvana's HUB concert contains 15 tracks and runs for just under 47 minutes. Table 14.1 lists the 15 songs from the performance, the commercial release on which the conventional version of each song is found and their durations. The songs are all relatively short, ranging from 2:15 to 4:15 minutes. I will provide a brief description of each song before discussing the set as a whole.

Table 14.1   Songs performed by Nirvana, University of Washington, 6 January 1990

Song	Commercial release	Duration (mins)
1. 'Scoff'	*Bleach*	4:15
2. 'Floyd the Barber'	*Bleach*	2.28
3. 'Love Buzz'	*Bleach*	3:21
4. 'Dive'	*Incesticide*	4:08
5. 'Polly'	*Nevermind*	2:27
6. 'School'	*Bleach*	3:27
7. 'Big Cheese'	*Bleach*	3:27
8. 'Sappy'	none	3:18
9. 'Spank Thru'	*From the Muddy Banks of the Wishkaw*	3:24
10. 'Molly's Lips'	*Incesticide*	2:31
11. 'About a Girl'	*Bleach*	2:49
12. 'Breed'	*Nevermind*	3:35
13. 'Been a Son'	*Incesticide*	2:15
14. 'Negative Creep'	*Bleach*	2:24
15. 'Blew'	*Bleach*	2:57
	Total time	46:46

'Scoff' is based on a straightforward, repeated groove. The drum part is very simple, essentially seven eighth notes and an eighth rest divided between the tom-toms and snare:

Beat	1		2	3		4		1		2	3		4	
Snare		*			*				*			*			
Tom	*	*		*	*	*			*	*		*	*	*	
Bass	*			*					*			*			

Over this pattern the guitar and bass play a three-note, E-string riff with the same rhythm as the drums. The chorus changes to a decorated drum part and two alternating chords. The lyrics are a simple, rebellious rant against an authority figure, possibly a parent. Yet, like many of the songs from *Bleach*, there is far more than this description suggests, because it does not address the overall sound quality. The bass and guitar – heavily distorted – thunder, rather than plod, which gives them a strong, low-range presence and a saturated tone, while their quick pace and clear attack give them a swift percussiveness. The power and energy communicated on stage by Cobain and Novoselic, combined with Cobain's raw and sarcastic vocals, create an unusual degree of musical intensity to a song that is, essentially, the pout of a wise-ass teenager. In this performance, Cobain is already demonstrating his prodigious ability to articulate to others the passion and intensity of everyday life for a disaffected youth. 'Scoff' is a model for how most of the songs in this show work and, as such, is an ideal opening number.

Like many early Nirvana songs, 'Floyd the Barber' is reminiscent of the music of the Melvins, an Aberdeen punk band that greatly influenced Cobain and Novoselic. The song is a silly, juvenile and mildly disturbing portrait of the town of Mayberry, from the television series *The Andy Griffith Show*. It takes the stylized, wholesome, rural image of Mayberry and inverts it into something dark and twisted. This performance *does* plod – but deliberately so, in a mocking fashion, combining sophomoric humour and musical intensity. It also demonstrates the accuracy provided by bootlegs: Cobain's guitar and vocals suddenly drop out during the second half of the first verse, the sort of blemish that is eliminated from commercially released live recordings, but which is, of course, an integral part of live performance.

'Love Buzz' is a cover of a Shocking Blue song that Nirvana released in 1988 as their first single. Here, it begins with a quasi-Middle Eastern bass riff; Novoselic's bass is overdriven, but not heavily, and has a thin tone with very little upper-midrange sound. This meshes nicely with Cobain's wall of distorted guitar noise, which arrives in a burst of feedback at the end of the bass intro, accompanied by Channing's solid but unspectacular drums. After a few bars of noisy jamming, the band reduces the levels of volume, distortion and activity, while continuing to play the same groove – revealing Nirvana's renowned, two-gear, dynamic strategy.

Cobain delivers his vocals in a goofy, mush-mouthed accent, mocking the song even as he performs it.

Coming from *Bleach*, these opening three songs were already familiar to the audience (the opening bass riff of 'Love Buzz', in particular, drew cheers of recognition). They are more humorous and sarcastic than passionate; this is 'class-clown' music, hard, fun and irreverent. Having gained the ears of the audience, it's time to try out some stronger, and newer, material.

The lyrics of 'Dive' as performed here differ from the lyrics of the version later to appear on *Incesticide*, suggesting a song still in the process of creation. For example, the fourth verse has these words:

Pick me, pick me yeah
Everyone is hollow.
At ease at least, yeah
You can even swallow.

In the commercially released recording, Cobain sings:

Pick me, pick me yeah
Everyone is waiting.
Hit me, hit me yeah
I'm real good at hating.[3]

While more sophisticated than the first three songs, 'Dive' is still heavy and relatively slow. The most interesting part of the song, however, is the chorus, 'Dive ... dive ... dive ... dive in me' (repeated four times). It is simple, memorable and, above all, relevant to its performance, since stage-diving had come to be expected not just at Nirvana's shows but at punk and hard-rock shows throughout the region.

Today, 'Polly' is well known (having appeared on *Nevermind*) and controversial (because of its subject matter). At the HUB performance, it was the first song in the set to clearly demonstrate Cobain's skill at writing in a pop style. Based around two different cyclical chord progressions, it is played at a fairly quick tempo with a solid backbeat; Channing's drums work much better on this brand of medium-intensity punk-pop than on Nirvana's harder-driving songs. The vocals are, unusually for Cobain (except on ballads), sung without any overdriving or mannerisms. The lyrics come from the true story of a rapist and torturer that Cobain read about, and are told from the torturer's point of view. What makes the song so effectively creepy is its combination of a medium level of intensity, a brisk tempo and a catchy pop appeal. It is horrifying and attractive at the same time.

'Polly' segues directly into 'School' which is, in some ways, an inversion of the previous song. The volume, dynamic and activity levels of 'School' are high and Cobain's vocals and guitar are heavily overdriven, producing a marked level of intensity. Yet the lyrics are little more than a complaint about 'no recess' and being back in high school again. Once again, the combination of strong passion and routine griping is disturbing, and points to the pain that can fill everyday life. It is interesting to compare Channing's busy drumming at this performance with the part played by Dave Grohl on the November 1991 recording released on *From the Muddy Banks of the Wishkah*. Grohl's part is also extremely active, but he uses the cymbals much more extensively than Channing. When Grohl does use the mid-ranged drums (tom-tom and snare), he prefers the snare, hitting it with great force, resulting in a loud snap rather than the thud of Channing's tom-toms. As a result, his style is brighter and higher because of the cymbal-work, and yet harder because of the explosive snare sound. Hearing the two, one can see that Grohl complemented Nirvana's fusion of punk sensibility, pop style and raw power much better than Channing.

'Big Cheese' is also heavily overdriven. Its quasi-industrial sound suits the subject of its virtually undecipherable lyrics which, in fact, present a parody of Sub Pop executive Jonathan Poneman. The highly regimented sound of industry is interrupted by the second half of the chorus, where Channing plays a hilariously overblown part, complete with rapid sixteenth notes on his double bass drums. However, the drums work well during the somewhat complicated instrumental break that follows each chorus. In a sense this song is a showcase for Channing's drumming but, as with many similar showcases, it primarily demonstrates the band's need for a better drummer.

Nirvana had recorded 'Sappy' in the studio just before the HUB appearance, although it was never commercially released. This omission is understandable because 'Sappy' is (by Nirvana's standards) a fairly conventional rock song. It is built on a chord progression that is cyclical in a self-generating manner, marking it as part of Cobain's later style. But it possesses neither the powerful dynamic range nor the pop melodicism of his songs from *Nevermind* and *In Utero* (1993). As with many of the songs in this set, the bass seems to disappear as the part Novoselic plays, and the sound he creates, mesh effectively with Cobain's more acoustically present guitar.[4] Channing is clearly happier to play in this mid-tempo rock style. The lyrics seem to offer a conventional warning about 'romantic entrapment' (Azerrad 1993: 137) but are written in a deliberately vague manner that does not actually specify any *romantic* relationship at all. It is equally plausible to suggest that they refer to a parental relationship or, for that matter, any relationship capable of extending to imprisonment:

> And if you save yourself
> You will make him happy
> He'll keep you in a jar
> And you'll think you're happy
> He'll give you breathing holes
> And you'll think you're happy
> He'll cover you with grass
> And you'll think you're happy now

You're really in a laundry room
You're really in a laundry room
The clue just came to you, oh.[5]

Given Cobain's personal history, it is likely that the song is about his difficult relationship with his father, which also represents a foreshadowing of his later, mature style. As I will discuss below, the specific *topic* of Cobain's lyrics was less important than the *feelings* expressed through them. Since many of his deepest feelings were generated by childhood trauma, Cobain would frequently write songs about those events. But he was intelligent enough to write them in such a way that listeners could supply the appropriate specific situation from their own lives to match the emotions Cobain expressed. This is a strategy he was still developing in early 1990, but one that he was coming to embrace more and more.

'Spank Thru' is an interesting composite of two very different parts. The first half opens with rhythmic guitar scrapes before breaking into a rapid, clean-channel, A-major guitar riff with a galloping eighth/sixteenth/sixteenth rhythm. One of the connections between Nirvana and the Melvins is that both enjoyed mocking Kiss, probably because of the band's status as icons of adolescent hard rock and cheap theatrics.[6] The opening guitar riff satirizes 'The Great White Buffalo' by Ted Nugent – another 1970s icon of adolescent hard rock – and the lyrics also mock the sentimental love poetry that many arena bands used to disguise songs that were really about sex. Cobain sings in a barely intelligible style, reminiscent of a stoned Elvis Presley, slurring the words 'soft, pretentious mountains' into three syllables. After ending the first part of the song with the line 'living without you girl, you'll only break my heart', Cobain lets loose a howl and the song abruptly shifts gear into a high-energy punk song about masturbation: 'I can cut it, I can taste it, I can spank it, I can beat it, ejaculate it!' Cobain's vocals are percussive and overdriven, his guitar is louder, distorted and frequently feeds back, he adds a wildly out-of-control guitar solo, and the drums and bass become far more active and energetic. While Cobain is mocking the heavy metal kids who regularly beat him in high school, the frenzied energy he displays simultaneously communicates a sense of the dumb, frustrated, angry state of mind that fuelled those beatings. While 'Spank Thru' is not exactly the sort of affectionate tribute to cretins that the Ramones were known for,[7] it is still a surprisingly sympathetic satire. It is also one of Cobain's oldest songs, dating as far back as December 1985.[8]

As the song ends, Novoselic tells the audience about the band that wrote the next song, 'Molly's Lips':

This is a cover song. There's a band out there that you should all … worship. They're called the Vaselines, they're from Scotland. If you ever heard of 'em, you'd be mowed over. Like a … steamroller! I'm serious, yeah, yeah! Kick out the jams, motherfucker!

This demonstrates Nirvana's habit of paying tribute to the (often obscure) bands they admired. Indeed, they seemed more comfortable promoting the music of the Vaselines, the Meat Puppets, the Melvins, Bikini Kill or Beat Happening than their own. 'Molly's Lips' is a simple, spirited, two-chord punk song. However, in this case it is performed with a noticeably slower tempo (164 beats per minute instead of 176) and in a less energetic vocal style than the studio recording on *Incesticide*. It is also missing the harmony vocals of the later version; the band only really began to incorporate back-up vocals in their live shows when Dave Grohl joined in September 1990.

'About a Girl' is often cited as the one song from *Bleach* that demonstrates Cobain's later style. It is certainly more pop-oriented than any of his earlier songs, and clearly influenced by the Beatles:

> 'About A Girl' was an important song in Kurt's development as a writer – it was his first straight-ahead love song, and even if the lyrics were twisted, it was so unabashedly melodic that in Nirvana's early live performances, audiences mistook it as a Beatles' cover. Kurt told Steve Schillinger that on the day he wrote 'About A Girl', he played *Meet the Beatles* for three hours straight to get in the mood. This was hardly necessary: ever since he was a toddler he'd studied their work, even though they were considered *passé* in punk circles (Cross 2001: 121).

The performance here is very different from the version on *Bleach*, however. The tempo is around 156 bpm, while the studio recording is around 140 bpm, but more important is the change in the overall sound. The studio version has Channing's skilful cymbal work placed much higher in the mix, while this live performance features more energetic drum fills. Novoselic's bass is quieter, the guitar is more distorted and Cobain's vocals, although not screaming, are also overdriven. The net result of all these changes is a faster, harder, and more intense performance, which reveals stylistic elements hidden in the studio version – particularly a quasi-rockabilly sound, reminiscent of the Cramps or Dead Moon. However, the beautiful, ascending pentatonic melody still stands out strikingly against this much harder background. A live, acoustic version of the song opened *Unplugged In New York* (1994), with a different arrangement and personnel: Grohl plays only on snare and cymbals, and with brushes instead of drumsticks; Novoselic plays a hollow-body acoustic/electric bass; Cobain and Pat Smear are on acoustic guitars. This performance was slower again, at around 132 bpm. What is remarkable is Cobain's ability to make the same melody and lyric work in three very different musical contexts, adjusting his vocals to achieve the right combination of intensity and urgency.

'Breed' is among Nirvana's most powerful songs, both sonically and rhythmically. Like 'Polly' it was recorded for *Nevermind*, by which time the band had become far more skilled, polished and ambitious. The live performance here contains some important differences, in music and lyrics. In both versions, 'Breed' begins with a burst of white guitar noise, followed by the main riff on guitar. On

Nevermind, this one-measure riff is repeated twice before the drums and bass join in (the bass doubles the riff an octave below). Grohl plays a sixteenth-note snare roll for six full bars, building up considerable momentum before breaking off to establish the main groove (which is still built upon the same guitar and bass riff). But here in Seattle, Channing enters after three and a half bars and only plays a snare roll for two beats. In other words, Grohl's introductory drum roll, which is also played with far more force, is twelve times as long as Channing's. Furthermore, Channing's drum part during the main groove is an embellished version of the same rhythm found in the guitar/bass riff (four eighth notes and two quarter notes). This leaves two dead spots in the groove, on the second halves of beats three and four, so that the perceived pace slows down in the second half of each measure. Grohl's part plays steadily throughout the entire bar, continuing to carry the momentum when the guitar and bass hesitate after the third and fourth beats. There is also one important timbral change in the *Nevermind* version: the bass is very heavily distorted, resulting in an extremely rich, but indistinctly articulated, timbre that recalls Larry Graham's influential bass lines on Sly and the Family Stone's records of the late 1960s. 'Breed' was a new song at the time of this concert, so its lyrics were in a state of flux. Some of the inconsistencies stem from Cobain's technique of deliberately mumbling or altering the words of his more intense songs (discussed below). But there are clear changes across the two texts:[9]

Seattle: January, 1990	*Nevermind*: May, 1991
I don't care (×5)	I don't care (×5)
I don't care if I'm old	I don't care if I'm sold
I don't mind (×4), mind,	I don't mind (×4), mind,
Mind if you know	Don't have a mind
I don't care (×5)	Get away (×4), away,
I don't care if I'm old	Away from your home
I don't mind (×4), mind …	I'm afraid (×4), afraid …
Yeah!	Ghost!
Even if you have	Even if you have
Even if you need	Even if you need
I don't even care	I don't mean to stare
We could have a tree	We don't have to breed
We could plant a house	We could plant a house
We could build a tree	We could build a tree
I don't even care	I don't even care
We could have all three	We could have all three
She said (×8)	She said (×8)[10]

'Been a Son' is another fast, riff-based song, which makes for an effective trilogy alongside 'Breed' and 'Negative Creep'. The lyrics are about a girl whose parents wish she had been a boy (possibly referring to Cobain's own sister Kim). Here, it lacks the dual-vocal parts which characterize the song as it appeared on later recordings. It begins and ends with several seconds of loud, very high-pitched feedback, probably generated by a microphone instead of a guitar. (Guitar feedback tends to take advantage of the strings, so it is usually constrained to the lower partials of an open or fretted string. Microphone feedback, however, can take advantage of the entire frequency range of the microphone and speaker combination, so it is frequently far higher pitched than guitar feedback.) The feedback at the end overlaps the introduction of the next song, 'Negative Creep'.

'Negative Creep' is among the most energetic and intense of Nirvana's songs. Its tempo is not especially fast (around 172 bpm) but it is a very *active* song – particularly in the guitar part.[11] The main guitar riff is simply a steady stream of eighth notes on the lowest open string. (The string is tuned down from E to D for the last two songs, a common technique for Nirvana.) But on the third and sixth of these notes – the ones on the second beat and the second half of the third beat – Cobain slides his hand from about a quarter of the length of the string (roughly the seventh fret, playing an A) up to its midpoint at the twelfth fret, which plays the D one octave above the open string. This metrically disruptive, yet symmetrical placement of glissando octave leaps easily draws our attention twice per bar. It also divides the steady pulse of the guitar into two registers, creating an effect similar to a drum part. Novoselic compounds this effect by playing Ds on his bass almost as if it were a tom-tom or bass drum. When added to a full, energetic drum part, the cumulative effect is a swirl of activity that is nonetheless highly predictable – an ideal hard-rock groove. Above this high-energy storm, Cobain sings some of his darkest lyrics in his most heavily overdriven vocal style, sounding more like Howlin' Wolf or John Lee Hooker than a rock singer. Most of the lyrics consist of two phrases: 'I'm a negative creep, I'm a negative creep, I'm a negative creep … and I'm stoned!' (repeated in groups of two); and 'Daddy's little girl ain't a girl no more' (repeated in groups of six). Although obviously filled with self-loathing and anger, the words are widely open to interpretation, again allowing the listener to apply them to any situation from his or her own life that matches the intense emotions being expressed.

The closing song, 'Blew', matches the intensity of 'Negative Creep' but is otherwise quite different. It has the slower tempo, heavier sound and nihilistic humour of the Melvins, or perhaps a punk version of an older Black Sabbath song. The chorus is both dark and self-mocking:

> Is there another reason for your stain?
> Could you believe who we knew was stress or strain?
> Here is another word that rhymes with shame.[12]

There are several reasons why 'Blew' sounds so heavy: the overdriven sound of the bass, guitar and vocals, the way those parts double the same melody, the relative slowness of that melody, and the fact that the lowest string on the guitar is tuned down a whole step (an old technique used by guitarists from Albert King to Corin Tucker to give the guitar a heavier sound). One of the most striking aspects of the song's performance is its conclusion. While not exactly a rave ending, it is merely a repeat of the first half of the main riff, accompanied by the words 'you could do anything' repeated eight times. In the studio version, this melody begins with an eighth rest on the downbeat; here on stage, however, that rest is replaced, in an ingenious manner, with a short, disconcerting burst of high-pitched feedback. After this passage, the song completely breaks down into random noise and feedback – a conventional ending for a Nirvana concert that is obviously derived from The Who.

Overall, the HUB concert appeared as five groups of songs. First, three fast and familiar songs from *Bleach*, positioned to grab the Seattle audience's attention and put them in a spirited mood. Second, two newer, darker and more sophisticated songs, taking advantage of the indulgent crowd to introduce more challenging material. Third, a pair of older, sarcastic favourites, to recapture the attention of anyone who had lost interest during the previous songs about alienation or torture. Fourth, a group of four 'lighter' songs, albeit with some serious lyrics. Finally, a group of four songs which formed the heart of Nirvana's set at this point in their career – serious, intense, powerful and well crafted. As a whole, the performance ebbs and flows but builds to a climax of great intensity and energy before ending in an archetypal punk display of auto-destruction.

The sound

The two most prominent aspects of Nirvana's sound are, as represented in the Seattle performance, the two aspects provided by Kurt Cobain: the voice and the guitar. Like most guitarist/singers, he used them in a highly coordinated fashion, but was able to extend this coordination beyond pitch and rhythm to include timbre and dynamics. Indeed, he carefully rehearsed the quality of sounds made by his voice:

> Kurt was very particular about his singing, and would get very angry if he couldn't make the sounds he wanted to make. 'He'd start smacking his chest and stuff', says Chad [Channing]. 'Not into it' (Cross 2001: 91).

By pushing his voice to the boundary between a coherent tone and a complete breakup, he developed a timbre that was rich as a result of its *impurity*, rather than its purity. The way he did this was to overdrive his voice.

Distortion, or overdriving, is not a timbral quality. It is a physical process, and it works in the same way for the voice as it does for electronic signals. Distortion is, simply put, the sound of a signal too powerful for the system transmitting it:

For people who use any sort of audio equipment, the relationship of distortion to power is familiar: a small radio turned on full blast, a portable cassette player booming cacophonously, a malfunctioning stereo system. This electronic distortion results when components are overdriven – required to amplify or reproduce a signal beyond their capacity to do so 'cleanly' (Walser 1993: 42).

The acoustic effect of this process is greater sustain and a richer timbre. This is why a single note played on an undistorted guitar has a thin, pure timbre that decays rapidly, while a note played on a distorted guitar has a dense, complex tone and can sustain for a very long time. Distortion operates in much the same way for the human voice:

> Not only electronic circuitry, but also the human body produces aural distortion through excessive power. Human screams and shouts are usually accompanied by vocal distortion, as the capacities of the vocal chords are exceeded. Thus, distortion functions as a sign of extreme power and intense expression by overflowing its channels and materializing the exceptional effort that produces it ... The vocal sounds of heavy metal are similar, in some ways, to the guitar sounds. Quite often, vocalists deliberately distort their voices, for many of the same reasons that guitar players distort theirs. Heavy metal vocalists project brightness and power by overdriving their voices (or by seeming to), and they also sing long sustained notes to suggest intensity and power (Walser 1993: 43–5).

However, distortion can have other effects on the voice as well, including multi-phonics and highly complex waveforms – both of which are generally interpreted as noise. But what is perhaps more important than noise level is the effect on linguistic articulation. An overdriven voice generally obscures the articulation of consonants and the clarity of pitches, but leaves vowel articulation, phrasing, dynamics and pitch contour relatively unaltered. In other words, distortion de-emphasizes aspects that contribute to a conventional, linguistically effective singing voice, and emphasizes aspects that contribute to non-linguistic forms of expression, such as screams, moans, wails, roars and shrieks. Because these are sounds that are generally associated with great duress, urgency or intense feelings, overdriven vocals can communicate duress, urgency or intense emotions, along with power.

Cobain also developed the ability to sustain an overdriven voice for extended periods and to control the timbre of his voice to a great degree. As a result, he had a remarkably wide timbral and dynamic range from which to choose. The most famous demonstration of this range is, of course, 'Smells Like Teen Spirit', in which Cobain's voice – in coordination with his guitar sound – shifts from a conventional, relatively pure, vocal sound during the verses, to a heavily overdriven, almost screaming sound during the chorus.

Cobain's vocal style had roots in both metal and punk. The timbre of his voice was more characteristic of metal or hard rock than punk. It had a similar timbre to the voice of Rob Halford, the influential and popular singer for Judas Priest – although Halford used heavy vibrato and Cobain generally did not.[13] Cobain's voice also shared similarities with the voices of both Bon Scott and Brian Johnson of AC/DC and of The Who's Roger Daltrey. But the manner in which he employed that instrument – particularly the conscious lack of control – was directly derived from the punk tradition.

Cobain worked extremely hard to develop a vocal sound that appeared to be honest and spontaneous. This is paradoxical but not contradictory: he carefully developed a range of sounds that accurately communicated emotional states and, once that range of sounds was under his control, spontaneously adjusted his vocal style to suit the emotional state that he wanted to express. The emphasis here is not on spontaneity – although that was important – but on directness of communication, on honesty.

His guitar style was a similar fusion of punk and metal. His guitar was often heavily overdriven, resulting in a thick, muddy timbre with complex interactions between multiple overtones. Dynamically, the result was longer sustain and compression. Any medium or loud notes became saturated and sustained for a long time, but quieter sounds were much less affected. Each note also had an explosive attack. The overall effect was a combination of the percussive rhythm style of punk, and the heavy, saturated, tone quality of metal.

As previously mentioned, Novoselic's bass sound seems lower in the mix at the HUB performance than usual, because of the nature of soundboard recordings. It is clear, however, that his tone is boosted in the high and low ranges, and decreased in the midrange. When combined with his very understated style, the result is a fusion of his sound with the sound of Cobain's guitar that can be quite hard to separate. However, Novoselic's primary role was not to draw attention, but to control the flow generated by the multiple, nested series of repeated figures found in every Nirvana song – to hold the songs together while Cobain and Channing moved from loud to quiet, rough to smooth, busy to empty.

Channing's role was to control the tempo and texture (the number of musical events occurring within a given time). He was not, however, the primary source of rhythmic/metric material, since so many of Nirvana's songs were built around Cobain's rhythm guitar parts. As this concert revealed, Channing's overall style did not mesh well with the music that Cobain and Novoselic were creating. He had difficulty in playing songs that changed styles (a trait that would ultimately become Nirvana's signature) and in smoothly interlocking with Cobain's increasingly complex rhythm parts.

In analysing the 15 songs that the band performed that night, the set as a whole and the roles of each musician in a live concert setting, one can note the existence of three important and distinctive traits, which worked together to effectively communicate intensity and directness of emotion: the deliberate use of chaos, the deliberate use of overdriven sounds (especially of *dangerously* overdriven sounds), and the use of inarticulation.

Nirvana thrived on chaos, promoted chaos, decorated themselves with chaos. It was a hugely important part of their identity. But ironically, their music is anything but chaotic in a larger sense. Cobain's songs and arrangements, even in January 1990, were sophisticated and well organized. But the music is organized *loosely* – at times, so loosely that it treads the boundary between organization and chaos. Higher intensity songs like 'Negative Creep', 'Breed' and 'Blew' threaten to break apart when Cobain's vocals or guitar work become especially wild or energetic. But they never actually fall apart, except at the one point where the music is specifically designed to do so: the end of the last song, when the entire musical system explodes.

The deliberate use of chaos within an organized context works because it effectively communicates spontaneity. Cobain worked inside organized frameworks, but within those boundaries he was free to express himself. The unpredictability of Nirvana's music told the audience that, whatever else they might be doing, the band wasn't following a script. The controlled use of chaos within boundaries is also a strategy that allows groups of artists to work together without losing their individuality.[14] The awareness that each of the musicians is free to express himself, at least within very general parameters, sends a strong signal to an audience: whatever these musicians play is a direct communication from them. The music is honest.

Nirvana's music did not, and does not, exist in isolation. Instead it arose from the combined influence of countless musicians and has, in turn, influenced many others. The use of overdriven sounds situates them in a long tradition of punk, metal and abrasively hard-rock styles. It also enables them to participate in traditional modes of discourse found in punk, counterculture and Pacific Northwest music scenes. But the role of distortion in Nirvana's music goes beyond tradition. Distorted guitar and bass, shouted or raspy vocals, uncontrolled or barely controlled feedback and an overdriven PA system are all examples of the same physical process described above: a signal too powerful for a given system to fully contain. It is true that in each of those cases, Nirvana did not saturate the system so much as to render the signal completely incoherent. But the signals *are* usually saturated enough that the signal can only be suggested or inferred, and they are often so powerful that they are *dangerously* overdriven. Cobain's guitar and vocals in particular were frequently pushed right to the verge of breaking down. If an overdriven system communicates power, as Walser (1993) asserts, then a dangerously overdriven system communicates power that is too great to be controlled.

The deliberate use of inarticulation – mumbled or mis-stated lyrics, fumbled guitar solos, loosely controlled tempos – can be interpreted in many ways. In the case of Nirvana, it is a part of their aesthetic. The inability to articulate what we think and feel is, in essence, the subject of 'Smells Like Teen Spirit' (if it can be said to have a single subject). This is why Kurt Cobain did not complete the lyrics to many of the songs on *Nevermind* until the night before the songs were recorded:

> The biggest problem of the session was Kurt's own procrastination: he still hadn't
> settled on lyrics for many of the songs, though a few tunes, like 'Polly' and 'Breed',
> the band had been playing for years. When he did finish a lyric, most were as
> paradoxical as they were revelatory. Many lines left the listener unclear as to whether
> he was singing about external or internal circumstances, defying explanation though
> communicating an emotional tone (Cross 2001: 182).

But, as he frankly admitted, the specific words mattered less to Cobain than the
intensity of the feelings being expressed:

> Most of the music is really personal as far as the emotion and the experiences that
> I've had in my life ... but most of the *themes* in the songs aren't that personal.
> They're more just stories from TV or books or movies or friends. But definitely the
> emotion and feeling is from me (Azerrad 1994: 35).

Nirvana often expressed emotion as powerfully in songs with lyrics that are silly
('Floyd the Barber', 'School') or sarcastic ('Love Buzz', 'In Bloom') as they did
in songs whose seriousness matches the intensity of the music. The feelings are
still powerful, whether the words to express them are there or not: 'Oh well,
whatever, nevermind ...'. Similarly, the specific notes generally matter less than
the communication of the song's intensity and the sense that it is organized just
enough to hold together:

> Cobain's railing screams and blurred delivery were as big a part of the emotion he
> conveyed as his words were – the sarcastic tilt of 'Smells Like Teen Spirit' and the
> raging, mad tones of injustice in 'Rape Me' ... Music and lyrics that powerful can't
> be feigned; there has to be some validity behind them (Ali 1994: 98).

The abrupt shifting of levels of chaos, distortion and inarticulation (while other
aspects of a song remain essentially the same) therefore distinguish the sound of
Nirvana. Again, the obvious example is 'Smells Like Teen Spirit', in which the
pitches and rhythms do not dramatically change from verse to chorus, but the
amount of chaos, distortion and inarticulation do. The band's two-gear dynamic
approach is consistent with someone who is trying to express thoughts and feelings
too powerful to be expressed: you can either communicate your thoughts clearly,
and lose the emotional intensity, or you can communicate the emotional intensity,
but lose the ability to be articulate.

This seems to be the main point of the sounds of chaos, distortion and
inarticulation in Nirvana's music: Cobain was trying to express the inexpressible.
This is not something new; most great songs are about thoughts or feelings too
great to be contained within a song. But Cobain *also* wanted to communicate his
inability to express the inexpressible – which is an important addition. This is
why Nirvana's unique, carefully balanced fusion of metal, punk and pop was so
effective. By playing in a chaotic, dangerously overdriven and barely articulate
style, they were able to depict the contemporary dilemma of a generation of

disaffected youth, like those in the Seattle audience, who were themselves struggling to honestly communicate thoughts and feelings that were simply too powerful to be expressed.

> 'That ambiguity, that's the whole thing', says *Nevermind* producer Butch Vig. 'What the kids are attracted to in the music is that he's *not* necessarily a spokesman for a generation, but all that's in the music – the passion and [the fact that] he doesn't necessarily know what he wants, but he's pissed. It's all these things working at different levels at once. I don't exactly know what 'Teen Spirit' means, but you know it means *something*, and it's intense as hell' (Azerrad 1994: 35).

Notes

1. Cobain and Novoselic grew up in the blue-collar city of Aberdeen, Washington, only 100 miles, but many worlds removed, from Seattle. Their early days as a band primarily took place within the rich, distinctive music scene in Olympia, Washington. However, because their first record company, Sub Pop, was based in Seattle and because it is by far the largest city in the region, Nirvana is often characterized as a Seattle band.
2. It was sold as *Supercolossal Big Muff* (1990).
3. 'Dive'. Words and music by Kurt Cobain and Krist Novoselic. EMI Virgin Music/The End of Music 1990.
4. This is also partly due to the acoustic properties of the ballroom. Soundboard cassettes do not pick up the sounds coming directly from onstage amplifiers or drum kits, which, particularly in a smaller room, can be a very large part of the sound. As a result they tend to de-emphasize bass and drum parts. The versions of 'Polly' and 'Breed' on *From the Muddy Banks of the Wishkah* were also recorded from a soundboard cassette, made in December 1989, and then remixed to bring the sounds into better balance. A comparison reveals that the bass and drums on these songs are much louder than at the HUB concert.
5. 'Sappy'. Words and music by Kurt Cobain. EMI Virgin Music/The End of Music 1990.
6. Nirvana recorded the Kiss song 'Do You Love Me?' for the tribute album *Hard To Believe* (1992). The Melvins performed Kiss's 'God of Thunder' on the same record.
7. For examples, listen to 'Pinhead' from *Leave Home* (1977); 'Cretin Bop' and 'Lobotomy' from *Rocket To Russia* (1977).
8. Cross provides an account of the song's performance at Nirvana's very first concert, at a house party in Raymond, Washington in 1987. The band had already mocked those hard rock fans at the party, who had requested Lynyrd Skynyrd's 'Freebird' and Led Zeppelin's 'Heartbreaker':

   > What happened next guaranteed it would be a party to be remembered. Shelli and Tracy [who were dating Novoselic and Cobain, respectively] decided to add to the freak show by rubbing their hands on Krist's chest and kissing each other. Kurt quickly introduced the next song: 'This one's called "Breaking the Law"'. They played what would later be titled 'Spank Thru', a song about masturbation. The Raymond crowd may not have been the most sophisticated audience, but they began to get the sense that they were the butt of some kind of joke (Cross 2001: 88).

9. The recording of 'Breed' on *From the Muddy Banks of the Wishkah* is from December 1989. Its lyrics are virtually identical to those sung at the HUB.

10. 'Breed'. Words by Kurt Cobain. Music by Nirvana. Virgin Songs Inc/The End of Music 1990.

11. For a discussion of the significance of the activity level of a song (the number of events to which the ear must attend within a given span of time, and the way that high activity levels can communicate a sense of high energy, even in slower songs), see Hughes (2003: 237–40).

12. 'Blew'. Words and music by Kurt Cobain. EMI Virgin Music/The End of Music 1989.

13. Judas Priest was one of the last heavy metal bands Cobain saw in concert, as a teenager in 1983 (Cross 2001: 47).

14. A similar strategy lies behind the controlled use of improvization in funk. See Hughes (2003: 107–267).

Chapter 15

The booing of Sinéad O'Connor Bob Dylan 30th Anniversary Concert, Madison Square Garden, New York, October 16, 1992

Emma Mayhew

In the beginning she was an enfant terrible who didn't even fit that properly, because at twenty-one she was also mother to a newborn baby boy. Later, she became a leftist radical with no clear political base, and a musical eccentric who fit no genre comfortably, especially not rock'n'roll. Shunned by American audiences, reduced to caricature by pundits and critics, O'Connor has wilfully continued on her way. Unlike other rock'n'roll bad girls, she's never been cool, never much fun … It's become awkward to talk about O'Connor, awkward, in a way, to be her fan (Powers 1997: 377).

Sinéad O'Connor as a celebrity and popular music performer has been the focus of both media and general public attention since her appearance on the world music charts with her hit single 'Nothing Compares 2 U'. In fact it is rather clichéd to say that her career and personality can be defined by the overarching adjective of 'controversial'. The booing of O'Connor at the Bob Dylan 30th Anniversary concert in 1992 represents one of the most notorious examples of her reputation as an outspoken 'bad girl'. This status has been accompanied by various other terms that seek to define her identity in a set of competing stereotypes. On the one hand, her behaviour and outspokenness on a number of social topics has branded her not only rebellious, but crazy and irrational, with a taste for publicity. On the other hand, she has been seen as an original and courageous performer, offering up her very personal self as the central focus of her protests against the power of the Catholic Church, child abuse, abortion and war. Her shaved head, a fairly stable hairstyle she has adopted over her career, has become a physical mark of this controversial and radical identity. In fact, her hairstyle and her identity as outspoken rebel have become one and the same thing, her baldness becoming a metaphor for eccentricity but also for strength and courage. It simultaneously reflected an alternative femininity, one that shocked, but also challenged, the parameters of what women in popular music could look like and, at the same time, be successful.

Recent appearances in the media, and another apparently new chapter in O'Connor's status as controversy queen, centred around her announcement that she would be retiring from the music industry, citing media intrusion and the need to be a private person rather than a public figure. In a statement released on her website in early 2003 she declared 'I would request that as of July, since I seek no longer to be a famous person, and instead I wish to live a normal life, could people please afford me my privacy' (www.sineadoconnor.com). This only added to her reputation as contradictory and rather irrational; in fact, her statements of retirement are often linked to her representation as slightly mad, 'an affable nut who enjoys pissing people off and making ludicrous statements of imminent retirement every six months' (Shanahan 2000).[1]

However, whatever the long-term status of Sinéad O'Connor as an active musical recording artist, it is the tension between the public and the private, as emphasized in her retirement statement, which has been the major theme of her career. Exploring this theme highlights how the identity of femininity is negotiated and challenged in the mainstream discourses that shape the meaning of musical protest for women performers. That is, private and public space, as feminism has demonstrated, has been defined along gendered lines, with 'normal' female and male behaviour and interests conceptualized within this dichotomy. Female musical performers have often challenged, but have also been described through, this dualism. This chapter explores the booing of Sinéad O'Connor and her star-text through understanding the continued existence of a patriarchal masculine/feminine dichotomy in popular music culture, especially in relation to the meanings of protest and rebellion. In identifying the discourse of authenticity and the construction of the persona of the diva, the following analysis of the representation of O'Connor seeks to understand how accounts from the media and the audience are negotiated through a private/public dichotomy which reflects a gendered divide.

The star-text, authenticity and the construction of Sinéad as diva

In this analysis, O'Connor's booing is conceptualized as part of a larger star-text. The star-text is a set of mediated descriptions, narratives and performances which locate the star as an identity or a subject. As the audience, we read the star or celebrity as a whole identity with intentions and behaviours which fit into a star type. She or he may be viewed through various social types ranging from the hero to the villain, including alternative or subversive types (Dyer 1979: 53–8). Dyer's work, and that of others exploring the modern celebrity, draws our attention to a construction of the public person that is mediated through institutions, media forms and styles. She or he is not a 'real' person, and we can never know or reveal the 'real' person behind the persona. Studying stars is about uncovering discourses and structures of meaning that shape our understanding not only of popular music performers, but also of more generalized meaning-making processes about groups of people whom we categorize in terms of gender, class, sexuality, ethnicity and so on. Sinéad O'Connor represents a case study in gender discourses; how fans, audiences, and the media talk about her can tell us something about gender relations in the context of popular music.

Certainly O'Connor's career has been seen through a shifting and competing set of recognizable gendered personae. In the context of her musical profession, one social type very relevant to this analysis is the diva; and more precisely, the way in which representations of O'Connor play with this stereotype in terms of her identities as rebel (social crusader and activist), abused child (fragile little girl), singer (vocally skilled) and a woman on the edge of madness (eccentric, self-absorbed, hysterical). As we will see, the diva, as a complex, stereotyped social type, has moved into the world of popular music from operatic origins, and is a useful concept through which to approach the meanings surrounding O'Connor as petulant, egotistical, tragic, emotionally charged and irrational. And yet, the diva, however excessive in her emotional displays, remains valued, in spite of such 'feminine' weaknesses, because of her haunting, beautiful and dramatic voice. In O'Connor's case, her extra-musical voice as social protester and the detailing of her own intimate life are contained, in many media accounts, through representations of her as a skilful and emotionally moving singer.

This skill is conceptualized through a discourse of authenticity which, in this analysis, is understood to represent a knowledge of the performer as emotionally honest, individually talented and original in the way she produces and presents her art. The definition of authenticity as 'the full development and expression of individuality' (Pratt 1986: 62) has significant roots within romanticism, and constructs the individual as central to artistic work. In fact, popular musical culture has grown out of an older romantic tradition of the notion of the artist and creativity as naturalized in the male/masculine subject. As one feminist study into the notion of artistic genius explains:

> Romanticism, which started out by opening a window of opportunity for creative women, developed a phraseology of cultural apartheid ... with women amongst the categories counted as not-fully human. The genius was a male – full of 'virile' energy – who *transcended* his biology: if the male genius was 'feminine' this merely proved his cultural superiority. Creativity was displaced male procreativity: *male* sexuality made sublime (Battersby 1989: 3).

Thus the meaning of the authentic song, performance or performer is rooted in previous ideas about male and female creative capacity. It is not that women cannot be seen as creative individuals in their own right, but rather that any creativity acknowledged is often couched in masculine forms and patriarchal interests. Thus, playing down traditional images of femininity can gain 'authentic points' for female performers. This has been especially true in rock. Sinéad O'Connor is an interesting performer because she challenges traditional, expected feminine behaviour and images, whilst at the same time she embraces the femininity (particularly the importance of mothering) of the private sphere, long seen as the silent domestic domain of women. Moreover, her performance at the Dylan concert tackled the difficult and ugly topic of child abuse – a very private experience in a very public space.

The Dylan concert, *Saturday Night Live* and competing perspectives of the audience

The crowd reaction in Madison Square Garden to O'Connor can partly be understood as the belated reaction to another O'Connor performance 15 days earlier, when she had been a guest on the long-running CBS television show *Saturday Night Live*. On that occasion, she sang a cover of Bob Marley's 'War', whose lyrics are based on a speech made to the United Nations by Haile Selassie. Earlier that day, she had rehearsed the song in the studio without any problems. However, at the conclusion of the live TV performance, she had produced a picture of the Pope, shouted 'Fight the real enemy' and tore up the picture, to the shock of the producer, causing instant switchboard gridlock to CBS.

A little over two weeks later, she appeared at the Dylan celebration (among a cast list of performers all scheduled to perform their own versions of Dylan's songs) intending to sing 'I Believe in You'. From the television tapes of the event, we can see O'Connor take centre stage, but some initial crowd noise, including booing, clearly disturbs her. She remains quiet and, instead of going into the song, waits in silence for several minutes. As the crowd does not quieten, the celebratory mood of the concert is clearly souring. Kris Kristofferson comes on stage and whispers something to O'Connor in support. The noise of the crowd does not diminish and she screams out the song 'War', changing some of the lyrics relating to racism to the plight of abused children. She leaves the stage, visibly shaken, Kristofferson seemingly taking her shoulder. In fact, in some accounts she is said to have 'burst into tears' while leaving the stage (Clarke 1998: 945).

Television seems to record and retell these 'facts', but this media event, like many in popular media history, cannot be approached as a single set of logically unfolding moments with clear actor intentions. Confusion around what actually happened, and why, is exemplified in the kinds of fan debates that have gone on since that night. In these debates we see a clash between the understanding of the circumstances of the event, the audience's identity and intentions, and the general 'meaning' of the event. There are also disagreements about what the event reveals of O'Connor's star-text or identity. Even though the initial concert was broadcast live to a global audience, the controversy over whether she did the 'right thing', and what it was that the crowd was actually reacting to has remained – for both the live and television audiences. For example, these website exchanges indicate the kind of details that remain contentious:

> Many people claim Sinéad O'Connor was booed at the 30th Anniversary Concert at Madison Square Garden, and while this may appear to be true a close examination of the existing tapes reveals some confusion; perhaps the set was too short, or the crowd was unable to hear her. Why are people so sure she was booed?

Another fan replies:

> I was there, She was definitely booed. A little at first, almost jokingly. But when she could not get the crowd to become absolutely silent she refused to begin her song and that resulted in heavy booing until she was literally booed off the stage.

Another audience member points out the different experience of being in the crowd, rather than the TV audience:

> What I want to bring up here is the idea that Sinéad 'could have stilled the crowd by singing her song'. I know the Pay-Per-View recording makes it seem like that was possible: the camera shows Booker T. as he clearly plays the opening notes of 'I Believe in You' at one point. But the sound mixed for broadcast and the actual sound in the building are very different – the crowd noise is turned way down (for good reason). Take it from one who was in the Garden that night; the booing and cheering was incredibly, outrageously, prohibitively LOUD. My comment to friends the next day was 'it sounded like a bomb went off'. Booker's piano and Kris' comment to Sinéad were not audible AT ALL, at least not to me. Her shouting of 'War' was just barely above the din. I really don't think it was possible for her to pull off 'I Believe in You' – though for the record, I wish she had tried. Also for the record: many in the crowd did stand and cheer, myself included, which only made the boobirds louder and made everything louder! I know that there were booing/cheering contests between audience members who had been getting along just fine up to that point. I will admit that I shouted 'Judas!' just once for historical continuity's sake. Yes, I agree Sinéad brought the debacle on herself and was being awfully immature all around (www.sinead-oconnor.com).

The issue of immaturity will be discussed later. However, these testimonies demonstrate the importance of recognizing the crowd's mood, and the opposition from some fans to the mainstream emphasis on the negative reaction; the singer herself has maintained that much of the crowd was supportive:

> I think at the time, for each person that didn't understand what I had done, there was a person who did. You would think the way the papers wrote about it that nobody understood it. At the Bob Dylan show, three quarters of the audience was cheering, but the newspapers would have you believe that everyone was booing (O'Connor 1998).

However, this analysis does not seek to reveal the 'truth' about these events, or to clear up the controversy. Rather, the Dylan concert represents a moment in media-recorded time where we can examine the discourses surrounding the event. The examples of internet discussions make it clear that the event represents a significant moment for her fans, and popular music audiences in general, to attempt to understand her as a personality. However, musically the event is also significant in its construction of O'Connor as star-text and figure of protest.

In good company

The booing off stage of Sinéad O'Connor at Madison Square Garden in 1992 is ironic if we look back at Bob Dylan's own career. In the mid-1960s, Dylan moved away from his acoustic folk roots into the electrified sounds of rock; on his subsequent tours of the US and Europe, after the release of the album *Bringing It All Back Home* (1965), he himself was booed off stage by angry folk purists. So O'Connor's controversial career sits in good company and parallels the romantic discourse of misunderstood artists, ahead of their time. However, whereas Dylan is now seen as one of the most influential white men in popular music, in the aftermath of the Madison Square Garden and *Saturday Night Live* events, O'Connor, especially in the US, has never repeated the success of her album *I Do Not Want What I Haven't Got* (1990). Comparisons between the two performers may seem absurd, but are essential in making the argument that O'Connor's representation of her 'personal' private experience of child abuse in the context of public and political protest is rendered meaningful through a gendered division of appropriate public and private self.

Her presence as part of the musical line-up that night reflected her affinity with Dylan; she has frequently identified him as a major influence on her work, and one of her first demo tapes included a cover of his 'Simple Twist of Fate' (Clarke 1998: 945). Her presence at the event was also significant as O'Connor has drawn on the folk genre, which Dylan so famously revived (musically and lyrically) in his musical commentaries on 'classic' protest themes such as poverty, class, oppression and societal hypocrisy. The irony of the evening's subsequent events was not lost on her fans nor on the popular music media:

> Who would have guessed the fans of Bob Dylan, the consummate rebel of his time, would turn on Sinéad O'Connor, the pop iconoclast of a new era? The crowd, filled with forty-somethings who three decades ago ushered in the era of protest music by hoisting their fists to the defiant tunes of a young Dylan, showed little patience with O'Connor (Morse 1992).

However, the spirit of the 1960s protest era was echoed in many of the artists set to perform that night. Tracy Chapman had recently had worldwide successes with her first two albums, exploring such topics as urban decay and working-class poverty, and fashioning new popular music anthems in socially conscious songs such as 'Talkin' Bout a Revolution'. Others on the list with socially conscious credentials included Johnny Cash, John Couger Mellencamp, Eddie Vedder and George Harrison. Female performers included Mary Chapin Carpenter and Roseanne Cash, while Chrissie Hynde and Sophie B. Hawkins represented a more contemporary, younger reference to rock and pop.

Her position as a singer within a white folk/protest tradition (Greig 1998: 173) is one which has become synonymous with women such as Joni Mitchell, Peggy Seeger and Joan Baez.[2] Indeed, O'Connor calls herself 'a protest singer' (Rayner 2000) and her Irish background gives her an authentic folk status. She has furthered this connection on record with her use of Celtic instruments, musicians and songs, and has drawn on a mixture of protest and Celtic folk music to present an image to the public as a recognizable Irish performer.[3] Thus, her inclusion in the Dylan concert re-emphasized the folk genre roots of her musical background, which has continued to the present day – her album *Sean-Nos Nua* (2002) consisted of her versions of traditional Irish folk tunes. In addition to the obvious folk/protest associations between Dylan and O'Connor, her choice of song that night and her vocal performance also need to be analysed.

O'Connor was set to sing 'I Believe in You' from Dylan's album *Slow Train Coming* (1979), produced at the time of his Christian conversion. The themes of religious redemption, healing and retribution, further connect Dylan and O'Connor; both have incorporated religious themes in their musical work and have seen their spirituality as part of, not separate from, their public musical output. The lyrics of 'I Believe in You' (there is an ambiguity about the identity of 'you' – a romantic love interest or an abstract god) can be interpreted as a narrative which expresses a spiritual faith.[4] Her selection of the song parallels her own public struggles with her Christian faith and her criticisms of the Church as an institution. In fact, several lines from the song provide a prophetic summary of her relationship with those seeking to boo her off stage, and her US audience:

> They'd like to drive me from this town,
> They don't want me around
> 'Cause I believe in you.

Even more ominous were the lines:

> They show me to the door,
> They say don't come back no more,
> 'Cause I don't be like they'd like me to.[5]

The lyrics allude to religious persecution, while also declaring a continuing faith in the face of opposition. However, whatever resonance the song may have had to the immediate situation, she chose to sing 'War'. Besides the conscious intertextual links she was making to her *Saturday Night Live* appearance, it also exemplified the musical influences of reggae and the social and religious themes of Rastafarianism that were also influential within O'Connor's career and work.[6]

Public/private voice and reggae roots

'War' originally appeared on Bob Marley's second solo album *Rastaman Vibration* (1976). Inspired by a speech made by Haile Selassie to the United Nations, the lyrics condemn racism, white imperialism and the destruction they have done to the black population of Africa. One verse directly raises the struggles of black Africa:

> Until the ignoble and unhappy regimes
> That hold our brothers
> In Angola,
> In Mozambique,
> South Africa,
> Sub-human bondage,
> Have been toppled,
> Utterly destroyed,
> Well, everywhere is war, me say war.[7]

Selassie is the central figure in Rastafarianism, Emperor of Ethiopia and regarded as the saviour of the African. Marley himself was a major political figure in Jamaica; not only did he write and perform songs about the political and social problems of his country, but he was also a symbol of peace and reconciliation within Jamaican politics. The message of 'War' is that until racism is abolished there will be conflict – and a state of war – between white and black, between oppressor and oppressed.

O'Connor's performance of the song re-appropriated the theme of racist oppression and transformed it into the oppression of child abuse. Her version changes the verse above to:

> Until the ignoble and unhappy regime
> Which holds all of us through
> Child-abuse, yeah,
> Child abuse, yeah,
> Sub-human bondage,
> Has been toppled,
> Utterly destroyed,
> Everywhere is war.

The reggae genre and the religious and political connotations combine in this performance with her vocal gestures to obliterate the private/public split that often seeks to contain private experience as outside of the political realm. In fact, her vocal style is central to understanding this rupture. In his study of Sinéad O'Connor, Negus identifies her two musical voices: 'a more private, confessional, restrained and intimate voice, and a harsher, declamatory, more public and often nasal voice that frequently slides into a snarl or shout' (1998: 181). He explains, through various examples from *I Do Not Want What I Haven't Got*, that she often uses the two voices in the one song, exploring a tension between vulnerable/ uncertain and imperative/assertive. This analysis is valuable in interpreting O'Connor's performance and understanding its representations in the media and by audiences. The vocal styles of public and confessional voice come together in a combination of singing style (declamatory and confessional), choice of song (reggae and Marley's connotations of radical protest) and lyrics (oppression of child abuse and its destructive consequences), and in the media's continuation of her rebel/protest career profile.

Thus, she appropriates the lyrical references to white imperialism and racist oppression, and the genre of reggae and its association with Marley as a political musician, by connecting the plight of abused children with racist oppression around the world. Furthermore, her use of the song goes beyond the concert event (and its re-affirmation of the *Saturday Night Live* moment) as it also stands for the religious eccentricity for which she has been famous.[8] Her identification with reggae is not simply a musical one, chosen 'on the basis of its aesthetically pleasing surface qualities' (Alleyne 2000: 15), but an engagement with music as a political/religious vehicle or force. Her cover of Marley's song is thus an example of the complexities of her performance in bringing the public voice of protest (coded in the reggae genre) to the private matter of child abuse. Her appropriation is a clear political one, and thus is represented at once both as authentic, but also as disconcerting and inappropriate.

Her choice of 'War' rather than the selected Dylan song was additionally interesting, in that by making this decision she was obliged to make her voice heard above the crowd, without accompaniment. Although apparently a spontaneous response to the crowd's hostility, this type of singing – known as a cappella – has been used by O'Connor elsewhere, and has a long history in various musical traditions to convey intense personal narratives and numerous religious connotations within spiritual communities. In the performance of 'War', it is a defiant public voice, which reconnects to her individual and personal protests against child abuse and institutions like the Catholic Church. It is a lone voice of protest against the many voices of the crowd. Within western musical traditions, the use of the unaccompanied voice is the exception (although the unaccompanied voice has been significant in the gospel and blues roots of rock). The connotations of the unaccompanied voice in the West 'tend to express extreme isolation and loneliness rather than "exclusive dominance"' (Van Leeuwan 1999: 72). Based on the representation of O'Connor as an outspoken individual, and the consequential media attention her behaviour attracted, this interpretation of her voice, as socially as well as sonically isolated, is significant.

The a cappella style also plays with the ideas of authenticity in performance. By stripping away the musical decoration, it gives listeners a sense that we are getting to the 'real person', or to the real human emotions of the song. It is intimate in that the accompaniment cannot cover up the silences and noises of the human body of the singer; in this sense, the listener feels a sonic visceral connection with the singer. Thus, O'Connor's rejection of the scheduled song, her ignoring of the backing band in its attempts to start playing over the crowd and the use of her lone voice to re-assert her protest stance and presence on stage put her, paradoxically, in a very authentic position as radical/rebel rock persona.

This persona and its defiant voice were established in her first solo album *The Lion and the Cobra* (1988), to many fans the high point of her musical output. Media reviews of the time clearly represented her vocal presence and star-text as rebellious: 'O'Connor is fond of dynamics and she loves to yell. That's just fine if she did so only at appropriate moments. No such luck' (Atkinson 1988). This comment not only connects her with a declamatory singing style but also frames her voice as both powerful yet inappropriate. This of course is the criticism that O'Connor has worn for much of her career and which was exemplified in Madison Square Garden. Her insinuation that the Church was intimately involved in the abuse of children, and her angry and shocked performance against the crowd has, in the main, been interpreted on a scale from misplaced good intentions to incomprehensible madness. And yet for some rock journalists it was a genuinely radical moment in rock history, even though it was still seen as a rather embarrassing personal display. The reaction of the *New York Times* was a mixture of praise and slight embarrassment at her personal outrage:

> It's clear that she has the attitude that afflicts all post-Romantic artists: the conviction that her private problems are the world's concern. From the unwillingness or inability to distinguish between private torments and public affairs come great statements and petty ones, raw nuttiness and carefully honed masterpieces. It's easy to disagree with O'Connor's latest outbursts.[9] But better the occasional passionate, off-the-wall eruption ... than a culture of safety and calculation (Pareles 1992).

While this highlights the dichotomy between serious protester and radical exhibitionist, what needs to be noted in O'Connor's case is the way in which patriarchal discourses often dominate her representation. The radical authenticity of her performance, as represented by Pareles, is negotiated through the gender relations of rock over the last 50 years. The romantic discourses that rock has drawn upon to construct the rebel rock icon have marginalized women as rebellious serious subjects. Sinéad O'Connor has challenged the definition of rebel-as-male, and brought into the world of popular music feminine and feminist issues (sexual and violent abuse) embedded in her own gendered experience.

Child abuse

The subject of child abuse and sexual abuse on which her protest was focused is a subject matter that clearly articulates the problems of the split between the private domestic sphere (the intimate body, the self, the family, emotions) and the public arena (politics, rationality, objectivity). O'Connor has been vocal in the media about her own experience of child abuse, which in particular represents the way she brings the personal into the public political world, and disrupts the divide, to the discomfort of many. Her personal re-telling of her abuse was doubly shocking as it was enacted by her mother:

> It was extremely violent but the abuse was sexual too. It need not always be about touching. Though that's not to say she didn't touch us. One thing she did regularly was make me take all my clothes off and force me to lie on the floor and she would stamp on my abdomen with the intention of bursting my womb. That's what she said, 'I'm going to burst you' (Sutcliffe 1994: 82).

In these retellings, and in her music ('Fire On Babylon'), O'Connor explores anger, hate and rage in the personal domain of the family. Her experience challenges one of the most naturalized loving relationships of the family, the mother/daughter bond:

> The mother–child dyad is meant to be a picture of domestic and sanctified bliss, not the image of hell. Moreover, because this is a case of mother–daughter hatred there is … a clear cultural blindness; it is virtually taboo for a mother to hate a daughter and for a daughter to hate her mother; and feminism in particular has difficulty in seeing this hatred (Kilby 2001: 115).

O'Connor's public declaration as a daughter abused by her mother is an image not easily appropriated into a mainstream popular culture. Of course, many of the audience that night would have been ignorant of the details of her protest and the context of Irish Catholicism. As one Irish fan states:

> Sinéad may be a bit petulant, but her ripping up of the Pope's picture was a dramatic statement against the Church. The statement was specifically intended for the catholic Church in Ireland, which Sinéad sees as an organization which oppresses us all over here. It was also against the protection the Church has given to paedophile priests and how for the last fifty years it's been trying to sweep it under the carpet. Sinéad being booed by a Dylan audience was one of the most ironic and disgusting things I've ever seen. American audiences condemn her, but they are largely ignorant of her background and the events in Ireland which have moulded her personality (www.sinead-oconnor.com).

It is clearly important to conceptualize the details of O'Connor's star-text within the representation of female anger and to expose the difficulty in which this anger may be represented within a patriarchally dominated media and popular culture. Although her protests have often been seen as rather silly and embarrassing, critics still maintain her ability to interpret and sing a song as her ultimate saving grace: 'Some people have questioned Sinéad O'Connor's sanity since she ripped up the Pope's picture on *Saturday Night Live* in 1992, but no one has ever questioned her talent' (Morse 2000).

When reading the critics' words over her career there is a sense that many would be contented if she just shut up and sang. In recent years her persona has been somewhat normalized, her youthful behaviour bracketed off to a past history. Outrage has been contained through an assessment of her behaviour within a romantic and patriarchal discourse that allows us to enjoy the singer's voice but tells us to ignore her other voices, or at least contain them. It is the established stereotype of the (operatic) diva that may help us most in understanding the representations of O'Connor's identity, her career and the events of *Saturday Night Live* and the Dylan concert.

The rebel diva

Leonardi and Pope explore two competing traditions of the diva. First, there is the masculinist discourse of the *prima donna*, concerned with her image, highly competitive, self-absorbed, with a dangerous, seductive voice. Her vocal fragility and highly strung nature often leads to a hysterical, demented madness which in turn leads her to a tragic end, often reflecting the operatic roles she once played. On the other hand, there is also the proto-feminist diva, her voice powerful and strong, competing in a public male dominated world. This 'diva's voice is a political force. It asserts equality and earns authority in the public, masculine world.' However, these qualities are 'one reason that … masculine discourse must diminish it, other it, confine it, label it and the woman who possesses and wields it as "unnatural" or "demented"' (1996: 19).

The persona of the diva frames the contradictions and tensions between the private and the public sphere, constructing at the same time a singing voice (understood as a physical voice) and a subjective voice (understood as representing the self), and conceptualizing them within one stereotype. As the diva carries these contradictions, the label can legitimize as well as condemn an artist's behaviour and image; the term denotes musical skill as well as an eccentric and difficult 'artistic temperament'. Thus, Sinéad O'Connor's extra-musical controversies have often been forgiven or put aside, because of her singing voice; her persona is presented as difficult and transgressive but ultimately musically rewarding. Her 'emotional rawness' (Edwards 2000) can be seen as an asset to her singing but, as we have seen, her extra-musical transgressions are less easily appropriated into an appropriate feminine subject. The label 'rebel diva' (Rayner 2000) has been used to sum up her star-text. In fact, many of the descriptions of her voice are couched in the discourse of musical authenticity: 'soulful' (Packer 2000), 'soul-baring' (Morse 2000), 'otherworldly' (Anderson 2000) and 'fervently impassioned' (Joyce 1994), all of which override her 'sometimes goofy rebellious attitude' (Violanti 2000).

At the same time, she has also been interpreted through the destructive and tragic themes of the diva's career. O'Connor's career, after the very public incidents of 1992, has been understood through a 'personal' biography of broken marriages, child abuse, suicide attempts and other extra-musical political comments and activities. All have added to her persona as an eccentric, misguided rebel. Media accounts have even voiced concern, in a rather paternalistic vein, for her mental and emotional well-being. In the *Irish Times*, journalist Kevin Courtney pleaded for the public to give O'Connor another chance with the release of *Universal Mother* (1994):

> We have kicked and spat at rock's Joan of Arc for so long now that our scorn is becoming gratuitous … it's time to stop the abuse and let this small, lonely but still lovely voice speak loud and clear once more (1994).

In such accounts, O'Connor's attempts at an extra-musical public voice, like the one she used at the Dylan concert, are portrayed as self-destructive, with her weak, vulnerable femininity incapable of resisting the vicious media onslaught. This perception has been strengthened by her literal withdrawal from a public life on several occasions since the booing incident, and her anger, represented in various performances, has been reconstructed in the past decade through a discourse of normalization. For example, the events of October 1992 have been sanitized and redefined as the angry, misplaced emotions of (her) youth, by media and fans alike. Press profiles in recent years have attempted to re-represent her as normal rather than mad, calm rather than angry, feminine rather than feminist:

> Far from being a 'bald-headed banshee', as London tabloid *The Sun* once described her, the tiny woman with the enormous reputation for trouble, has been agreeable, throughout and unflappably calm. Eccentric, certainly, but not, apparently, nutty (Herrick 2000).

Thus her mad persona has been redeemed to some extent by accounts of her as 'ordinary'. The underlying tone of this maturing narrative warns against such rebellion in the first place, because of the consequences, made real in O'Connor's own personal struggle to maintain a public image. She apparently sees herself as less angry and more mature: 'I love that girl who was courageous enough to take so many risks … but I learned that if I'm going to communicate to people, I need to learn to communicate in a way that is non-threatening, that's calmer' (Farber 2000). These confessionals are a powerful technique in closing off and containing female protest and anger. It is hard to imagine any male rock figure from the last 30 years having to explain his youthful behaviour in such a way.

Ironically, her apparently quieter and less angry style denotes, for some critics, a less interesting performer. Her normalization into a contented individual is linked to her domestic role as mother, her move from angry youth to thirty-something parent, and the portrayal of her femininity as the death of her rock authenticity:

The birth of O'Connor's second child and her own thirtieth birthday have seen her reach a degree of contentment at last, and her music has adjusted accordingly. Whatever the onstage rant or offstage controversy, her defence has always been that she was only being true to herself: angry equals angry music. And, while one must be very, very careful before wishing any more trouble on her, this formula means that better life equals worse music. On Monday she played nothing from her first album, *The Lion And The Cobra*, and she softened up the songs from her second. Mostly she played simple, repetitive ballads, swaddled in thick cello, penny-whistle sounds from a keyboard, and layers of harmony from her four backing singers (Barber 1997).

The above description constructs a feminine sentimentality (countering the rebellious authenticity of her first album) that represents her music as too soft, wrapped in musical layers like 'swaddling' (a direct reference to mothering and, more obscurely, to her religious convictions). O'Connor has, in her music, been developing and exploring the theme of motherhood, which is not a topic that has had much serious or complex time in the past. However, for some critics the mothering/mother theme is tainted with the feminine, and thus remains domestic, personal, outside the 'real world' of street culture and masculine concerns.

What these critics are suggesting in such profiles is the incompatibility of traditional femininity with musical rock authenticity. The great rock/pop divide, though musically difficult to define, continues to organize performers and texts into authentic/inauthentic. O'Connor has challenged this divide, mixing up her music through combinations of rock, folk and reggae, and bringing the private world of relationships into the public world without containing them inside a pop discourse of romantic love or a masculinist discourse of heterosexual 'cock rock' (Frith and McRobbie 1978). In doing so, she has mobilized the radical and political nature of the female singer's voice, establishing her own voice as a protest singer and as a social activist outside the comfortable, commercial music world.

Conclusions

The booing of Sinéad O'Connor is a moment in media history that demonstrates the problems encountered by female performers who wish to protest and rebel in mainstream popular music arenas. However, it is not a story of absolute patriarchal oppression. Paradoxically, she draws on the romantic authenticity that rock has employed since the 1960s to position its male performers as iconic heroes of youth and the disaffected. She has the rock credentials of a rebellious youth and has rejected the use of a traditional, feminized, sexualized image to sell records. This has allowed her to achieve and maintain a sense of authenticity; and the booing incident served to reinforce this authenticity and established her identity, on a global media scale, as a spontaneous and emotionally honest performer.

At the same time, this event, and others throughout her career, have undermined her serious artistic status, because of an (apparent) inappropriate radicalism and personalized anger that are linked to her own abuse. Her performance of 'War' on *Saturday Night Live* and at the Dylan concert made many rock journalists, mainstream media, fans and public uncomfortable. As a female who challenged male authority, she broke the 'taste-boundaries' of protest; consequently, her career and her star-text have been understood through the image of a slightly comical and unhinged rebel. As a woman in the public eye, her behaviour was perceived as inappropriate, inexplicable, extreme, and she took her place in a long line of divas: tragic, mad, but vocally compelling. However, as we have seen, this image has been 'softened' through an alternative narrative of feminine normalization – as a mother, a wife and a more feminized singing style. She is also contained through the presentation of her career and personal failures, which warn the observer of the pitfalls associated with public protests of a personal nature.

And yet, this attempt to explain, and thus normalize, Sinéad O'Connor has been continually challenged by competing representations of her as a defiant and unique performer who possesses an eclectic mix of musical styles and references. Her (potential and real) ability to disrupt, exemplified in her performance at the Dylan concert, carries with it old patriarchal baggage and beliefs about the hysterical feminine, but it was also a moment when those old stereotypes were challenged and confronted. Her recent retirement makes it still 'awkward' to be a fan and, without any new material or public events to remain current and new, she may well fade into media and musical history. However, her appearance at the Bob Dylan 30th Anniversary concert remains a touchstone to the specific constraints and challenges faced by the female performer who dares to speak, sing and scream the house down.

Notes

1. Several of the press and magazine extracts in this chapter were accessed online, without the pagination details of the original source. To locate these, and many other Sinéad O'Connor-related articles, there are a number of useful sites. The *Universal Mother* website at www.members.tripod.com/dcebe is a valuable source of information; so too is the *Jump in the River* discussion group at jitr@postmodern.com.
2. It is interesting to note that none of those women, influential singer/songwriters of the 1960s folk revival, were included in the line-up that evening. In fact, all the women who appeared on the live broadcast were not from Dylan's generation but were younger and represented succeeding daughters of that generation.
3. For example, she has teamed up with various Celtic/Irish performers, including the Chieftains, and has contributed versions of traditional folk songs to a number of compilation projects, such as *Common Ground: Voices of Modern Irish Music* (1996).
4. For a discussion of the lyrics of 'I Believe in You', see the fan website www. pool.dylantree.com. This contains archives of various online discussions about the 'meanings' of Dylan's songs.
5. 'I Believe in You'. Words and music by Bob Dylan. Special Rider Music 1979.
6. O'Connor has mentioned in interviews that she sees herself as a Rastafarian.

7. 'War'. Words and music by Allen Cole and Carlton Barrett. Fifty-six Hope Road Music Ltd/Odnil Music Ltd/Blue Mountain Music Ltd 1976.
8. One of the most 'outrageous' examples of her image as a religious eccentric came in 1999, when it was widely reported that she had been ordained as a female priest through the Tridentine Church, a breakaway Catholic group.
9. Here, Pareles is referring to an interview in *Rolling Stone* in which O'Connor claimed that the boxer Mike Tyson 'was used by the woman he raped'.

Bibliography

Albiez, Sean (2003) 'Know History! John Lydon, Cultural Capital and the Prog/Punk Dialectic', *Popular Music* 22.3, pp. 357–74.

Ali, Lorraine (1994) 'He Screamed Out Our Angst', in Rolling Stone (eds) *Cobain*, Boston: Rolling Stone Press, pp. 96–8.

Alleyne, Mike (2000) 'White Reggae: Cultural Dilution in the Record Industry', *Popular Music And Society* 24.1, pp. 15–30.

Allison, Bill (1987) 'Bob Dylan's Neglected Newport Year: 1964', in Michael Gray and John Bauldie (eds) *All Across the Telegraph: A Bob Dylan Handbook*, London: Futura, pp. 32–8.

Altman, Billy (1985) 'The Guillotine, Please', *Creem*, January, pp. 47–8.

Andersen, Christopher (1991) *Madonna Unauthorized*, New York: Simon & Schuster.

Andersen, Christopher (1994) *Michael Jackson: An Unauthorized Biography*, revised edition, New York: Simon & Schuster.

Anderson, Brett (2000) 'With Faith, a New Wisdom: Sinéad O'Connor Finds Joy in Self-Acceptance', *Washington Post*, June 21.

Atkinson, Terry (1988) 'Winter Album Roundup', *Los Angeles Times*, February 14.

Auslander, Philip (1999) *Liveness: Performance in a Mediatized Culture*, London: Routledge.

Austin, J.L. (2003) 'Lecture I', in Philip Auslander (ed.) *Performance: Critical Concepts in Literary and Cultural Studies, Volume 1*, London: Routledge, pp. 91–6.

Azerrad, Michael (1993) *Come As You Are: The Story of Nirvana*, New York: Doubleday.

Azerrad, Michael (1994) 'Inside the Heart and Mind of Nirvana', in Rolling Stone (eds) *Cobain*, Boston: Rolling Stone Press, pp. 33–9.

Badman, Keith (2000) *The Beatles Off the Record*, London: Omnibus.

Bailey, Beth (1994) 'Sexual Revolution(s)', in David Farber (ed.) *The Sixties: From Memory to History*, Chapel Hill: University of North Carolina Press, pp. 235–62.

Bailey, Beth (2002) 'Sex as a Weapon: Underground Comix and the Paradox of Liberation', in Peter Braunstein and Michael William Doyle (eds) *Imagine Nation: The American Counter-Culture of the 1960s & 70s*, New York: Routledge, pp. 305–24.

Bangs, Lester (1987) 'Thinking the Unthinkable about John Lennon', in Greil Marcus (ed.) *Psychotic Reactions and Carburetor Dung*, New York: Knopf, pp. 298–300.

Bangs, Lester, Reny Brown, John Burks, Sammy Egan, Michael Goodwin, Geoffrey Link, Greil Marcus, Eugene Schoenfeld, Patrick Thomas and Langdon Winner (1970) 'The Rolling Stones Disaster at Altamont: Let It Bleed', *Rolling Stone*, January 21, pp. 18–34.

Banks, Jack (1996) *Monopoly Television: MTV's Quest to Control the Music*, Boulder: Westview.

Barber, Nicholas (1997) 'A New, Happy, Rather Dull Sinéad', *Independent on Sunday*, August 3.

Barthes, Roland (1972) *Mythologies*, New York: Hill & Wang.

Battersby, Christine (1989) *Gender and Genius: Towards a Feminist Aesthetic*, London: Women's Press.

Bayton, Mavis (1998) 'Women and the Electric Guitar', in Sheila Whiteley (ed.) *Sexing the Groove: Popular Music And Gender*, London: Routledge, pp. 37–49.

Beatles, The (2000) *The Beatles Anthology*, London: Cassell.

Bego, Mark (1992) *Madonna: Blonde Ambition*, New York: Harmony Books.

Belz, Carl (1972) *The Story Of Rock*, New York: Oxford University Press.

Bennett, Marty (1969) 'Fistful of Dollars: Do $1-Mil Gates generate Violence?', *Variety*, July 16, pp. 1, 73.

Black, Johnny (1999) *Jimi Hendrix: The Ultimate Experience*, New York: Thunder's Mouth Press.

Boehlert, Eric (1996) 'Did Radio Kill MTV's Video Star?', *Rolling Stone*, May 2, pp. 18–20.

Boehlert, Eric (1998) 'The "Pop-Up" Backlash', *Rolling Stone*, May 28, pp. 49–50.

Boone, Graeme M. (1997) 'Tonal and Expressive Ambiguity in "Dark Star"', in John Covach and Graeme M. Boone (eds) *Understanding Rock: Essays in Musical Analysis*, Oxford: Oxford University Press, pp. 171–210.

Booth, Stanley (1984) *The True Adventures of the Rolling Stones*, New York: Random House.

Bordwell, David and Christian Thompson (1993) *Film Art: An Introduction*, New York: McGraw-Hill.

Bowles, Jerry (1980) *A Thousand Sundays: The Story of the Ed Sullivan Show*, New York: Putnam.

Bowman, Rob (1995) 'The Stax Sound: A Musicological Analysis', *Popular Music* 14.3, pp. 285–302.

Boyes, Georgina (1993) *The Imagined Village: Culture, Ideology and the English Folk Revival*, Manchester: Manchester University Press.

Bracewell, Michael (2003) *The Nineties: When Surface Was Depth*, London: Flamingo.

Brackett, David (1995) *Interpreting Popular Music*, Berkeley: University of California Press.

Bright, Spencer (1999) *Peter Gabriel: An Authorized Biography*, New York: Macmillan.

Bristol Recorder 2, January 1981.

Brossard, Nicole (1991) 'Green Night of Labyrinth Park', in Betsy Warland (ed.) *InVersions: Writings by Dykes, Queers and Lesbians*, Vancouver: Press Gang Publishers, pp. 93–204.

Brown, Peter and Steven Gaines (1983) *The Love You Make: An Insider's Story of the Beatles*, New York: McGraw-Hill.

Burks, John and Loraine Alterman (1969) 'Free Rolling Stones: It's Going to Happen!', *Rolling Stone*, December 2, p. 1.

Butler, Judith (1990) *Gender Trouble: Feminism and the Subversion of Identity*, New York: Routledge.

Cameron, Gail (1964) 'Yeah! Yeah!Yeah! Beatlemania Becomes a Part of US History', *Life*, February 21, p. 34B.

Campbell, Joseph (1949) *The Hero with a Thousand Faces*, Princeton: Princeton University Press.

Carpenter, John (1969) 'Mick Jagger Says ...', *Los Angeles Free Press*, November 21, pp. 33, 39.

Castleman, Harry and Walter J. Podrazik (1980) *Watching TV: Four Decades of American Television*, New York: McGraw-Hill.

Charlton, Katherine (2003) *Rock Music Styles: A History*, 4th edn, Boston: McGraw-Hill.

Clarke, Donald (ed.) (1998) *The Penguin Encyclopedia of Popular Music*, 2nd edn, London: Penguin.

Coleman, Ray (1984) *John Lennon*, London: Sidgwick & Jackson.

Connell, John and Chris Gibson (2003) *Sound Tracks: Popular Music, Identity and Place*, London: Routledge.

Connell, R.W. (1995) *Masculinities*, Berkeley: University of California Press.

Courtney, Kevin (1994) 'Sinéad O'Connor: Universal Mother', *Irish Times*, September 23.

Cresap, Kelly M. (1999) 'New York School's Out': Andy Warhol Presents Dumb and Dumber', in Patricia Juliana Smith (ed.) *The Queer Sixties*, London: Routledge, pp. 43–61.

Cross, Charles R. (2001) *Heavier Than Heaven*, New York: Hyperion.

Crowe, Cameron (1986) *Biograph* booklet, Special Rider Music.

Curtis, Deborah (1995) *Touching From a Distance: Ian Curtis and Joy Division*, London: Faber & Faber.

Dalton, David (1999) 'Altamont: An Eyewitness Account', *Gadfly*, November. http://www.rocksbackpages.com/article.html?ArticleID=219

Davies, Hunter (1996) *The Beatles*, 2nd rev. edn, New York: Norton.

DeBoer, Jennifer (1999) 'Queen, the Rock Press and Gender', MA thesis, McMaster University.

DeCurtis, Anthony (1994) 'Kurt Cobain 1967–1994', in Rolling Stone (eds) *Cobain*, Boston: Rolling Stone Press, p. 8.

Deleuze, Gilles and Constantin V. Boundas (1990) *The Logic of Sense*, New York: Columbia University Press.

Dempsey, David (1964) 'Why the Girls Scream, Weep, Flip', *New York Times Magazine*, February 23, pp. 15, 69–70.

Denisoff, R. Serge (1988) *Inside MTV*, New Brunswick: Transaction.

Denselow, Robin (1989) *When the Music's Over: The Story of Political Pop*, London: Faber & Faber.

Dollimore, Jonathan (1993) 'Different Desires: Subjectivity and Transgression in Wilde and Gide', in Henry Abelove, Michele Aina Barale and David M. Halperin (eds) *The Lesbian and Gay Studies Reader*, London: Routledge, pp. 626–41.

Donahue, Tom (1969) 'Metonomena: The Rolling Stones', *Cashbox*, November. http://www.rocksbackpages.com/article.html?articleID=2311

Duncan, Robert (1984) *The Noise: Notes From a Rock'n'Roll Era*, New York: Ticknor & Fields.

Dunning, David and Scott F. Madey (1995) 'Comparison Processes in Counterfactual Thought', in Neal J. Roese and James M. Olson (eds) *What Might Have Been: The Social Psychology of Counterfactual Thinking*, Mahwah, NJ: Lawrence Erlbaum Associates, pp. 103–32.

Dyer, Richard (1979) *Stars*, London: BFI.

Dyer, Richard (1999) 'It's Being So Camp Keeps Us Going', in Fabio Cleto (ed.) *Camp: Queer Aesthetics and the Performing Subject*, Ann Arbor: University of Michigan Press, pp. 110–16.

Dyer, Richard (2004) *Heavenly Bodies: Film Stars and Society*, 2nd edn, New York: Routledge.

Dyson, Michael Eric (1993) *Reflecting Black: African-American Cultural Criticism*. Minneapolis: University of Minnesota Press.

Early, Gerald (1995) *One Nation Under a Groove: Motown and American Culture*, Hopewell: Ecco Press.

Echols, Alice (1999) *Scars of Sweet Paradise: The Life and Times of Janis Joplin*, New York: Holt.

Edwards, Mark (2000) 'Sinead O'Connor: Faith and Courage', *The Sunday Times*, June 11.

Ehrenreich, Barbara, Elizabeth Hess and Gloria Jacobs (1986) *Re-Making Love: The Feminization of Sex*, Garden City, NY: Anchor Press.

Farber, Jim (2000) 'Spirit of Sinéad', *New York Daily News*, June 11, 2000.

Fast, Susan (2001) *In the Houses of the Holy: Led Zeppelin and the Power of Rock Music*, Oxford: Oxford University Press.

Fein, Esther R. (1985) 'Stands and Phone Lines Jammed for Aid Concert', *New York Times*, July 14, p. 14.

Ferguson, Niall (1997) 'Virtual History: Towards a 'Chaotic' Theory of the Past', in Niall Ferguson (ed.) *Virtual History: Alternatives and Counterfactuals*. London: Picador, pp. 1–90.

Fitzgerald, Jon (1995) 'Motown Crossover Hits 1963–1966 and the Creative Process', *Popular Music* 14.1, pp. 1–11.

Ford, Simon (2003) *Hip Priest: The Story of Mark E. Smith and The Fall*, London: Quartet.

Friedlander, Paul (1996) *Rock and Roll: A Social History*, Boulder: Westview.

Frith, Simon (1980) 'Formalism, Realism and Leisure: The Case of Punk', in Ken Gelder and Sarah Thornton (eds) *The Subcultures Reader*, London: Routledge, pp. 163–74.

Frith, Simon (1988) *Music for Pleasure*, Cambridge: Polity.

Frith, Simon (1996) *Performing Rites: Evaluating Popular Music*, Oxford: Oxford University Press.

Frith, Simon and Angela McRobbie (1978) 'Rock and Sexuality', *Screen Education* 29, pp. 3–19.

Fuchs, Cynthia (1995) 'Michael Jackson's Penis', in Sue-Ellen Case, Philip Brett and Susan Leigh (eds) *Cruising the Performative: Interventions into the Representation of Ethnicity, Nationality and Sexuality*. Bloomington: Indiana University Press, pp. 13–33.

Gardner, Paul (1964a) '3000 Fans Greet British Beatles', *New York Times*, February 8, p. 49.

Gardner, Paul (1964b) 'The British Boys: High-Brows and No-Brows', *New York Times*, February 9, p. 19.

Garofalo, Reebee (1992) 'Understanding Mega-Events: If We Are the World, Then How Do We Change It', in Reebee Garofalo (ed.) *Rockin' the Boat: Mass Music and Mass Movements*, Boston: South End Press, pp. 15–36.

Garofalo, Reebee (1997) *Rockin' Out: Popular Music in the USA*, Boston: Allyn & Bacon.

Garofalo, Reebee (2002) *Rockin' Out: Popular Music in the USA*, 2nd edn, Englewood Cliffs, NJ: Prentice-Hall.

Geldof, Bob (1986) *Is That It?*, London: Sidgwick & Jackson.

George, Nelson (1986) *Where Did Our Love Go? The Rise and Fall of the Motown Sound*, Sydney: Omnibus.

George, Nelson (1988) *The Death of Rhythm and Blues*, New York: Plume.

Gilbey, Ryan (2002) 'Kinky Bio', *Sight And Sound* 12.4, pp. 21–2.

Gillett, Charlie (1971) *The Sound of the City*, London: Sphere.

Gleason, Ralph J. (1970) 'Aquarius Wept', *Esquire*, August, pp. 48–9, 82–92.

Goffman, Erving (1979) *Gender Advertisements*, New York: Harper & Row.

Goldberg, Michael (1985) 'The Day the World Rocked', *Rolling Stone*, August 15, pp. 22–6, 31–2, 34.

Goldberg, Michael, Lisa Hendrickson and Robert J. McNamara (1985) 'The Media Missed the Message', *Rolling Stone*, August 29, p. 26.

Goldstein, Toby (1985) 'Inside the MTV Awards: The Media Glitz', *Creem*, January, pp. 36–8.

Goodwin, Andrew (1992) *Dancing in the Distraction Factory: Music, Television and Popular Culture*, Minneapolis: University of Minnesota Press.

Gordy, Berry (1994) *To Be Loved: The Music, the Magic, the Memories of Motown*, New York: Warner Books.

Gottdiener, Mark (1997) 'Dead Elvis as Other Jesus', in Vernon Chadwick (ed.) *In Search of Elvis*, Boulder: Westview Press, pp. 189–200.

Gould, Jack (1964) 'TV: The Beatles and Their Audience', *New York Times*, February 10, p. 53.

Graham, Bill and Robert Greenfield (1992) *Bill Graham Presents*, New York: Delta.

Greig, Charlotte (1998) 'Female Identity and the Woman Songwriter', in Sheila Whiteley (ed.) *Sexing the Groove: Popular Music and Gender*, London: Routledge, pp. 168–77.

Grein, Paul (1985) 'A Show That Had Something For Everybody', *Billboard*, July 27, pp. 3, 70.

Guralnick, Peter (1986) *Sweet Soul Music*, New York: Little, Brown.

Guralnick, Peter (1994) *Last Train to Memphis: The Rise of Elvis Presley*, New York: Little, Brown.

Guralnick, Peter (1999) *Careless Love: The Unmaking of Elvis Presley*, New York: Little, Brown.

Hadleigh, Boze (1991) *The Vinyl Closet: Gays in the Music World*, San Diego: Los Hombres Press.

Hammontree, Patsy Guy (1985) *Elvis Presley: A Bio-Bibliography*, Westport, Conn.: Greenwood Press.

Harker, Dave (1980) *One For the Money: Politics and Popular Song*, London: Hutchinson.

Harper, Philip Brian (1996) *Are We Not Men? Masculine Anxiety and the Problem of African-American Identity*, New York: Oxford University Press.

Harvey, Mike (2002) 'The Ziggy Stardust Timeline: The Early Beginnings', *The Ziggy Stardust Companion*, http://www.5years.com/early.htm

Harwood, Ronald (1984) *All the World's a Stage*, London: Methuen.

Haslam, Dave (2000) *Manchester, England: The Story of the Pop Cult City*, London: Fourth Estate.

Head, Sydney W. (1976) *Broadcasting in America: A Survey of Television and Radio*, 3rd edn, Boston: Houghton Mifflin.

Hebdige, Dick (1979) *Subculture: The Meaning of Style*, London: Routledge.

Herrick, Stefan (2000) 'Mother of Mercy', *Wellington Evening Post*, July 22.

Heylin, Clinton (1991) *Bob Dylan: Behind the Shades*, London: Penguin.

Heylin, Clinton (2000) *Bob Dylan: Behind the Shades Take Two*, London: Viking.

Hillmore, Peter (1985) *Live Aid World-Wide Concert Book*, Morris Plains, NJ: Unicorn.

Hiram's Report (1964) 'The Talk of the Town', *New Yorker*, February 22, pp. 21–3.

Hoffmann, Dezo (1985) *The Beatles Conquer America: The Photographic Record of Their First American Tour*, New York: Avon.

Hollinghurst, Alan (1983) *Robert Mapplethorpe 1970–1983*, exh. cat., London: Institute of Contemporary Arts.

Holmes, Peter (1996) 'Gay Rock', in Elizabeth Thomson and David Gutman (eds) *The Bowie Companion*, New York: Da Capo, pp. 77–8.

Home, Stewart (1995) *Cranked Up Really High: Genre Theory and Punk Rock*, Hove, Sussex: Codex.

Hopkins, Jerry (1969a) 'The Stones Tour: Is That a Lot?', *Rolling Stone*, November 15, pp. 16–17.

Hopkins, Jerry (1969b) 'Kiss Kiss Flutter Flutter Thank You Thank You', *Rolling Stone*, December 13, pp. 1, 6.

Hopkins, Jerry (1971) *Elvis*, New York: Simon & Schuster.

Hoskyns, Barney (1998) *Glam! Bowie, Bolan and the Glitter Rock Revolution*, New York: Pocket Books.

Hoye, Jacob (ed.) (2001) *MTV Uncensored*, New York: Pocket Books.

Hughes, Tim (2000) 'Greil Marcus's "Invisible Republic: Bob Dylan's Basement Tapes"', *Contemporary Music Review* 18.4, pp. 159–69.

Hughes, Tim (2003) 'Groove and Flow: Six Analytical Essays on the Music of Stevie Wonder', Ph.D. thesis, University of Washington.

Hutchinson, John (1986) 'From Brideshead to Shrunken Heads', *Musician* 93, July, pp. 68–78.

Jackson, Michael (1988) *Moonwalk*, London: Heineman.

Jones, Lesley-Ann (1997) *Freddie Mercury: The Definitive Biography*, London: Hodder & Stoughton.

Joyce, Mike (1994) 'Sincerely, Sinéad O'Connor', *Washington Post*, September 21.

Kahn-Harris, Keith (2003) 'The Aesthetics of Hate Music', http://www.axt.org.uk/HateMusic/KahnHarris.htm

Kamin, Philip and Peter Goddard (1984) *Genesis: Peter Gabriel, Phil Collins and Beyond*, New York: Beaufort.

Kaplan, E. Ann (1987) *Rocking Around the Clock: Music Television, Postmodernism and Consumer Culture*, New York: Methuen.

Kemal, Salim and Ivan Gaskell (1999) 'Performance and Authenticity', in Salim Kemal and Ivan Gaskell (eds) *Performance and Authenticity in the Arts*, Cambridge: Cambridge University Press, pp. 1–11.

Kendall, Brian (1997) *Our Hearts Went Boom: The Beatles' Invasion of Canada*, Toronto: Viking.

Kilby, Jane (2001) 'Tracking Shock: Some Thoughts on TV, Trauma, Testimony', in Anu Koivunen and Susanna Paasonen (eds) *Conference Proceedings For Affective Encounters: Rethinking Embodiment in Feminist Media Studies*, University of Turku, Finland, pp. 112–17.

King, Jason (1999) 'Form and Function: Superstardom and Aesthetics in the Music Videos of Michael & Janet Jackson', *The Velvet Light Trap* 44, pp. 80–96.

Kooijman, Jaap (2002) 'From Elegance to Extravaganza: The Supremes on 'The Ed Sullivan Show' as a Presentation of Beauty', *The Velvet Light Trap* 49, pp. 4–17.

Laing, Dave (1985a) *One Chord Wonders: Power and Meaning in Punk Rock*, Milton Keynes: Open University Press.

Laing, Dave (1985b) 'Music Video: Industrial Product-Cultural Form', *Screen* 26.2, pp. 78–83.

Lee, C.P. (2002) *Shake, Rattle and Rain: Popular Music Making in Manchester 1955–1995*, Ottery St Mary, Devon: Hardinge Simpole.

Leonardi, Susan J. and Rebecca A. Pope (1996) *The Diva's Mouth: Body, Voice, Prima Donna Politics*, New Brunswick: Rutgers University Press.

Lewisohn, Mark (1986) *The Beatles Live!*, New York: Holt.

Lewisohn, Mark (1988) *The Beatles Recording Sessions: The Official Abbey Road Studio Session Notes 1962–1970*, New York: Harmony Books.

Lhamon Jr, W.T. (1990) 'Dylan's Living Lore', *The Telegraph* 37, pp. 102–31.

Lydon, Michael (1967) 'Where's the Money From Monterey Pop?', *Rolling Stone*, November 9, p. 1.

Lydon, Michael (1970) 'The Rolling Stones: At Play in the Apocalypse', *Ramparts*, March, pp. 28–53.

McLeod, Ken (2001) 'Bohemian Rhapsodies: Operatic Influences on Rock Music', *Popular Music* 20.2, pp. 189–203.

McRuer, Robert (2002) 'Gay Gatherings: Reimagining the Counter-Culture', in Peter Braunstein and Michael William Doyle (eds) *Imagine Nation: The American Counter-Culture of the 1960s & 1970s*, New York: Routledge, pp. 215–40.

Mann, William (1963) 'What Songs the Beatles Sang', *The Times*, December 27, p. 4.

Marcus, Greil (1969) 'The Woodstock Festival', *Rolling Stone*, September 20. Repr. in Jann S. Wenner (ed.) (1987) *20 Years Of Rolling Stone: What a Long, Strange Trip It's Been*, New York: Straight Arrow, pp. 49–56.

Marcus, Greil (1991) *Dead Elvis*, Cambridge, Mass.: Harvard University Press.

Marcus, Greil (1992) 'Anarchy in the UK', in Anthony DeCurtis and James Henke (eds) *The Rolling Stone Illustrated History of Rock and Roll*, 3rd edn, New York: Random House, pp. 594–608.

Marcus, Greil (1997) *Invisible Republic: Bob Dylan's Basement Tapes*, London: Picador.

Marshall, Lee (2000) 'We Want Folksingers Here', *The Bridge* 7, pp. 31–44.

Martin, George (1983) *Making Music*, London: Pan.

Mercer, Kobena (1994) *Welcome to the Jungle: New Positions in Black Cultural Studies*, New York: Routledge.

Middles, Mick (1996) *From Joy Division to New Order: The Factory Story*, London: Virgin.

Middleton, Richard (1990) *Studying Popular Music*, Milton Keynes: Open University Press.

Middleton, Richard (2000) 'Locating the Popular Music Text', in Richard Middleton (ed.) *Reading Pop*, Oxford: Oxford University Press, pp. 1–19.

Moore, Allan (1997) *Sgt Pepper's Lonely Hearts Club Band*, Cambridge: Cambridge University Press.

Morley, Paul (2000) 'Shot By Both Sides', *Uncut* 42, November, pp. 72–5.

Morse, Steve (1992) 'Sinead O'Connor's Career at Risk', *Montreal Gazette*, October 19.

Morse, Steve (2000) 'Sinéad O'Connor: Faith and Courage', *Boston Globe*, June 13.

Muncie, John (2000) 'The Beatles and the Spectacle of Youth', in Ian Inglis (ed.) *The Beatles, Popular Music and Society: A Thousand Voices*, New York: St. Martin's Press, pp. 35–52.

Murray, Charles Shaar (1972) 'David at the Dorchester: Bowie on Ziggy and Other Matters', *New Musical Express*, July 22. Accessed online at www.rocksbackpages.com/writers/murray.html

Murray, Charles Shaar (1989) *Crosstown Traffic*, New York: St Martin's Press.

Nava, Mica (1992) *Changing Cultures*, London: Sage.

Negus, Keith (1998) 'Sinéad O'Connor: Musical Mother', in Sheila Whiteley (ed.) *Sexing the Groove: Popular Music and Gender*, London: Routledge, pp. 178–90.

Nolan, David (2001) *I Swear I Was There: Sex Pistols and the Shape of Rock*, Bury: Milo.

Noland, Carrie Jaures (1995) 'Rimbaud and Patti Smith: Style as Social Deviance', *Critical Inquiry* 21.3, pp. 581–611.

Norman, Philip (1981) *Shout! The True Story of the Beatles*, London: Hamish Hamilton.

O'Brien, Lucy (1995) *She Bop: The Definitive History of Women in Rock, Pop and Soul*, London: Penguin.

O'Connor, John J. (1983) 'Sound of Motown Celebrated', *New York Times*, May 16, p. C18.

O'Connor, Sinéad (1998) 'Sinéad O'Connor Transcends Her Troubled Past', *Request Magazine*, February.

Packard, Vance (1964) 'Building the Beatle Image', *Saturday Evening Post*, March 21, p. 36.

Packer, Nigel (2000) 'Faith and Courage', *BBC Online News*, June 11.

Palmer, Robert (1995) *Rock & Roll: An Unruly History*, New York: Harmony.

Pareles, Jon (1992) 'Why Sinéad O'Connor Hit a Nerve', *New York Times*, November 1.

Pegley, Karen (2002) 'Multiculturalism, Diversity and Containment on MuchMusic (Canada) and MTV (US)', *Canadian University Music Review* 22.2, pp. 93–112.

Petrozzello, Donna (1998) 'Video Music Awards is Big Winner For MTV', *Broadcasting & Cable*, August 31, pp. 26–30.

Pond, Steve (1983) 'Former Motown Stars Return For Birthday Bash', *Rolling Stone*, May 26, pp. 56–7.

Porterfield, Christopher (2003) 'Feb 9, 1964: Yeah, Yeah, Yeah!', *Time*, March 30, p. 47.

Powers, Anne (1997) 'Sinéad O'Connor', in Barbara O'Dair (ed.) *Trouble Girls: The Rolling Stone Book of Women in Rock*, New York: Random House, pp. 377–81.

Pratt, Ray (1986) 'The Politics of Authenticity in Popular Music: The Case of the Blues', *Popular Music And Society* 10.3, pp. 55–78.

Rawlings, Terry (2003) *Harmony in My Head: Steve Diggle's Rock and Roll Odyssey*, London: Helter Skelter.

Rayner, Ben (2000) 'Sinéad O'Connor', *Toronto Star*, June 11.

Rettenmund, Matthew (1995) *Encyclopedia Madonnica*, New York: St. Martin's Press.

Rich, Frank (1995) 'Ticket to Ride: Beatlemania Before the Hype', *New York Times*, November 18, p. 21(L).

Ricks, Christopher (2003) *Dylan's Vision of Sin*, London: Viking.

Riley, Tim (2002) *Tell Me Why: A Beatles Commentary*, 2nd edn, New York: Da Capo.

Rimmer, Dave (2003) *The Look: New Romantics*, London: Omnibus.

Rinzler, Alan (1964) 'No Soul in Beatlesville', *The Nation*, March 2, p. 221.

Riordan, James and Jerry Prochinichy (1991) *Break on Through: The Life and Death of Jim Morrison*, New York: William Morrow.

Rodman, Gilbert R. (1996) *Elvis After Elvis*, New York: Routledge.

Rogan, Johnny (1993) *Morrissey and Marr: The Severed Alliance*, London: Omnibus.

Rolling Stone (1969) 'The Stones and the Gathering Madness', December 13, p. 8.

Ross, Ron (1972) 'David Bowie: Fleeting Moments in a Glamorous Career', *Phonograph Record*, October. Accessed online at www.5years.com/pr.htm

Sanders, Charles L. (1983) 'Diana and Michael' *Ebony*, November, pp. 29–36.

Sandford, Christopher (1998) *Bowie: Loving the Alien*, New York: Da Capo.

Savage, Jon (1991) *England's Dreaming: Sex Pistols and Punk Rock*, London: Faber & Faber.

Scaduto, Anthony (1996) *Bob Dylan*, London: Helter Skelter Books.

Schneider, Steve (1986) 'MTV Aims to Improve Awards Show', *New York Times*, August 31, Section 2, p. 20.

Sedgwick, Eve Kosofsky (1985) *Between Men: English Literature and Homosocial Desire*, New York: Columbia University Press.

Seideman, Tony (1984) 'Hancock Stars at MTV Awards', *Billboard*, September 29, p. 96.

Selvin, Joel (1992) *Monterey Pop*, San Francisco: Chronicle Books.

Shales, Tom (1983) 'Motown at 25: Yester-me, Yester-you', *Washington Post*, May 16, pp. B1–B8.

Shanahan, Brendan (2000) 'Sinéad O'Connor Profile', *Sydney Sunday Telegraph*, July 2.

Shapiro, Harry (1991) *Electric Gypsy*, London: St. Martin's Press.

Sheff, David (1981) 'Playboy Interview: John Lennon and Yoko Ono', *Playboy* 28.1, January, pp. 75–114, 144.

Shelton, Robert (1986) *No Direction Home: The Life and Music of Bob Dylan*, London: Penguin.

Shuker, Roy (1998) *Key Concepts in Popular Music*, London: Routledge.

Shuker, Roy (2001) *Understanding Popular Music*, 2nd edn, London: Routledge.

Silber, Irwin (1964) 'An Open Letter to Bob Dylan', *Sing Out!* 14.5, November.

Small, Michael (1984) 'What Can It Mean When a Video Awards Bash Draws the Superstars of Rock? MTV's Coming of Age', *People Weekly*, October 1, pp. 57–8, 63.

Smith, Mark E. and Mick Middles (2003) *The Fall*, London: Omnibus.

Smith, Suzanne E. (1999) *Dancing in the Street: Motown and the Cultural Politics of Detroit*, New Haven: Yale University Press.

Sounes, Howard (2001) *Down the Highway: The Life of Bob Dylan*, London: Black Swan.

Spencer, Neil (1976) 'Don't Look Over Your Shoulder, But the Sex Pistols Are Coming', *New Musical Express* February 18. Repr. in *NME Originals: Punk 1975–1979*, vol. 1, Issue 2, 2002, p. 38.

Spizer, Bruce (2003) *The Beatles Are Coming! The Birth of Beatlemania in America*, New Orleans: 498 Productions.

Sragow, Michael (2000) 'Gimme Shelter: The True Story', *Salon.com*, August 10. http://www.dir.salon.com/ent/col/srag/2000/08/10/gimme_shelter/index.html?sid=944041

Street, John (1986) *Rebel Rock: The Politics of Popular Music*, Oxford: Blackwell.

Strongin, Theodore (1964) 'Musicologically …', *New York Times*, February 10, p. 53.

Sturken, Marita (1997) *Tangled Memories: The Vietnam War, the Aids Epidemic, and the Politics of Remembering*, Berkeley: University of California Press.

Sutcliffe, Phil (1994) 'This Time It's Personal', *Q Magazine* 69, pp. 80–83.

Sutherland, Steve (1989) 'Acid Rain: Woodstock/Woodstock II', *Melody Maker*, May 6, p. 34.

Sweeting, Adam (2003) 'The Boy Looked at Bowie', *Uncut*, March. Accessed online at www.btinternet.com/~s.essom

Taraborrelli, J. Randy (1991) *Michael Jackson: The Magic and the Madness*, New York: Lane.

Tarmarkin, Jeff (2003) *The End of the Beginning: Jefferson Airplane at Altamont*, London: Helter Skelter.

Tate, Greg (1987) 'I'm White! What's Wrong With Michael Jackson' *Village Voice*, September 22. Repr. in Greg Tate (1992) *Flyboy in the Buttermilk: Essays on Contemporary America*, New York: Simon & Schuster, pp. 95–9.

Taylor, Derek (1987) *It Was Twenty Years Ago Today*, London: Bantam.

Taylor, Ian and David Wall (1976) 'Beyond the Skinheads: Comments on the Emergence and Significance of the Glamrock Cult', in Geoff Mungham and Geoff Pearson (eds), *Working Class Youth Culture*, London: Routledge, pp. 105–23.

Terry, Ken (1984) 'Rockit, Thriller, Big Winners in MTV Music Video Awards', *Variety*, September 19, pp. 115–16.

Toynbee, Jason (2000) *Making Popular Music: Musicians, Creativity and Institutions*, London: Arnold.

Ullestad, Neal (1992) 'Diverse Rock Rebellions Subvert Mass Media Hegemony', in Reebee Garofalo (ed.) *Rockin' the Boat: Mass Music and Mass Movements*, Boston: South End Press, pp. 37–54.

Urry, John (1995) *Consuming Places*, London: Routledge.

Van Leeuwen, Theo (1999) *Speech, Music, Sound*, London: Macmillan.

Vermorel, Fred and Judy Vermorel (1985) *Starlust: The Secret Life of Fans*, London: W.H. Allen.

Violanti, Anthony (2000) 'Sinéad O'Connor: Faith and Courage', *Buffalo News*, July 7.

Wallace, Michelle (1990) *Invisibility Blues: From Pop to Theory*, London: Verso.

Walser, Robert (1993) *Running With the Devil: Power, Gender and Madness in Heavy Metal Music*, Hanover: Wesleyan University Press.

Ward, Ed, Geoffrey Stokes and Ken Tucker (1986) *Rock of Ages: The Rolling Stone History of Rock & Roll*, New York: Summit Press.

Watts, Michael (1996) 'Oh You Pretty Thing', in Elizabeth Thomson and David Gutman (eds) *The Bowie Companion*, New York: Da Capo, pp. 47–51.

Weinstein, Deena (1999) 'Art Versus Commerce: Deconstructing a (Useful) Romantic Illusion', in Karen Kelly and Evelyn McDonnell (eds) *Stars Don't Stand Still in the Sky: Music and Myth*, New York: New York University Press, pp. 56–69.

White, Avron Levine (1987) *Lost in Music: Culture, Style and the Musical Event*, London: Routledge.

Whiteley, Sheila (ed.) (1998) *Sexing the Groove: Popular Music And Gender*, London: Routledge.

Whiteley, Sheila (2000) *Women and Popular Music: Sexuality, Identity and Subjectivity*, London: Routledge.

Whiteley, Sheila (2003) *Too Much Too Young: Popular Music, Age and Gender*, London: Routledge.

Williams, Paul (1990) *Bob Dylan: Performing Artist*, (Vol. 1), London: Xanadu.

Williams, Richard (1985) 'Grains of Hope from the Gods of Pop', *The Times*, July 15, p. 6.

Willis, Ellen (1999) 'Crowds and Freedom', in Karen Kelly and Evelyn McDonnell (eds) *Stars Don't Stand Still in the Sky: Music and Myth*, New York: New York University Press, pp. 152–9.

Wills, Geoff and Cary L. Cooper (1988) *Pressure Sensitive: Popular Musicians Under Stress*, London: Sage.

Wilson, Tony (2002) *24 Hour Party People: What the Sleeve Notes Never Tell You*, London: Channel 4 Books.

Index